CAR
LENOIR RHYNE COLLEGE

P9-ARD-020

378.74827
Swlh

97410

DATE DUE			

WITHDRAWN

A History of Muhlenberg College 1848—1967

Dr. Erling N. Jensen

A History of Muhlenberg College

1848–1967

JAMES E. SWAIN

CARL A. RUDISILL LIBRARY
LENOIR RHYNE COLLEGE

Appleton-Century-Crofts

DIVISION OF MEREDITH PUBLISHING COMPANY, NEW YORK

378.74827
Swih
97410
Jue 1976

Copyright © 1967 by Meredith Publishing Company.
All rights reserved.

This book, or parts thereof, must not be used or reproduced in any manner without written permission. For information address the publisher, Appleton-Century-Crofts, Division of Meredith Publishing Company, 440 Park Avenue South, New York, N.Y. 10016.

657–1

Library of Congress Catalog Card Number: 67–24976

PRINTED IN THE UNITED STATES OF AMERICA

85800

Preface

THIS HISTORY OF MUHLENBERG COLLEGE is written to commemorate the hundredth anniversary of the naming of the College. The first twenty-five years are recounted in S. E. Ochsenford's *Quarter-Centennial of Muhlenberg College*, the only other published history of the College. However, I have interpreted my assignment to present the story from the inception of the Allentown Seminary in 1848 to the present. Further, it is my intention to relate the history of Muhlenberg College to those national and international events that affected the College.

The true spirit of an institution of learning is difficult to capture. "When you put your hand in a flowing stream," wrote Leonardo da Vinci, "you touch the last that has gone before and the first that is still to come." Such is the experience of one who seeks the pulse of a college—ever moving, ever changing. While what is past can sometimes be documented, and while the present may be observed—the future can only be surmised.

Like individuals, no two colleges are alike. Though each may have its thumbprint, may leave its impression, such unique characteristics are often only the tip of the iceberg. One must probe beneath the surface to find the sources of strength and endurance.

I am aware of the challenge in undertaking to write this history. If endurance is a virtue, my virtue is assured; for I have been here forty-two years, forty years longer than I planned to stay when I arrived on campus in 1925 at the behest of Dr. Edward P. Cheyney of the University of Pennsylvania, one of my greatest and most influential teachers. Frankly, I was hurt when he insisted that I come to a place entirely unknown to me; for my background (Harrison Fellow in History and Ph.D. at the University of Pennsylvania) had spawned ambitions to remain in the Ivy League. I began the two-year sentence much as a prisoner enters jail. Mrs. Swain and I didn't even move to Allentown. But when the sentence was served I stayed on and gradually a completely changed attitude emerged. I was engulfed in something that now means so much, and which I am at a loss to define satisfactorily. In time I continued my research, wrote books, and for twenty-five years was chairman of the History Department.

There is a feeling, I hope well founded, that the trained historian has an important role in analyzing the problems of education. Herbert Baxter Adams, of Johns Hopkins University, called attention to the development of schools as a part of local history from which national history should grow. In a report of findings of a distinguished committee for The Fund for Advancement of Education, Paul H. Buck wrote: "the history of educational forces in this country, both in and out of the classroom, has been shamefully neglected by American historians . . . and the imperfect knowledge of the history has affected adversely planning of curricula, the formation of policy, and the administration of educational agencies in the continuing crisis of American education."

I have received information and ideas for this book from many people and many sources. Indeed there have been so many willing workers that it is not possible to list them all here. I am deeply grateful to my colleagues, the Board of Editors,* for their invaluable assistance. They examined the manuscript minutely on various occasions. Their advice saved me from many mistakes.

Any list of co-workers, no matter how abbreviated, must include Dr. J. Conrad Seegers, Mr. Howard MacGregor, Mr. John Phillips, Mr. Charles Ettinger, Dr. Harold K. Marks, Mr. John Davidson, and the late Mr. Walter L. Reisner. Mrs. Dewey L. Brevik did the secretarial work and compiled the faculty list.

I acknowledge a special debt to my former students in Historiography. For three years, majors in history worked on assigned topics in Muhlenberg history. Some very fine papers were pre-

* Dr. Preston A. Barba, Judge James F. Henninger, Dr. Erling N. Jensen, the Reverend Theodore L. Fischer, Mr. Alan M. Hawman, Jr., Mr. Jon F. LaFaver, and Mr. Richard K. Brunner.

sented and extensive use was made of them. I salute the following: Raymond D. Bauman, Mr. and Mrs. William H. Becker, Richard H. Benveniste, Edward Bonekemper, Kay Christoffersen, Barbara Fretz Crossette, George H. Darby, Wilson E. Dewald, Edwin M. Goldsmith, Matthew John, Florence E. Kahmar, Dolores Lipham, David Mayer, Edward P. Paules, Thomas Petro, Carol Baumgartner Reeves, Jr., and Larry Weikel.

In the end, however, the author must assume the responsibility for this book. It cannot be otherwise. The result is not perfect, but it was achieved with enthusiasm and devotion.

JAMES E. SWAIN

Allentown, Pennsylvania
April, 1967

Contents

Preface   v
Introduction   xiii

1   AN IDEA EMERGES   1
2   THE FIRST QUARTER CENTURY   9
3   MUHLENBERG COLLEGE AT THE TURN OF A CENTURY   19
4   ON A CHARTED COURSE   29
5   "NOW WE HAVE BECOME A COLLEGE"   38
6   THE CHARTED COURSE HAS DIFFICULTIES   56
7   GROWING PAINS AND FINANCIAL BURDENS   69
8   DARKNESS BEFORE DAWN   85
9   IN THE FIRST STAGES OF MATURITY   101
10   GROWTH: SPIRITUAL, INTELLECTUAL, AND PHYSICAL   109
11   MIRTH, MYTH, AND MIRACLE   132
12   RETROSPECT   147
13   PROSPECT   167

APPENDICES   177
   College Presidents   177
   Deans of the College   177
   Presidents of the Board of Directors   177
   Board of Trustees (1966–1967)   177
   Members of the Faculty   180
BIBLIOGRAPHY   203
INDEX   205

Illustrations

Dr. Erling N. Jensen

Frontispiece

Between pages
46 and 47

Four distinguished members of the Muhlenberg
  family
Frederick Augustus Muhlenberg
Theodore Lorenzo Seip
Benjamin Sadtler
Early faculty group
Laying the foundation stone of the Administration
  Building, 1903
Receipt for tuition and board, 1904
The baseball team, 1894
Muhlenberg vs. Indians, 1906
Varsity football squad, 1908
Report card, 1903
The German Recitation Room
Euterpia Hall
College buildings at Fourth and Walnut Streets
  and some of the faculty

Between pages
78 and 79

Statue of Peter Muhlenberg on the College
  grounds is desecrated in a protest against
  coeducation, 1957
Faculty play *The Boor*, May 17, 1935
Undefeated tennis team, 1942
The College basketball team plays Long Island
  University at Madison Square Garden, 1947

ILLUSTRATIONS

John A. W. Haas
Levering Tyson
J. Conrad Seegers
Seegers Union
Interior, Seegers Union
The interior of the Chapel
Navy V12 Unit in front of the Chapel
Women's Dormitory Council
Three Presidents: Dr. Jensen, Dr. Tyson,
    Dr. Seegers

Between pages
142 and 143

Martin Luther Hall
Memorial Hall
Prosser Hall
The President's House
Student Health Center and Infirmary
Walz Hall
Benfer Hall

Introduction

As MUHLENBERG COLLEGE approaches the one hundredth anniversary of the naming of the institution, it seems appropriate to publish this volume. The only other published history of the College covers the period up to 1892.

Muhlenberg College is the product of the hopes, inspiration, contributions, and dedication of many individuals and groups, including its faculty, administration, students, alumni, the church, the community, and its friends. It is necessary to assess the past, and to become better acquainted with the present institution, to be better prepared to serve higher education and the church in the world of the future. These are some of the reasons why Dr. James Edgar Swain was commissioned to write the history of Muhlenberg College.

Dr. Swain is a distinguished teacher, historian, and author, who is well qualified for this assignment. He came to Muhlenberg in 1925 and has served the College with distinction for forty-two years, twenty-five of them as Chairman of the History Department. In 1965 he was named Senior Professor of History.

Dr. Swain has written a number of books, including the well-known *History of Civilization,* one of the first in its field. A respected academician and citizen, he has been honored both by Muhlenberg College and the Allentown community. In June, 1967, when he retired from active teaching, Muhlenberg conferred upon him an honorary Doctor of Laws degree.

Like many other institutions of higher education, Muhlenberg has grown out of small beginnings. The Allentown Seminary was founded in Allentown, Pennsylvania, in 1848, to be succeeded in 1864 by the Allentown Collegiate Institute and Military Academy.

In January of 1867, the name was shortenend to Allentown Collegegiate Institute, and since September of 1867, the institution has been known as Muhlenberg College.

It is coincidental that the one hundredth anniversary of the naming of the College should occur at a time when major developments are taking place in higher education. The explosion of knowledge is tremendous. Increased recognition of education's contribution to our complex life is made evident by the increased demand for more education. There have been significant developments in financial aid to students and to educational institutions by both federal and state governments, to try to insure that all qualified young people have an opportunity to pursue higher education, regardless of financial status, and to insure a free choice in the type of institution they want to attend.

This history of Muhlenberg College is published at a time when the role of private education, particularly in the church-related college, is being re-examined and reassessed in light of the many serious problems facing higher education, which includes the fact that a larger percentage of students are attending public institutions. With these developments, the place of the private college becomes even more important than it has been in the past.

Conditions today are greatly different from what they were a century ago. In the past, Muhlenberg College was able to adjust and adapt its programs to the needs of the time. It must continue to do so in the future. In the immediate past, the College has conducted various studies, to provide a firm foundation and to be better prepared for the course it is to follow in the future. Long-range plans for the academic area and for physical resources were made. Studies on the future of the College and on the curriculum, including an honors program, were conducted. A projected building program was formulated, and a study made of the endowment fund. These programs are already underway. The College has tried to set the objectives, and to chart its course for tomorrow. This, too, is appropriate, as we recognize the centennial anniversary.

In the spring of 1966, the institution was evaluated for a possible Phi Beta Kappa Chapter. In August, 1967, the College was informed that the Phi Beta Kappa members of the faculty have been authorized to establish a chapter at Muhlenberg. It is indeed most fitting that in the one hundredth year of its naming Muhlenberg College has received this valued recognition of the academic progress of the institution.

In behalf of the Muhlenberg community, I want to express my sincere appreciation to the many dedicated men and women whose contributions, in so many different ways, made it possible for Muhlenberg College to serve, in a meaningful way, higher education, the church, and our society. Muhlenberg College hopes to be able to perform an even greater service in the future.

Particular and special thanks are due the members of the Board of Editors who assisted Dr. Swain in his task, and I acknowledge with gratitude the assistance of the Muhlenberg College Alumni Association for its support and encouragement in the preparation of this volume.

ERLING N. JENSEN
President
Muhlenberg College

September 1, 1967
Allentown, Penna.

A History of Muhlenberg College 1848—1967

1

An Idea Emerges

MIGRATION of western Europeans to the eastern fringe of North America and from there westward created a phenomenon called the "great frontier," which eventually made possible the United States of America. Motivations of the pioneers were varied: material gain, lure of adventure, and freedom of thought and action. The urge was sufficiently strong for a break with comforts of home, friends, and relatives to face a frontier without culture or religion and, in many instances, without facilities to promote them. The establishment of schools and churches, with trained personnel, was difficult and demanded another type of pioneering.

A large group of Germans from the Palatinate, Würtemberg, and Alsace, some after a brief sojourn in England, formed a settlement in the Lehigh Valley of eastern Pennsylvania, practically isolated from the rest of the world. The Pennsylvania Germans, as they soon were known, prospered from tilling the fertile soil and became specialists in thrift, cleanliness, and simplicity. They clung to their own dialect and gave little heed to amusements and luxuries. The majority were Lutherans, served principally by ministers trained in Germany. However, replacements for ministers too old to continue, and the increased demand because of rapid growth, created problems. Reports of this clerical shortage reached Philadelphia, were eventually relayed to England, and finally to Germany.

Those interested were few in number and those willing to respond were still fewer. A conspicuous exception existed at the Francke Institute, located in an ancient Saxon town on the River Saale. Dr. Gottlieb August Francke, son of the illustrious organizer Augustus Herman Francke, was an influential sponsor of a revivalist movement among German Lutherans. He emphasized a personal religious life and Christian character, apart from close control of a governing political system, that became common practice in Germany. In fact, it was Henry Melchior Muhlenberg, patriarch of the Lutheran Church in America, who believed in a free church in a free state, who brought this spirit into the New World. From Halle outstanding clergymen were sent to the British American colonies where large groups of German Lutherans were located.

By strange coincidence or Divine Providence, Henry Melchior Muhlenberg visited Dr. Francke on his way to another prospective call. It was his thirtieth birthday and he took advantage of the opportunity to seek advice and guidance. During conversation at dinner a letter, recently arrived from America, was read by the congenial host: "We live in a country that is full of heresy and sects. As far as our religious interests are concerned, we are in a state of greatest distraction; and our means are utterly insufficient to effect necessary relief. . . . It is truly lamentable to think of the large numbers of a rising generation who know not their right hand from their left; and, unless help be promptly afforded the danger is great that, in consequence of the great lack of churches and schools, most of them will be led into ways of destructive error."

The call was from "dispersed Lutherans in Pennsylvania" and Dr. Francke advised Muhlenberg to accept it for a trial period of two years. Young Muhlenberg replied: "If it be God's Will, I shall go." He did not leave Germany in search of freedom, adventure, or worldly possessions but on a very special mission of service. Had this call gone unanswered, America would have been deprived of the services of a family distinguished in religion, education, science, statesmanship, and the military. Henry Melchior Muhlenberg arrived in Philadelphia on November 25, 1742.

His lot was not an easy one. The first encounter outside Philadelphia was at New Hanover Church near Reading. Here he met Count Zinzendorf, who had attracted the greater part of the Lutheran congregation to the Moravian faith. The rest were being served by a German who had been dismissed from a pastorate in Germany. This situation was mastered with dispatch and new adventures were undertaken. Henry Melchior Muhlenberg was responsible for building at least three churches, including St. Michael's and Zion in Philadelphia and Augustus Church at Trappe. The Lutheran Synod of Pennsylvania was his handiwork, and a liturgy, or order of service, was prepared and brought into use which for many years remained virtually unchanged.

While on duty as pastor, Muhlenberg met and married Anna Maria, daughter of Conrad Weiser, famous Indian Agent. To the union were born eleven children. Among them were John Peter Gabriel, the most flamboyant and immortalized clergyman of the American Revolution; Frederick Augustus Conrad, the statesman; and Gotthilf Henry Ernest, the scientist. The latter's grandson, Frederick Augustus, became the first President of Muhlenberg College. Muhlenbergs of later generations continued to serve their adopted country brilliantly as soldiers, statesmen, ministers, and teachers.

Traditionally, as part of the heritage from Martin Luther, Lutherans insisted upon a well-educated clergy. Unlike certain denominations that believed preaching was merely a God-given faculty and needed no augmentation, they insisted on careful scholarly preparation and examined candidates before they were accepted as "their rightful teachers." Even ministers in charge of frontier congregations, far removed from seats of learning, were well versed in classical languages as well as theology—part of the inspiration engendered and brought to America by Henry Melchior Muhlenberg. A meeting of the Ministerium at Philadelphia in 1769 went on record: "Be it resolved that each member write out his thoughts concerning best methods to proceed in training of ministers and send them in." Four years later, when Pastor J. C. Kunze asked the Ministerium for support for his newly established elementary school, Henry Melchior Muhlenberg expressed the opinion that training for school teachers, catechists, and country preachers should be included. Further effort to advance this cause was made in the organization of a "Society for Propagation of Christianity and Useful Knowledge among Germans in America." There was also clear intimation of need and intent to provide college training. One thing they needed was a college.

The newly established University of Pennsylvania (1779) gave expression to the desire for training German Lutherans when it made Dr. Kunze a Trustee and Professor of German philology. This was a step in the right direction, but even so Lutherans had little to compare with Presbyterians (Princeton), Congregationalists (Yale), Unitarians (Harvard), Baptists (Brown), and Anglicans (Columbia and William and Mary).

It was the hinterland that caused real concern. Travelers reported a large German population in east central Pennsylvania: "Prosperous and progressive, a large percentage Lutherans, yet not a single institution of higher learning other than an academy, that could confer a literary degree." Clearly, there was nothing adequate to train the German population for service to either church or state. Furthermore, no one was being prepared to replace the earlier recruits from Germany, as they became older and as multiplicity of duties increased. The available training was limited to overworked pastors who took apprentices into their own homes. In spite of the obvious drawbacks of this practice, several outstanding ministers were trained through this procedure.

The late eighteenth and early nineteenth centuries witnessed a number of efforts to establish institutions of higher learning in Pennsylvania. Dickinson College (1784) provided for prominent Lutherans on the Board of Trustees. The Charter of Franklin College (1787) allowed fifteen of forty-five Trustees to be Lutherans. German was taught along with English and Classical languages and degrees were granted in liberal arts and sciences. Principals were to alternate between Lutheran and Reformed; not a happy combination—there was too much room for friction and not enough grounds for effective cooperation.

The idea for a school suggested by Patriarch Muhlenberg before the American Revolution was not successful. Gettysburg College (1832) was the first major independent effort to establish such an institution. The Charter decreed: "A College for education of

4

youth in languages, arts, sciences, and useful literature." No pupil was to be denied admission, and no person to be excluded as patron, Trustee, teacher, or officer because of religious beliefs. Further facilities were made available in the creation of a Lutheran seminary in the same locale.

The failure of Gettysburg College and Seminary to satisfy the desires and needs for eastern Pennsylvania soon was evident. Frederick A. Muhlenberg expressed an opinion: "We are of German ancestry, and Lutheran in our belief and practice, and none [of the colleges already in existence] in our neighborhood is calculated to train our children in the faith of our forefathers." Not enough students from the eastern area attended Gettysburg Seminary to supply the need for new pastors. One reason given—although not too convincing—was distance and a strange environment. Travel was difficult but not prohibitive; a more likely explanation was the possibility of homesickness.

There was, however, a more fundamental reason—a growing difference in sentiment and principle, not easily distinguishable. During meetings of the newly organized Lutheran Ministerium and General Council of Pennsylvania, questions were raised whether Gettysburg Seminary was the proper place to train ministers who "would be faithful to doctrine and usages of Lutheranism." Subsequently a Synodical Lutheran Theological Seminary (1864) was founded in Philadelphia. A revival of the demand for a college to provide preliminary training was more realistic and in line with the desire expressed by Henry Melchior Muhlenberg a generation or two earlier. The Philadelphia Seminary was unable to attract enough students; a fact freely admitted by the first President of Muhlenberg College, Dr. Frederick A. Muhlenberg.

Philadelphia seemed to be a logical location for a college but it would not serve the particular needs of the Lehigh Valley. Indeed, the distance separating the proposed College from the Seminary continued an annoying problem. Meanwhile, a series of incidents, ascribed by those high in authority to Divine Providence, brought Allentown into focus as a center for a college to serve a providential purpose.

The Reverend Samuel K. Brobst, a citizen of Allentown and an

5

influential member of the Ministerium and vitally interested in education was instrumental in forming the Allentown Seminary (1848). This he described in his own newspaper as in line with objectives already advanced in Philadelphia. Dreams of what became Muhlenberg College were in the making. According to the Reverend Mr. Brobst: "This institution is especially designed to train teachers; however, it is easily seen that they can attend the institution with advantage who propose studying either theology, jurisprudence, or medicine and wish to prepare themselves for one of the higher classes of college and those who are seeking important acquisitions in knowledge and a higher culture."

Reports of success or failure vary. Only eleven prospective teachers registered for the first term; in fact, so little interest was shown that the curriculum was changed to emphasize the classics. Personnel was not entirely Lutheran; the first Principal was Reformed. There was a brief period of apparent success; the enrollment showed promise, new buildings were constructed, others improved, and prominent people served as faculty members and administrators. But the financial depression of 1857–58 and the Civil War had disastrous effects which further accentuated inherent problems. In 1864 a reorganization gave rise to the Allentown Collegiate Institute and Military Academy, chartered by the Commonwealth of Pennsylvania to grant degrees.

The Allentown Collegiate Institute and Military Academy became the Allentown Collegiate Institute (January 8, 1867). In turn this corporate name was transformed into Muhlenberg College (May 21, 1867). The petition was signed by F. A. Muhlenberg, President. At this time, events and ideas converged that gave rise to Muhlenberg College. True, the material basis was a defunct institution, but it was something on which to build. Ideas and plans formerly without anchorage were accepted and for some time were in process of formation. The hope of a few farsighted people who prayed for realization was long-standing. However, this is the actual date when Muhlenberg College took definite if precarious form.

Transition from imagination to blueprint and then to realization was supported by a spirit of determination and abiding faith that existed before the College was a reality. This thread, thin at times, made the institution what it is and around it clustered buildings, curriculum, administration, faculty, and alumni. Buildings deteriorate unless they are kept in repair or new ones are built, personnel grow old and must be replaced, and curricula need change to keep pace with the times. The task is never finished and the need for intelligent pioneering never ceases.

Part of the drama unfolded in Allentown and the chief proponent was Samuel K. Brobst, who nurtured his school with a vision of something bigger and better—a real collegiate institution of learning. He kept in touch with the Ministerium, argued in favor of church support, and offered all the services at his disposal. A crucial situation came when the Institute closed (1867) and the properties were offered for sale.

The Ministerium moved slowly. Dissatisfaction with Gettysburg grew and the need for an institution to serve the Germans in the Lehigh Valley was discussed at the meeting held in Philadelphia (1860). A deciding factor was the founding of the Philadelphia Lutheran Seminary four years later. The need for a collegiate institution for preliminary training grew steadily, largely because of lack of students for the Philadelphia Seminary. It was suggested that: "The design in having an institution in our midst cannot be realized by present arrangements with the school in Allentown. General satisfaction can only be given by placing this institution under direct supervision of the Synod." A committee was appointed to investigate but it was warned to act "in such a way as not to place the Synod under any pecuniary responsibilities." Fortunately the Reverend Mr. Brobst was made chairman. A joint stock company was formed. Its stockholders and the Evangelical Lutheran Ministerium of Pennsylvania and Adjacent States elected a Board of Trustees. The properties of the defunct Institute were purchased, the first material step in the direction of a Lutheran College at Allentown.

Announcement was made at the Ministerium meeting in Lebanon (1867) that seven years' effort "have resulted in the attainment of its chief object . . . to secure the continuation and advancement of the school established nineteen years ago for the promotion of

7

Christian education, to bring the institution under the supervision of our Church, and to raise it to the grade of a full college. Muhlenberg College can and will soon be formally opened with fair prospects for success."

Under an amended Charter, Muhlenberg College was declared a reality, and under the laws of the Commonwealth of Pennsylvania "to do all and singular, the matters and things which may be lawful for them to do for the well being of the institution and due management and ordering of the affairs thereof." The Board of Trustees elected the Reverend Frederick A. Muhlenberg, D.D., President of the institution, which would be known as Muhlenberg College in honor of his great grandfather, Henry Melchior Muhlenberg. Induction services were held May 21, the first faculty meeting in August, and the College opened in September, 1867.

2

The First Quarter Century

MUHLENBERG COLLEGE emerged from a somewhat uncertain background, cautiously backed by the Ministerium with little more than theoretical interest, and in an environment not particularly enthusiastic about education and culture. However, it was backed by a few people with genuine interest in perpetuating a German heritage and a true Lutheran faith as transplanted from Germany to America by Henry Melchior Muhlenberg.

It took time and effort for the institution to become a credit to the name it bore. There was much more agony than ecstasy; great need for financial support, facilities, and personnel, and there were only a few promising students. Never, however, was there a complete absence of College personnel with capabilities and determination to wage battle. Indeed, from time to time, there were stalwarts of such stature that it is perplexing to know why they remained. In some way, an intangible spirit was engendered, became a part of the College, and carried on through discouragements to ultimate success.

There were many Lutherans who, from the beginning, questioned the feasibility of another college and seminary when those at Gettysburg were available, and comparatively prosperous. Many times both sentiment and logic supported their doubts. However, competition between Muhlenberg and Gettysburg continued.

President Frederick Augustus Muhlenberg met this challenge.

He spent seventeen years teaching at Gettysburg and spoke with feeling and conviction: "This schism which has developed within the two factions and which has developed within the Church and the factions cannot conform in one institution in spite of seventeen years' effort.

"We have, directly or indirectly, contributed upwards of forty-thousand dollars to its support; have been sending our representatives and students there; and we have made use of every effort to unite our entire Church in Pennsylvania in its support, but we are compelled, more in sorrow than anger, to lament that all our efforts to conciliate, consolidate, and assimilate have most singularly failed, and that we have met with bitter disappointment. . . . We are therefore compelled to organize a college for ourselves, to make proper provision for the education of our children, and to furnish a sufficient number of students for our Theological Seminary in Philadelphia, and adequate to the growing demands of our church in Pennsylvania and elsewhere."

No institution could have a better qualified leader than the first President of Muhlenberg College: a scholar of note with a wide range of experiences in teaching and administration, and the proud possessor of a name prominent in the annals of American Lutheranism. He was a pioneer in religion and education in an environment which could not have been to his liking, except as a servant performing the commands of his Master. He was a giant among pygmies, with so much to do and so little with which to work—financially and otherwise. One can imagine the intellectual gulf between Dr. Muhlenberg and his students and most of his associates. The Allentown community, with all its virtues, was lagging in cultural facilities. Provincialism, in which a great majority took pride, was deep-seated. Compared with his position at Gettysburg, it was a step down. The College faculty and administration staff were exemplary but not extraordinary. Most of the teachers had scholastic training as theologians and ministers.

The aims and ideals advocated by Dr. Muhlenberg in his inaugural address are clear indications of his Halle background and that of his famous great grandfather. A genuine desire was expressed to perpetuate German concepts of culture and Lutheranism: "to train our children in the faith of their forefathers." Talents for church and state which otherwise would be lost were primary objectives. Facilities for children humble in origin were to be furnished: "Which will be more valuable than gold and fit them to stand unabashed in the presence of kings."

Abiding faith in the classics was clearly stated. Ancient languages and mathematics—with emphasis on the former—were supplemented with modern languages, natural and physical sciences, history, and "polite" literature. "A general culture must always have the precedence over a special one, for it takes a comprehensive view of all the facilities of the mind and the powers of the soul, and endeavors to bring them all out by a suitable development." Religious training had equal significance with intellectual training: "We do not regard an education as complete that aims only at improving the intellect." Thus he defined "a Christian education."

The closing sentence is long and complicated but meaningful: "We have this day made a renewed beginning in this great work; let not sneers of those opposed to us chill the warmth of our feeling; let us under the influence of the truths we have been considering, with united hearts and hands, give ourselves, our money as it may be necessary, our children, our labors, our prayers to the noble cause of religion and education, until this part of our state, in this higher culture, shall be as attractive to the eye of the beholder as its rich and fertile valleys and as enduring as the everlasting hills by which we are surrounded."

Thus was born, one hundred years ago, in the midst of unimpressive physical surroundings, Muhlenberg College. At its head was a man of unusual ability with courage and conviction. The original Charter called for ". . . an Academy to consist of a primary school, college, and other appropriate departments as the patrons and managers of said Institute shall find themselves able to maintain, by the name, style and title Muhlenberg College. . . ." The College enrollment (1867) consisted of twenty-five students—four seniors, two juniors, six sophomores, and thirteen freshmen—most of whom came with Dr. Muhlenberg from Gettysburg. One building housed the College as well as the Secondary and Primary Departments. Many members of the faculty also taught in the lower departments.

Courses listed in the first catalogue reflect the President's guidance. Greek, Latin, German grammar, English Rhetoric, and Mathematics predominated. The language requirements continued except that English was not required of sophomores. The junior year offered certain courses to be given in English: chemistry, mineralogy, botany meteorology, composition, declamation, and natural theology. Seniors were offered geology, political economy, moral philosophy, evidences of Christianity, and forensic disputation—in English.

How all these courses were taught by a faculty of eight, including the President and the Principal of the Academic Department, is a wonder of wonders. A general basic principle was that with a thorough knowledge of the classics and a proper mental attitude, almost any field of teaching endeavor could be mastered.

Teaching was by no means the only responsibility of the faculty. Since the Ministerium refused to assume material responsibilities, one of Dr. Seip's chief assignments was to collect funds, in addition to being Professor of Greek and Principal of the Academic Department. Practically everyone, including the President and some students, was expected to visit congregations, preach sermons, and perform other duties; always seeking funds with hat in hand and a wistful expression.

"There is really nothing quite so poor as poverty." The College endowment fund at the first year's end was $4,000, collected with great effort. The Ministerium was in a position to offer only permission for solicitation among congregations. It even hesitated to accept ownership of the College which was offered by the Trustees. After six years of effort the sum for endowment was $38,000—a noteworthy accomplishment. The depression of 1873 temporarily retarded progress.

In the dark days of the Depression, when it seemed that all progress had come to a halt, an inspiration came unexpectedly. The lack of sponsorship by the Ministerium was a great disappointment, and since sufficient support from other sources was convincingly inadequate, the future of Muhlenberg College was not bright. In fairness it should be noted that lack of financial aid from the Ministerium was not due to a lack of interest, at least from that small but vigorous minority who never ceased their efforts. The

Ministerium had many responsibilities. It was committed to support a recently established Orphan's Home, a Theological Seminary, and a publication house, together with its well-recognized responsibility for missionary work. There was a ceaseless cry for more help from everyone. Ultimately action was taken—a mere beginning but nevertheless a beginning. At a meeting of the Ministerium of Pennsylvania in Allentown (June 23–24, 1874), it assumed responsibility for the entire management of Muhlenberg College and the Board of Trustees was authorized to employ means to secure funds to pay the indebtedness and to increase the endowment. Changes were made in the Ministerium's Charter, to give Muhlenberg College "its moral and material support and maintain the same, as a literary institution in Allentown." The year following, the annual meeting of the Ministerium agreed to plans for a Synodical College. The following objective was stated: to aim constantly to reach "the securing of the broadest literary and scientific education of the best collegiate institutions, so as to give a thorough general culture and the preparation for all the professions and occupations in which learning is useful."

The importance of the action was beyond doubt. The change was not only sudden but also complete—from a hands-off policy to complete control. As could be expected, a change so fundamental aroused differences of opinion. There was, nevertheless, the end of doubt and frustration, and it is difficult to imagine what would have happened had this action not taken place. Muhlenberg College became a church-related institution with corresponding privileges, immunities, and responsibilities.

One of the first tangible acts under the new order was the appointment of the Reverend Dr. Theodore L. Seip, a member of the faculty, as agent for securement of funds. In one year $30,000 was secured for endowment and current expenses. In addition students were attracted and interest in the College grew.

The real intent and purpose of the institution still was undecided. Frequent mention was made of the need for preliminary training for the Theological Seminary, and hope for preservation of the German background with particular reference to Lutheranism. "The discipline shall be in accordance with her doctrinal and spiritual life. Provision shall be made for preliminary studies of special importance to those contemplating the ministry of the Lutheran Church, and others who may desire to pursue the studies, and so far as may be necessary to this end, certain studies may be made *elective*." The extent to which emphasis should be given non-theological subjects, whether or not they could be compatible, and whether a multiple purpose would prevent financial support from sources other than the church, were moot questions. As the story of Muhlenberg College unfolds some interesting and important facts on this subject come to light.

For those close to the institution, with serious difficulties overcome, a brighter day dawned. The resignation of Dr. Muhlenberg, September 11, 1876, on the eve of opening a new school year, came as a shock to the Ministerium, Board of Trustees, faculty, student body, and community. He accepted a Professorship of Greek at the University of Pennsylvania, an outstanding offer in line with one of his fondest desires. He was primarily a scholar and teacher rather than a pastor or administrator. The acceptance of the Presidency of Muhlenberg College was in line with a call to duty similar to the case of his illustrious great grandfather when he consented to come to America. Perhaps he considered his services at Muhlenberg in the line of duty fulfilled and that in his declining years he had the right to consider himself. Not all of his time at the University was devoted to teaching since he served in many capacities to aid Lutheran institutions. Another contribution, unforeseen at the time but of inestimable value, lay in teaching and inspiring John A. W. Haas, later acclaimed as one of the "greats" in Muhlenberg history.

Dr. Benjamin Sadtler, a gentleman of high repute and a recognized Lutheran churchman, was elected to succeed Dr. Muhlenberg. He was less a public figure and not as renowned a scholar, but he was a minister with unusual appeal and an indefatigable worker. He may have lacked something in originality but he carried through on many things just started and added lustre to others that needed attention. He assumed leadership just as the College became accepted by the Ministerium and he made the transition remarkably smooth. His acceptance speech was noteworthy because of its high ideals and lofty sentiments and for its practical principles and concepts. He aided in promoting an aim of the College to "harmoniously combine the Christian element in education with a sound and comprehensive culture."

Two basic pronouncements were made: a commitment to keep Muhlenberg a small college, and a rigid opposition to an elective system for choice of subjects by students. Regarding the former he quoted a President of one of the few genuine universities in the land: "A small college, well manned and thoroughly administered, has many advantages over one that is larger, in respect to the intimacy of acquaintance and intercourse between officers and pupils and also in respect to the vigor with which a few studies, wisely selected, may be thoroughly enforced." Concerning the elective system: "We frankly mistrust the elective system of study . . . if applied to undergraduates of average age and judgment of those attending them. There is not a branch of the curriculum that can be spared without detriment."

Continued shortage of funds was an ever-present problem. It proved very difficult to get much money from congregations since most of them were hard-pressed to take care of their own needs. Attempts to endow a Professorship in honor of the Reverend Samuel K. Brobst (a leader in backing a college in Allentown) had to be abandoned because of poor response.

Basically, however, an institution of learning emerged with healthy, vigorous characteristics. A great boon came in 1879, in a gift of $30,000 from industrialist Asa Packer to endow a Professorship of "Natural and Applied Science." This prevented a neglect of science which would have been a serious handicap for a liberal arts college. The following year James K. Mosser and Thomas Keck gave $20,000 to endow a Chair of Greek Language and Literature. The amounts are significant, and in addition Asa Packer, not a Lutheran, set a precedent for support outside the church. The Asa Packer endowment was sufficient to interest Edgar Fahs Smith, Ph.D., in coming to Muhlenberg. He enjoyed a reputation as a distinguished chemist and later became Provost of the University of Pennsylvania. His interest in Muhlenberg continued; one of his students, N. Wiley Thomas, Ph.D., followed his former teacher and gave outstanding service for two years. The combined length of service for these men was only three years but the prestige they gave the College was immense.

A painful accident and poor health forced President Sadtler to retire (1886). The Reverend Dr. Theodore Lorenzo Seip was chosen as third President of the College. He was a graduate of Gettysburg College and a member of the first class at Philadelphia Seminary. He never served as a full-time pastor but was an excellent teacher and served in many fields in various departments.

Dr. Frederick Augustus Muhlenberg, Professor of Greek at the University of Pennsylvania, returned for the inauguration of President Seip. He delivered the charge to the President-elect and his presence added dignity and prestige to the ceremony. At least three important statements of future policy were expressed in Dr. Seip's inaugural address: a clear-cut definition of liberal arts, the meaning of a church-related college, and the desirability of more emphasis on English.

Muhlenberg College was described as "not a school for children, nor a university, nor a theological seminary, nor a medical school; but it is a College, a teaching body, a training school for all those whose aim is to lay the foundation broad and deep, upon which the professional student, and the liberally-cultured man of any calling or pursuit may afterwards rear the solid structure of his own particular life work. Liberal Arts," Dr. Muhlenberg continued, are to educate men, "so that when they engage in business or professional life they may be men of deep, broad, and liberal culture, who can appreciate professions and occupations other than their own, and who do not magnify their own particular pursuit out of all due proportion to everything else and hold it so close to their eyes as to shut out from their view the wide world of knowledge that lies beyond. Its aim, so far as it can, is to stem the current of narrowness and illiberality of crudity and superficiality, that are the result of arrogant specialism on the one hand, and of a showy but unsubstantial curriculum on the other."

The function of religion in an educational program and the reality of "liberal arts" were avoided, just taken for granted, or accepted as rhetorical verbiage. Dr. Seip made it clear where he stood: "A college that is to accomplish its proper work . . . should be under the auspices of some portion of the Christian church, in order for harmony of direction and teaching and to exert a positive religious influence on its students and the community which it intends to reach."

Futhermore, he clearly indicated where Muhlenberg College stood in his personal convictions. "It is the College of the Evangelical Lutheran Ministerium of Pennsylvania and occupies the same confessional position with it. All the members of the faculty are members in regular standing of this Ministerium, or of congregations in connection with it. While sectarian bias and illiberality will have no place and influence in the religious teaching of the College, its most solemn obligations and aim bind it to unswerving loyalty to Christ and the truth." Certainly, there is no lack of specific intent and motivation here expressed.

The question of linguistic and cultural motivation, particularly in the light of later history, is worth analyzing. Next to Lutheranism, the most frequently mentioned promotional argument for a college was to preserve the German language and cultural background. The extent to which this should be done in the United States, with an English heritage, had to be decided. The German language and culture preserved and practiced in the Lehigh Valley were far removed from what scholars in Halle, Germany, and their agents abroad had in mind. Pennsylvania German was a far cry from Classical German and there were few evidences of other aspects of German culture in the locality. The lower grade pupils, from which the College mainly recruited a student body, spoke a dialect. Instruction in the College was largely in German. The first catalogue even lists separately courses given in English. Dr. Seip had erudite remarks on the subject: "Though a high place of honor is given in our curriculum to the ancient classics, yet no less attention is devoted to the modern languages, especially English and German. English, pure and undefiled, is taught in an appreciative manner. . . ."

The extent to which this statement is valid is questionable but still an encouraging beginning. Muhlenberg College began to take on stature and recognition beyond the limits of the Lehigh Valley.

It was no longer a local Pennsylvania German institution—a local oasis of German culture in America.

Finances continued as an ever-present handicap. A degree of optimism instead of unadulterated pessimism cautiously was expressed. A report to the Ministerium included a ray of light: "In a few years the debt can be entirely liquidated and the institution freed from burden of indebtedness." However, optimism was not in order as income indicated. Most of the contributions were in driblets of only a few dollars. The two endowed Professorships were the most promising improvement. Various forms of appeal were used. One that is somewhat telltale provided that individuals or congregations that contributed $1,000 to the endowment fund be given a permanent scholarship with "perpetual right of educating a student in the institution free of expense for tuition throughout his collegiate course." Twenty individuals and four institutions responded.

Maturity was shown in an increased number of students recruited from a wider circle, beyond the scope of the Ministerium, and for training in professions other than the ministry. President Seip was well known and active among collegiate institutions. He was instrumental in founding The College Association of Middle States and Maryland and took an active part in meetings. Muhlenberg College received commendation from The American Society of Church History for outstanding service in religious services, at a national meeting held in Washington, D.C., December 31, 1890. The United States Commission on Education credited Muhlenberg College as especially proficient in the classics.

3

Muhlenberg College at the Turn of a Century

THE first twenty-five years of Muhlenberg College were Commemorated at Commencement exercises in the spring of 1892. It is worth noting that the founding date 1867 was accepted rather than 1848, that of the Allentown Seminary or the Collegiate Institute and Military Academy. S. E. Ochsenford's *Quarter-Centennial Memorial Volume* is a storehouse of information and very obviously a labor of love. It is a ready reference for reports and participants in College affairs, including Board of Trustees, Administration, faculty, and students.

The commemoration was a celebration in a true sense. Well might those who spoke declare that progress during those twenty-five years, from an inauspicious start, was the work of an unseen hand, often identified as God's Will. Coincidentally, 1867 was the 350th anniversary of Martin Luther's posting the Ninety-five Theses on a church door in Wittenberg, and, to add more local color, it was the twenty-fifth year of President Seip's affiliation with the school.

For the Baccalaureate sermon, Dr. Seip chose the text, "Hitherto hath the Lord helped us" (I Samuel VII, 12). He presented a review and preview of the College with appropriate credit to individuals and organizations and indicated guidelines for the future: "We think we remain within the bounds of modesty when we claim that Muhlenberg College has done a great work for the

Church and the world, during the first twenty-five years of its existence, in comparison with limited means which have been placed at its command. But, is it not a burning shame that a Church so rich should keep its College so poor, and that too, when the College is necessary for the education of its own pastors, to say nothing of Christian training of its lay members? Is it not credible either to the intelligence or piety of those who profess to be Lutherans, we will not say Christians, who show no interest in its prosperity and work, and are unwilling to contribute of their means to the cause of educating ministers in their own College for their own pulpits?"

Past President Sadtler was present to share reflections and to point out some dangers that might be encountered. Science, he believed, was neglected for theology and the humanities. President Andrews of Brown University was quoted: "We are coming to see the terrible and needless loss suffered by neglecting studies like botany, mineralogy, physiology, and elements of physics till the pupil has passed the age of special observational power."

Dr. Sadtler was much interested in the methodology of education: "All learning procured from observation, book, or teacher must be digested and you learn to think." In further elaboration he added: "The sorriest specimen of a student is the one that has a parcel of disassociated facts floating about in his mind, like the loose ends in a dried-up gourd. . . . It is a better conception of the educated mind that it should be a workshop rather than a mere bin, a productive power rather than a receptive reservoir, rather a mill than a mill-dam."

The elective system came in for renewed attack. He opined that experienced educators stand for a set course of study as indispensable to a good education. Those who opposed should be held up to scorn. "The number of electives Harvard offers is so large . . . it would require one hundred thirty-five years for any one student seriatim to take them all up and take a diploma for each."

Ochsenford was present and recorded details of the festivities including the dinner menu. Under each tempting course was a quotation from Shakespeare. Little Neck Clams on Shell—"He

hath eaten me out of house and home" (II Henry IV); Claret
Wine—"Good wine is a good, familiar creature, if it be well used;
exclaim no more against it" (Othello, II, 3); Cheese and Crackers—
"You shall nose him" (Hamlet IV, 3); and Cigars—"O thou weed
who are so lovely fair, and smellest so sweet, would thou hadst
Ne'er been born" (Othello, IV, 2).

Historian Ochsenford summarized: "Thus ended the most enjoyable, interesting, and successful Commencement Exercise ever
held at Muhlenberg College. The institution has been placed, more
prominently than ever before, to the attention of its friends and
supporters. It starts out on its second quarter centenary under very
favorable auspices; and it is not improper to express the hope that
all future efforts at advancement may be crowned with success."

For proper evaluation, a more detached point of view than that
of participants and eyewitnesses is needed—as a matter of course,
they lack perspective. Afterthought, while more subtle than
prophecy, is not infallible, but is of some value. Periodizing by
specific dates can be both misleading and inaccurate. Immediate
and drastic changes, except in rare instances, and they are almost
always bloody revolutions, do not occur. By the same logic, when
progress is considered a constant trend, one may lose himself in
the stream of history, ignoring changes and forces that prove valuable. The specialist may become hopelessly entrenched and a
general survey could be highly superficial.

Great changes were taking place throughout the world as the
twentieth century approached. The United States became a world
power. The Industrial Revolution, with all its ramifications—
economic, political, and social—affected almost everyone. The
frontier remained but was moving rapidly westward and there was
a gradual transition from rural to urban—from agriculture to industry. The country was no longer an appendage to western
Europe. The little red school house was still present but unobtrusively about to disappear. Colleges were few and a college
education was rare—perhaps no one foresaw the changes in store.

Muhlenberg College felt the impact and responded, hesitatingly
at first, but with increased momentum. It is futile to set a definite
time when it was certain the Rubicon was crossed, after a life span

of a quarter century, but there was enough evidence of accomplishment and sufficient promise for the future to be analyzed and evaluated. Curriculum, personnel (administration, faculty, and students), and physical plant constitute the core of an educational institution.

The most illusive, controversial, and maligned part of the College program was the curriculum, which entailed courses given, degrees granted, and the extent to which they collectively constituted an effective program.

While curricula in American colleges were changing as the nineteenth century ended, the traditional classical and prescribed pattern of courses remained. Latin and Greek were prominent, valued not only for subject matter but also for intellectual discipline. Mathematics, philosophy, and logic, largely for the same reasons, were prominent. Support came with importations from Europe, by-products of the Age of Enlightenment and the Industrial Revolution. Various forces that would require the whole span of history to describe were involved. However, at least two—religion and education—belong in a category for particular attention because of the role played at Muhlenberg College.

Harvard University and the University of Virginia pioneered innovations which became general trends: the abandonment of prescribed courses to an elective system and a gradual substitution of modern languages for classical. This may be considered the first deviation from the originally designated liberal arts. It has never been entirely the same since.

A crucial question persists: where does, or can a church-related and liberal arts college fit into the picture? Before jumping to a conclusion, it is well to remember that moving too far or too fast is dangerous. Recourse may be provided in pioneer efforts somewhere between the two extremes.

Muhlenberg College was founded with certain clear-cut objectives in mind: to train Lutherans for entrance into Philadelphia Seminary; to fulfill a desire to serve the large German population in or near the Lehigh Valley; and to emphasize German culture. If these objectives had been perpetuated with disregard of the American heritage, the future would have been uncertain. The compromise effected is a great tribute to those who labored, are laboring, and will labor in the College. This is one of the qualities that made Muhlenberg College great in the past and promising for the future. The curriculum reflects the efforts expended. Those who faced this eternal task, who sat in committees and presented reports know the story well. They are the unsung heroes of the forward movement.

A strong religious influence permeated the atmosphere in the early days at Muhlenberg. Daily work began with chapel service. Church attendance was compulsory on Sundays and teaching a Sunday School class was highly recommended. Christian conduct was expected of everyone. There is no reason to believe, however, that fun, mild roughhouse, and off-moment frivolities were unduly suppressed.

As previously indicated, the early curricula were classical and prescribed. More courses in classics were offered and taught by more teachers, including the President, than any other two subjects. English received scant attention. Under an English language classification, science courses, logic, and history of civilization were listed. While the language suffered, it must be recognized as a clever way of introducing, somewhat camouflaged, controversial subjects. The Ministerium belatedly recommended (1882) that more emphasis be given the English language.

Progress in introducing science at Muhlenberg, when compared with other institutions, including some universities, makes an impressive story. President Seip discouraged specialization but did not oppose introducing the sciences: in fact, they prospered under his direction. A major inducement, of course, was the $30,000 bequest from Asa Packer. An issue of *The Muhlenberg Weekly* (1883) included a plea from the students for more science courses.

Opposition to teaching science came from church organizations and theologians: anti-Darwinism flourished. A survey (1880) revealed that eight college Presidents (Yale, Rochester, Princeton, Lafayette, Amherst, Union, Hamilton, and Brown) were opposed to teaching evolution. The pollster did not include Harvard, Johns Hopkins, and the University of Pennsylvania. Another survey revealed that nine-tenths of the pre-Civil War college Presidents were ordained ministers.

Gradually, changes were made in the Muhlenberg curriculum.

23

A few electives, French, Hebrew, economics, political economy, and history, crept in but liberal arts remained a much discussed principle. However, there were variations, modifications, and additions that dimmed earlier prospects. Thence began what was destined to be a never-ending and ever-increasing effort to cling to something obviously and ideologically good but which necessarily had to be changed to keep in line with progress.

Extracurricular cultural activities provide a good barometer of the quality of college accomplishments. Changing environment alters the situation constantly. While Muhlenberg was at Fourth and Walnut Streets in Allentown, town attractions were available, although carefully, if not altogether satisfactorily, censored. Campus life for a student body without record players, radios, television, pool tables, bowling lanes, and motor cars now seems primitive, as indeed it was. Therefore, more time was available for writing, oratory, theatrical productions, vocal and instrumental music. These performances, given not only for student amusement but also for the general public, were well patronized and provided income for the College.

When President Muhlenberg came to the College, several students, also from Gettysburg, accompanied him. They were leaders in development of various entertainment and extracurricular activities—many on a very high level. Two were in the form of literary societies with high-sounding names—*Euterpea* and *Sophronia:* both were formed within a week after the official opening of the College. Obviously they were intended as inclusive rather than exclusive. The original selection for membership was by lot. The Societies were carefully supervised. College regulations required: "No literary or other society shall exist in the College, except by permission of the faculty—and approval of its Constitution." The expressed aim of these Societies was to cultivate appreciation for good literature, to provide training in speaking, and for informal meetings.

Once elected to membership there was no resigning. If dismissed, a student might or might not be elected to another Society. Complete ostracism was a very sorry state of existence. As the student body increased, the Administration ruled that only three-fifths of the incoming class each year should be chosen to membership in both Societies, making them more selective and competitive.

Both Societies charged membership dues; *Euterpea* had a $5 initiation fee and dues of fifty cents per term. Each group had commodious meeting rooms used exclusively by members and faculty. Much time was spent here between classes, in the evenings, and on weekends. Recreation was limited; no card-playing was permitted; conversation, reading, and rehearsals for performances—debates, oratorical contests, musicals, and theatrical productions—consumed most of the time. The two Societies cooperated on important projects including the Glee Club, orchestra, sponsorship of a Junior Oratorical Contest, and publication of the first College paper, *The Muhlenberg*. The first *Ciarla* was produced by the Class of 1893, which was a noteworthy cooperative effort. An excellent review of the College was presented in the 1896 edition.

One of the most remarkable experiments of the Societies was to develop individual libraries, important because existing facilities of the College were limited. Early College announcements rarely mentioned a library. In fact, the books inherited from the Seminary and Collegiate Institute, one hundred in all, were divided equally between the two Societies. The Constitution of *Euterpea* set forth its plans. "The object of this association shall be the diffusion of liberal principles and the promotion of social, intellectual, and moral improvement of its members by the establishment of a Library, Reading Room, and so forth, and have ample power to perform such acts as may be necessary to these objects." Within a year, possession of 390 books was reported; in 1892, there were 2,151 listed and available for circulation.

Sophronia had less publicity than its rival but seems to have been ahead in many ways. The library was smaller but better organized. The Librarian's job carried heavy responsibilities: "he shall be held personally responsible for any books or other property of the Society. . . ." In 1892, there were 1,700 books in the library. Titles indicate high quality, with particular emphasis in English and American literary classics. It is worth noting that the combined collections in the libraries of the two Societies in 1892 totaled 3,851 books, while the College listing was only 2,500.

Obviously, such an arrangement could not be called efficient and pointed to a weakness in the general College setup. However, it was an ingenious combination that served a purpose, without which the College would have been handicapped. The later story will reveal how changes for the better ultimately came. However, those who remember the College Library when housed on the second floor of the Administration Building recall how insufficient it remained until very recently.

These two Societies functioned and prospered many years. In 1904 a reunion was held which was attended by distinguished graduates. It was the last meeting held at Fourth and Walnut Streets. The Societies were given quarters in the new Administration Building on the third floor, *Euterpea* at the east end and *Sophronia* at the west. Interest dwindled, and shortly after World War I they disbanded.

A third Society that deserves consideration existed at Muhlenberg from the beginning and lasted for more than twenty-five years. It was called the Franklin Society and aimed "to furnish members with newspapers and periodicals of the day." Students were expected to sign the constitution and pay fees. They were not expected to engage in any form of activity and held only three meetings a year. Members of other Societies might belong. It is interesting that students supplied most of their own books, newspapers, and periodicals. They paid an average of $28 for four years' membership, while a full-year's tuition was only $45.

The Missionary Society was a fourth organization which prospered and was highly respected. It was organized in 1888, to promote a missionary spirit among students and to engage in practical work within necessary limitations. One hundred and twenty-two names were on the roll the first year. A missionary school was established in the northwestern part of the city, called St. Stephen's Lutheran Sunday School. A lot was purchased and plans were drawn to build a chapel. Prominent names listed as officers and members were those of George Gebert, A. L. Breinig, F. C. Oberly, J. B. Heil, William Wackernagel, J. H. Raker, and F. T. L. Keiter.

Another worthwhile student intellectual contribution was the creation of a publication called *The Muhlenberg Monthly*. It superseded the unsuccessful *Collegian* and represented a desire of the Class of 1883 to leave an appropriate memorial. Volume I, issue 1, was well received and still stands as a good example of a student publication. In 1886 the Commencement issue ran to a thousand copies and contained a very creditable coverage of President Seip's inaugural.

The Muhlenberg Monthly, later changed to *The Muhlenberg*, compares favorably with publications of other schools, older and larger. Editorials, with few criticisms and no clashes but numerous suggestions, literary articles by professors and students, and alumni notes dominate. All in all, the literary publications give a good impression of the College from the inside during twenty-five years.

A dignified status for organized athletics was not recognized in the nineteenth century. The lure of gate receipts, the inspiration to "die for good old Alma Mater," requirements for brawn, yards gained, and touchdowns in high school were not recognized as competition with high I.Q.s for admission. Organized gymnastics were emphasized only slightly except for lectures on good health secrets. It was up to the student to get exercise: walking, rough-housing, touch football, and boxing. There was no place in the College budget for stadiums, gymnasiums, uniforms, and equipment. A high-spot event that by some stretch of imagination might be listed under athletics was the faculty-student baseball game.

Existing evidence does not establish the faculty at Muhlenberg College as outstanding. Compared with other church-related small institutions, it was no more than ordinary. However, it should be remembered that graduate schools in this country were few in number. On the credit side, many who trained for the ministry, in the fashion prescribed at Halle, were well versed in subjects other than theology. Several were highly intelligent and could perform creditably through self-education. Records indicate that on the faculty before 1900 there were twelve D.D.s (predominantly honorary), eight M.A.s (also predominantly honorary), and three Ph.D.s, one from the University of Pennsylvania and two from New York University.

Finances proved the Achilles' heel, both before and after 1900.

Pangs of poverty can and do produce sterling qualities. Lack of funds not only limited material accomplishments, but also imposed low salaries and heavy teaching loads. Some taught courses in the Preparatory Department as well as in the College. The list of subjects taught is appalling. President Muhlenberg taught Greek, mental and moral sciences, evidences of Christianity, rhetoric, English literature, and political economy.

An additional matter pertaining to finance and the College future was the appointment of the Reverend Charles J. Cooper as treasurer and business manager. He was not a graduate of a business college but he did his work admirably. The report given to the Board of Trustees at the twenty-fifth anniversary meeting was short, concise, and revealing: really a new experience. He was able to relieve Administration and faculty of duties such as collecting funds, keeping accounts, and supervising management.

The turn of the century was no more a breaking point in the history of the College than it was in the records of time. Changes, at first indistinguishable, increased, and some, both good and bad, faded away or were absorbed. The physical setting of the College was not impressive, confined as it was to a city block without room for expansion. This very well might have created a dead end for a greater Muhlenberg, but a few people with sufficient foresight saw the problem and, taking a risk, did something about it.

Great things were in store as the new century arrived, and progress had been made in preliminaries. In spite of poverty and lack of facilities, notable advance was apparent in the student body and faculty, and a start came in creating a stimulating College atmosphere.

4

On a Charted Course

CELEBRATION of the Quarter-Centennial of Muhlenberg College gave an opportunity to assess, reminisce, and predict. In limitless time, twenty-five years is only a part of one generation. Some founders of the College, many former students, most of the faculty, past and present, and both ex-Presidents came to view the fruits of their efforts, bask in the glory of reality, and dream of what was in store. Dr. Frederick Augustus Muhlenberg reviewed the background and Dr. Benjamin Sadtler outlined what he thought an education should include. It was a legitimate exposition of satisfaction and hope. However, contemporary opinion is not always dependable.

From the vantage point of time and with temperate regard for sentiment, Muhlenberg's first quarter century was mainly an exposition of objectives, aims, and ideals. The celebration speakers presented plans reaching for the stars. What they said was a revelation to many, propagated renewed faith in religion, and engendered expectation of miracles. Renewed effort kept hope alive when there was little for the senses to realize and provided an attraction for leaders in whose hands implementation rested, for churchmen in the Synod who needed persuasion, and for possible benefactors. Also, it was an allurement for prospective students who had visions of grandeur: future ministers, lawyers, doctors, and presidents.

As a matter of cold fact, there was little more than promise based on faith and determination, and many disappointments were in store. What could be done when available means fell far short of heartfelt desires? Well-trained teachers at established institutions found little to attract them to Muhlenberg, with its poor library, no modern laboratories, inadequate living and teaching space, excessive teaching loads, and burdensome extracurricular assignments.

Actually, patience and ultimate signs of progress can add to the credit and glory prevalent in most worthwhile pioneering. If there had not been dreams, prayers, and patient effort, even by only a small minority, Muhlenberg College would not be what it is today.

Assessment of progress provided a soothing antidote for disappointments. Muhlenberg College, in its origin and struggle for existence, embodied ideas transplanted from the University of Halle by Henry Melchior Muhlenberg and was a part of the development of Lutheranism in the New Republic. Furthermore, the College became an important factor in a national trend in education.

Dr. Seip's apprenticeship for the Presidency of Muhlenberg College was unusual. He was an enthusiastic student and a proficient scholar in classical languages, thus following a precedent set by his two predecessors and continued by a successor. The Civil War forced him into military service, which he accepted with characteristic energy and enthusiasm. After the battle at Gettysburg he volunteered for the United States Commission for Military Hospitals, visited battlefields, and participated in General Sherman's March to the Sea. The effectiveness of his work was demonstrated when a mortally wounded German soldier, in appreciation of Dr. Seip's services, made a substantial bequest to the Lutheran Orphans' Home in Germantown. Furthermore, sermons were preached to German soldiers in their own language. Many of these acts of kindness made friends and later brought contributions to Muhlenberg, when news of Dr. Seip's Presidency became known.

He had entered the first class at Philadelphia Seminary. He proved to be an excellent student, found time to give lessons in organ and piano, and taught part-time at Rugby Institute in Philadelphia. During vacations he served as supply pastor, and showed another of his talents by organizing Ladies Aid Societies in most of the Lutheran parishes in Lancaster County.

The last term of the Collegiate Institute in Allentown afforded Dr. Seip an opportunity to teach, little knowing that in a short time he would serve Muhlenberg College at the same location. He was closely associated with President Muhlenberg, taught Greek, German, English literature, and filled a vacancy in mathematics. He served as Secretary to the faculty until elected President (1886), was head of the Academic Department until 1872, and was designated by the Board of Trustees to solicit funds. Hundreds of families were visited and numerous sermons preached. Very few parishes in the Synod were not visited; Muhlenberg College was familiar to most Lutherans because of these contacts. The sum of $33,000 was collected in one year and five months and the Mosser-Keck endowed Professorship in Greek Language and Literature provided another accomplishment largely due to his efforts.

Dr. Seip's background covered practically every type of experience that was useful in preparation for his lifework. Everything he did was performed with such enthusiasm that success was assured. Greek was a favorite study, and in spite of a busy program, he never gave up its pursuit.

His working relations promoted mutual respect between Muhlenberg College and the Ministerium of Pennsylvania. He served on the examining and executive committees, as a delegate to the General Council, and, for two years (1895–97), as its President. Truthfully it can be said that the College was no longer just a hat-in-hand beneficiary; through its President much needed support was given to the Ministerium. Dr. Seip's multiplicity of activities—secular, local, and national in character—raised the stature of the College appreciably.

Another prominent inscription in Dr. Seip's epitaph is recorded in mortar, stone, and spacious grounds; a rescue from the limited quarters at Fourth and Walnut Streets to the new campus in the West End of Allentown.

The first location was looked upon by the College's founders as not just temporarily adequate but as a permanent home for the foreseeable future. Allentown, at the time, was only a small city; the five acres of land, beautifully situated in a natural setting, were pronounced ideal. Improvements left by the Allentown Seminary and Collegiate Institute with dormitories for a hundred students, a president's home, and classrooms were there when the College took over.

Within a quarter century very few realized that this location, so highly cherished, would prove inadequate. Moreover, this very environment was considered a serious handicap to the College's future. First mention of need for a new setting met with skepticism and disdain. Dr. Seip issued a plea and a warning in the introduction to Ochsenford's *Quarter-Centennial Memorial Volume* (1892). "While we have educated many most excellent scholars in the past twenty-five years under the present limitations as to building and equipment, and can educate many more in the future under the same limitations, if God so wills, still our sphere of usefulness can be greatly enlarged, and the Church reap richer harvests if the sowing and planting were on a more liberal scale, if the College plant and equipment were larger. . . .

"We have in view at present a suburban property of over one-hundred acres, beautiful for situation, conspicuous from every point of view, accessible, and in every way suitable and ample for all the future requirements of the institution. . . . From time to time, building after building could be added, as the growth of the institution and liberality of its friends permitted. . . . Thus the past, with all its traditions so dear to the old college student, would be linked with the future with all its hopes and possibilities of development. What an opportunity for the princes of Israel, the rich men of our Church, both to do good perpetually with their money, and to erect for themselves monuments more lasting than brass and more sublime than the royal structure of the pyramids.

"May God move the hearts of some of His servants to signalize this quarter-century year, not only by the debts, but by devising liberal things for the speedy development of this larger sphere of usefulness for Muhlenberg College."

We do not know the extent of his quest or the number that worked with him before plans for a new setting were brought to light. There were grumblings, voices of dissent, and lamentations. However, in this instance, favorable response from most important sources came quickly and emphatically.

A spokesman for the Ministerium declared: "The old Mother Synod's self-respect was at stake. It could no longer do its educational work in an out-of-date building without inviting the contempt of the public. It had to enlarge its equipment or forfeit its self-respect. . . .

"Another reason for change is the Synod's debt to Reformation history. The Reformation was born in a University and the most distinguished schools in the world today are found in Lutheran lands. The Synod owes it to her mother to be like her and to follow in her footsteps. If it hides its educational light under a bushel, or permits it to shine dimly, it forfeits the right to be named after the mother it professes to love."

Support for a new location grew as opposition died. What the Synod did was an outstanding factor in quick realization. This did much to erase early indifference toward Muhlenberg College and set a good example; it also initiated an increased interest among church-related institutions.

The Synod established a Central Committee, composed of the nine conference members, to take charge of College affairs. Through appeals, $200,000 was subscribed and the Philadelphia English Conference furnished the west wing of the new Administration Building.

The move to the new location (1904) was quite an affair—a combination grind with headaches and sore muscles, within a carnival spirit. It must be remembered the new campus was beyond city limits, with only a few farmhouses and a vast expanse of open fields and wasteland; there were no public transportation facilities. With a true pioneer spirit, albeit without Conestoga wagons (although they could have used a few), Kentucky rifles, or Indians, there was real adventure, especially for the students who took part and for those who saw further fulfillment of hopes.

There were sentimental tears, nostalgic stories, and reverent last looks at the old home about to be deserted. The new place was not a paradise—an Administration Building surrounded with scaffolding, an uncompleted dormitory, and a combination powerhouse and chemistry laboratory. There were less than a hundred students, and only ten professors—no more than were adequately

33

cared for in the old location. But it was part of the vision of the future and gave prestige and hope.

Preston A. Barba, a student who took part in the moving and the first occupant of the dormitory, records his reactions:

Hardly a man is now alive (said the poet in quite another connection) who remembers being a freshman at Muhlenberg College in the year 1902. The students were no longer happy in the dismal dormitory rooms at 4th and Walnut streets, with their upper and lower bunks where sleep was frequently interrupted by invading members of the *Cimex Lectularius*.

But great changes were in the offing. Persistent rumors were about to become reality. The Trustees had purchased fifty acres of farmland somewhere west of Allentown, whose limits were then 17th Street.

On April 20th, 1903, ground was broken for the main building, and on June 18th the cornerstone was laid in the presence of the President, Dr. Theodore L. Seip, the Trustees, and dignitaries of the Lutheran Church. On June 24th, 1904, the President-elect (Dr. Seip having died November 28th, 1903), was installed and on the very next day the main building was dedicated, with the program concluded in the grove just north of Berks Hall. But neither of the two buildings was completed.

The College year 1904–05 opened in the old building. Students and faculty waited impatiently to take possession of the new quarters, but it was early winter before the power house was ready to function with light and heat. There was no official moving day, but some time shortly before the Christmas recess classroom furnishings and equipment that were not discarded, and the library, were gradually removed and taken to the administration building.

Before the Christmas holidays the students were given their choice of rooms in the new dorms. The writer was then a student resident of Allentown. Upon the death of his mother in 1904, the household was broken and discontinued, and so it was that during the Christmas recess 1904–05 he took such of his home furnishings that could be used and moved them into his new quarters. When the other students returned on January 3, 1904, he was already settled in 105 West Berks and only later fully realized that he thus came to be the first student to live in the new dormitory of "Greater Muhlenberg."

For the students, coming for the most part from simple homes,

34

now living in Berks Hall, in a beautiful new study with open fireplace, an adjoining bedroom, and hot showers nearby, was indeed sheer luxury. And to look from his study windows over billowy fields of farmland and the distant South Mountain, a lovely landscape not yet cluttered with new houses and automobiles, was an inspiring experience that lured to introspection and self-appraisal.

What then did the student receive and what remains from those ancient days? Little more perhaps than curiosity, awe and reverence instilled in him, but these have remained his steadfast companions down through the years.

All this—and much more—we remember, for was it not but yesterday that we lived in 105 West Berks?

A college with prestige must have more than buildings, grounds, and a President. Ochsenford's record, published in 1892, listed the names of teachers, benefactors, and one hundred and ninety-six graduates with "distinction." Memory of a few has survived in one form or another. Here are some of them: Davis Garber, Matthias Henry Richards, William Wackernagel, George F. Spieker, Edgar Fahs Smith, and N. Wiley Thomas. The names of ninety members who served on the Board of Trustees were listed. Included also were names of two hundred and seventy-four graduates, with photographs, and a forty-three-page listing of nongraduates. There are prominent names, notable accomplishments, and praiseworthy statements of aims and objectives. However, from a vantage point which brings into focus institutions of learning generally, Muhlenberg cannot be credited, on the basis of realities, as particularly outstanding. This does not in any way detract from what was done under stringent circumstances and actually provided a good foundation for workers who followed. The sum total is a Muhlenberg College that can stand on its own merit; a promising institution.

Dr. Seip's eventful career ended suddenly with his death on November 27, 1903. He was beloved, respected, and dependable. His career was fruitful and plans for the future were ever present and constantly growing. People were trained under his tutelage, but, as is generally the case, no adequate substitute was immediately available. The Reverend William Wackernagel was made Acting

35

President; not an envious position and not a healthy situation for the College.

The role of college president, as we know it, is essentially an American contribution. European colleges, particularly in England, were administered by boards of directors, with presidents or executive officers acting as liaison between faculty and directors. Conditions on this side of the Atlantic made such a practice impractical. Directors were not available or were too engrossed in other things to be effective. Consequently, there was an authority vacuum which the president had to fill. He served two groups, board and faculty, and was, in a real sense, the leader of both.

Eight of the nine first colleges in America were founded by religious groups. The Harvard University seal includes *Christo et ecclesia* (for Christ and Church). Before the Civil War nine-tenths of all presidents were trained for the ministry. Dependency for funds, students, and leadership was through religious contacts. While ministers were principally chosen as presidents and administrative officers, a change took place in composition of boards, with the selection of lawyers, bankers, and businessmen. A projection of the trend nationally shows that by 1930 only 7 per cent, compared with 39 per cent in 1860, were clergymen. Muhlenberg College reacted to the change more slowly but in some respects more fortunately than others. Again, looking into the future, the wholesale shift to secularization and to professional educators, trained in the new discipline, had some unfortunate consequences.

The terrific burden placed upon the president was, and still is, everywhere evident. Dr. Seip's career was a living manifestation. Only a man with diversified talents, with proficiency in all, could have done what he did. He made some progress in securing assistance—the Reverend Charles Jacob Cooper as Business Manager, an Academic Dean, a part-time Chaplain, and a Librarian eased the burden and made the task of his successor easier. Nevertheless, filling the void created by Dr. Seip's death was a difficult task.

For several months the search continued. At last a decision was reached (1904) in the choice of Dr. John A. W. Haas as fourth President of Muhlenberg College. With evident confidence and general satisfaction the following introduction was made to the Board of Trustees:

"Dr. Haas is forty-one years of age, with the best years of his life before him and a capacity for Biblical scholarship of the highest rank and for hard practical work in the executive line, which are extraordinary. He combines in himself the accomplishments of the learned scholar, the popular orator, and the personal and warm-hearted friend."

The *Muhlenberg* recorded: "The new incumbent seems a man well adapted to assume control at this critical step in the College's history and doubtless will imbue it with additional vigor for its advance with other institutions of a similar nature. . . . With such a personage at the head, the dim future of a greater Muhlenberg brightens."

Dr. Haas had an impressive background. He was a graduate of the Episcopal Academy in Philadelphia, the University of Pennsylvania, and the Lutheran Seminary at Philadelphia. In line with what would have pleased the early American Lutheran Church Fathers, he studied Philosophy at the University of Leipzig in Germany. He served two parishes in New York City, took an active part in editing the *Lutheran Cyclopedia*, and published two scholarly books—*Bible Literature* and *Biblical Criticism*—before assuming duties at Muhlenberg College.

5

"Now We Have Become a College"

As the nineteenth century faded and the twentieth dawned, Muhlenberg College was in a new location—although the campus was an open field except for four unfinished buildings—and it had a new President, Dr. John A. W. Haas.

The pioneer spirit must have been strong in the young President: he was brilliant, well educated in this country and abroad, accustomed to a metropolitan environment, in charge of a large congregation with a beautiful church in New York City, and used to being near libraries where his intellectual interests could be pursued. He certainly envisaged building a chapel, foresaw the challenge, and relished the possibilities of guiding a struggling young institution into maturity.

It was evident that he would promote innovations but those in fear of revolution soon were calmed. His inaugural address was not a glorification of the past or a promise of predestined glory. It was neither lamentation nor plea for sympathy, but a statement of principle and plans. Some who listened were disappointed and many were skeptical. Could this seemingly uninspiring person grapple with the demons of poverty and a Herculean task that could not be avoided?

He presented a clear-cut picture of purpose: "A graduate of Muhlenberg College should have the intellectual foundations well and broadly laid, the aesthetic sensibilities carefully and soundly adjusted, the intrinsic moral character strongly and harmoniously developed, and a religion truly chastened, sound, and honest." Relations between College and Ministerium, which he believed so important, were defined. "But now in the greater change of surroundings and equipment, in the larger demands of the present, in the growth of greater ideals of the Church, there is a call, not unjustified, for more marked progress and change. Such a call, however, needs to be taken up not as a quick inspiration, which shall work revolutions, but which shall hasten further evolution. . . . The Ministerium ought never to forget its child, but it ought not to so dominate it that the real freedom and highest development of the child is dwarfed." He further urged: "If the Church hampers true advance, or if my policy shall seem disadvantageous, then it is time for this presidency to cease."

Thus began a career destined to last over three decades (1904–36). During the long years of distinguished service Muhlenberg College history cannot be dissociated from Dr. Haas's personality, actions, and appearance. With the possible exception of Dr. Frederick Augustus Muhlenberg, there was no more profound individual influence on the College than Dr. Haas.

His personal appearance was unusual. He was bald, diminutive in size, and had a carefully trimmed goatee; he often dressed in a Prince Albert coat and striped pants. Except in guarded moments and to strangers, he was flamboyant, impractical, almost erratic, abrupt, and intolerant. There was a disarming disregard for established rules and regulations, and even for those who knew him well there were moments of expectancy that some colossal blunder would ruin everything. Faculty meetings were unpredictable and lacked democratic procedure. On one occasion, after a long discussion and an impressive affirmative vote, Dr. Haas declared vehemently: "It won't work" and dismissed the matter completely. In his later years, his class performed more like cheering sections at football games, without rhyme or reason in content or procedure.

But these were extreme and off-the-cuff demonstrations. The other side of his character was kindly, serious, and impressive. In the pulpit and on the platform he was a dynamo, a fount of learning, and unusually persuasive. The accomplishments of his long career demonstrate sound objectives; he was not just a devotee of luck and blind optimism. He had an abiding faith in God, an abundant self-confidence, and was stalwart in defense of principle and loyal to those in whom he had confidence. The number of sermons preached, classes taught, public lectures delivered, and articles and books written was prodigious. He served as College Chaplain for many years and taught courses in religion and philosophy. As late as 1916, a report to the Board of Trustees indicated a teaching load of twelve hours a week; again in 1925, seven; and in 1931, four. He wrote and published seven books in a ten-year period.

While Dr. Haas's technique was paternalistic, he sought and followed advice from friends, Board of Trustees, alumni, and faculty. When he took office there were only four buildings, ten faculty members, and just over a hundred students. He implemented and presided over changes which required a break with traditions and commitments and gradually moved the College into a new orbit. He represented both the traditional and modern. There were few sudden changes, but improvements were made in curriculum, administration, faculty, student body, physical plant, and athletics. He presided over the transition from a small, provincial, denominational, ultraconservative (things which caused many church-related institutions to close) College to a modified liberal arts institution. If it had clung to outmoded concepts with disregard for elements of progress, the College would not have emerged, at least not so painlessly, into what it is today. The fact remains that in a crucial period in the history of Muhlenberg College, Dr. Haas was a fortunate choice as President.

The President's responsibility as teacher consumed much time but this was common practice in church-related colleges. His course, required of seniors, was a summation of moral and intellectual philosophy intended to climax a general preparation for life: to set the pattern of thought, summarize the problems, and fortify against heresy. In summation, to provide a reconciliation of Enlightenment (reason and natural law) with sound and acceptable Judaeo-Christian concepts, and to harmonize or influence an age impregnated with evolution and technology. Dr. Haas as preacher, teacher, and author advocated "a return to orthodox Christianity in order to resist brute world force, embattled nationalism, mercenary human culture, and selfish commercialism."

Necessity for a well-trained faculty became increasingly important. Here the church-related denominational institution faced a challenge. Formerly, competence and training in particular fields were overlooked when religious beliefs, theological training, and honorary degrees were accepted as sufficient. Several church schools failed because they clung too closely to strict denominationalism and religious training. They could not fulfill the demands of a changing society and were unable to exist solely on church patronage and contributions. Muhlenberg moved slowly but persistently in a fashion that ensured survival and attainment of success.

Considerable emphasis on qualification for faculty members was expressed by the Board of Trustees. No positive statement of requirements was recorded, yet the general agreement was that faculty and administration should be Christians, not necessarily Lutherans. The Charter (1891) stated: "One of the duties of the faculty is to teach regularly and fully the doctrine of the Lutheran Church." However, there was expressed opposition to Roman Catholics, Jews, and Unitarians. Evangelicalism as a requirement was revoked when it was learned that a highly respected faculty member was a Quaker and would thereby be disqualified. There was no stated opposition to non-Lutheran students. However, Lutherans were given preference in admission but, at times, in the student body they were only a slight majority. Non-Lutherans from the beginning gave distinguished service to the College. Dr. Reuben J. Butz, a member of the Reformed Church, was President of the Board of Trustees for many years.

Muhlenberg College was never completely lacking in well-trained and distinguished faculty members. Early examples were scientists, partly explainable because of the Asa Packer endowed Professorship. Dr. Haas came with an earned Doctor of Philosophy degree, and Dr. Ettinger, before him, had a Ph.D. from New York University. Dr. Robert C. Horn, although his advanced degree was not received until 1926, served many years and in many capacities: Dean, Assistant to the President, Acting President, and distin-

41

guished teacher and scholar. They were an indispensable trilogy among the college personnel.

Dr. Haas maintained a staunch search to improve the teaching staff, careful in choice but relentless in support of anyone selected who proved himself worthy. On one occasion he remarked, after the Board of Trustees had approved the appointment of three new faculty members in whom he had special confidence: "Now we have become a College."

Demands for advanced training from industry, medical schools, and other disciplines indicated that the science department was inadequate in teachers and laboratory equipment. There was hesitancy and latent opposition to science from many clergymen because of abhorrence of evolution and the persistency of a few but vocal advocates of a conflict between the scientific and classical approaches to learning. Generally, the supporters of liberal arts saw danger in scientific intrusions. According to existing records, there was no heated discussion within the Board of Trustees; Dr. Haas was encouraged and supported in an effort to make desirable changes. The extent to which the Ministerium, Board of Trustees, and President edged forward in promoting science in the College curriculum and adequate facilities to teach it—ahead of general feeling in faculty, student body, and general public—was a praiseworthy accomplishment. Its significance in the history of Muhlenberg College is beyond doubt; also a good reason for its continuance as a church-related liberal arts college of note, when dropouts among similar institutions were numerous.

Changes in attitude toward accepting science in the curriculum were underway before Dr. Haas's term of office began. As indicated, mathematics was highly regarded and generally considered in the same category as the classics. Some instruction in scientific matter was given in lectures labeled in the catalog as English. In 1882 the Board decided that students could take science, with parental consent. Degrees of Bachelor of Science were conferred in 1883 and 1884. Three years later, the faculty called attention to the fact that Muhlenberg graduates were not properly prepared for medical schools and proposed a greater degree of emphasis in science.

Dr. Haas, in his inaugural address, gave expression to the value of natural science "to men living in the twentieth century." He did however, make a significant reservation that "certain studies in Anatomy and Histology . . . cannot be taught successfully in a college." Since evolution was closely related to science, his opinion was noteworthy. "I accept the process of evolution, but not that everything started with evolution; that man was purely a material being—the divine spirit in man must not be ruled out. . . . Christianity can allow an evolution as the continuation of creation."

The need for change was obvious. The courses at Muhlenberg were taught principally through lecture and demonstration rather than by laboratory experimentation and by teachers who were primarily naturalists, important for cultural purposes, but not sufficient preparation for graduate courses in natural science. A scientific revolution came with provision of new equipment and personnel. A modern science building was erected (1926) and well-trained teachers, including John V. Shankweiler, George Brandes, Ira Zartman, and Luther Deck were engaged. These men needed support in a new adventure and equipment with which to work. They received both.

Changes, somewhat less sensational, came in other fields: John D. M. Brown in English; Preston A. Barba, Harry H. Reichard, and Anthony S. Corbière in Modern Languages; and Henry R. Mueller and James H. S. Bossard in History. These, and of course many others to follow, gave new life to the faculty, the heart of the College.

The aims and objectives of any college, upon which the curriculum depends, are in essence a commitment to society and to students. They are difficult to phrase, must be constantly reconsidered, and must contain a promise of success. The curriculum, by nature and necessity, must be realistic, yet illusive; meaningful, but intangible; constant, although variable; and specific, but indefinable. It includes a listing of courses, requirements for graduation, and rules of procedure. Yet, if it is only these, it is wholly inadequate, just a matter of routine; an accumulation of credit hours and quality points for which a diploma is awarded.

A properly constituted and correctly implemented curriculum

results in a process, not an end in itself. Concepts change; old ones must be discarded and new ones introduced. The story of Muhlenberg College reflects a series of questions: was it to be an institution mainly for ministerial students? should it be strictly denominational? was the maintenance of a German culture in the Lehigh Valley a major purpose? and was it to be classical and nonprofessional?

Dr. Haas and his associates took an active part in formulating a course of study which pointed toward a College policy for the future. His position on making Muhlenberg a German center is typical of a general policy. He was a great admirer of German culture, especially philosophy and theology, and knew the language thoroughly. He was enthusiastic about the nineteenth century German cultural revival in America, being one of more than ten thousand Americans who studied in German universities. Freedom in teaching and thought—*Lernfreiheit* and *Lehrfreiheit*—was encouraged and practiced at Muhlenberg College.

However, enthusiasm was tempered and prejudice moderated to fit the occasion. German principles were adopted but not to the extent of domination. In his inaugural address he warned: "We are Americans, and English is our common tongue." In Allentown, the German spoken was a curruption of the two languages, and Germanic influences were found principally in social and occupational areas.

The College was deeply impregnated with classicism, and Greek and Latin continued to dominate the curriculum. There were recognized dangers that such limitations would impede demands arising from modern trends which called for teacher training, preparation for admission to graduate schools in law and medicine, and for service in industry. There was a growing resentment against emphasis on the "Dead Languages" as outmoded and unattractive to prospective patrons and students. This feeling was not new but it was growing in strength. Benjamin Franklin once remarked that "the study of Greek and Latin is a detriment to practical English education."

But classical studies were too well entrenched and too important to be eliminated. They were, and still are, too much a part of the liberal arts tradition to be obliterated. This idea is well expressed in Dr. Haas's rhetoric: "Greek thought and Greek spirit are best found through a medium of the Greek tongue. Nevertheless, even this study must be supplemented by reading in English to gain the wider understanding of what Hellas was and is for the world. . . . A certain knowledge of English should be a main requirement of entrance to college. . . . The ultimate best of real culture in American life is and will be the possession of undefiled English."

The extent to which the classics dominated the early curriculum is shown also in requirements for admission stated in the first catalog (1867). The candidate was expected to pass examinations in Caesar, Virgil, and Greek and Latin grammar. Gradual alterations followed, but the Muhlenberg curriculum remained close to the classical with emphasis on Greek, Latin, Mathematics, and Religion. College entrance requirement of Greek was dropped (1898), because it was no longer given in most secondary schools. In 1903, science students were allowed to limit Latin and Greek to the freshman year and were given the opportunity to substitute French for Latin. The elective system, still limited, was mentioned in the 1904–06 catalog. The degree of Bachelor of Philosophy (1909) required no Greek or Latin and extended the range of electives. However, the catalog announcing the change contained this appeal: "Muhlenberg College offers such courses based upon the study of masterpieces of Roman literature, as will afford an accurate and comprehensive survey of the character, the history, and the achievement of these wonderful people, the important part they played in the development of the human race and their contributions to the modern languages, literature, jurisprudence, and government in general."

Preprofessional work for law, medicine, and teacher training produced a challenge for curriculum architects and a threat to the original concepts of liberal arts. The changing society, which Dr. Haas recognized, would not support an institution of higher learning without more concrete practical training than cultural subjects alone could offer. In fact, although not openly recognized, the liberal arts, as originally conceived, were adequately handled by teachers without extensive training. But preparation for graduate

45

work in science and law needed background training. Science produced the greatest immediate challenge. The field was so broad and requirements for graduate school were so stringent that training at the undergraduate level had to be appreciably advanced in order to attract students. The manner and means in which Muhlenberg College met the challenge, not only in science but in other fields as well and without discarding the liberal arts, remains an impressive part of its history.

Teaching was one of the most responsible, far-reaching, and neglected of all professions. It was not highly rated or adequately compensated and the general attitude prevailed: "Those who can, do; those who can't, teach." Teacher training, when finally recognized and given status, made a threatening intrusion into the curriculum. In the first place, it was largely undergraduate and terminal. Secondly, politicians and harried legislators, in seeking a solution for certification, resorted to emphasis on methodology at the expense of subject matter.

Normal schools were established in Pennsylvania by act of the Legislature in 1857. Colleges, in need of students, added Normal Departments as appendages to the general curriculum. Muhlenberg College Trustees announced (1877) a teacher training program described "as the same as in our State Normal Schools." In 1893, the Department of Pedagogy was made a part of the regular course offering.

Meanwhile, state requirements for teachers, including those already in service, were upgraded. This created an additional demand for college aid outside the regular student body. An Extension Division was organized, with Professor Reese in charge. The Ministerium minutes recorded (1910): "During the past year a Saturday Course for Teachers has been organized at the College with fairly gratifying results. The matter is an experiment which, however, promises to be a successful undertaking and may mean a great deal for the institution in years to come." Nevertheless, the early years were not rewarding. In 1913 the Summer School had an enrollment of only twenty-five students and accumulated a deficit of $50. Not until Dr. Isaac M. Wright was made Chairman of the Extension Division in 1917 did the idea make headway. He

HENRY MELCHIOR MUHLENBERG, D. D.
The Patriarch of Lutheranism in America

HON. FREDERICK AUGUSTUS MUHLENBERG
The Statesman

GEN. JOHN PETER GABRIEL MUHLENBERG
The Patriot

GOTTHILF HENRY ERNEST MUHLENBERG, D. D.
The Pastor, Scientist

Four distinguished members of the Muhlenberg family

Frederick Augustus Muhlenberg   Theodore Lorenzo Seip

Benjamin Sadtler

Early faculty group. *Seated, left to right:* President Theodore L. Seip, Professor M. H. Richards. *Standing, left to right:* Professor John A. Bauman, Professor William A. Wackernagel, Professor David Garber

Laying the foundation stone of the Administration Building, 1903

MUHLENBERG COLLEGE,
Allentown, Pa., Sep 5 — 1904

Mr. P. A. Barba

To Muhlenberg College, Dr.,

To Tuition 121 Session   20 00
" Room Rent, Care, Heating,   -   -   -   -   8 80
" Material and use of Instruments in the Scientific Course.
" Deposit for Breakages in Chemistry, (The unused amount will
   be refunded at the close of the year.)   -   -   5 00

                                                           33 80

Received Payment, Sep 23 190 4
                                                    Treasurer.

Muhlenberg College,
ALLENTOWN, PA.

THE COLLEGIATE YEAR is divided
into THREE SESSIONS of 16, 14 and
9 week, (charges proportioned) making
an aggregate of THIRTY-NINE WEEKS
of Instruction, commencing on the first
Thursday of September, and closing on
the Thursday preceding the last Thursday
in June.

New STUDENTS are admitted at the
beginning, or at any time during the session, entering as a condition of admittance
always not less than half a session. No
deduction is made for absence or prema-
ture withdrawal or removal of a pupil
from the Institution.

PAYMENTS

The College charges of each term must
be paid in advance or satisfactory arrangements made for payment, before a student
will be allowed to recite with his class.
REV. C J. COOPER,
East Wing College Building, Treasurer.

Receipt for tuition and board, 1904

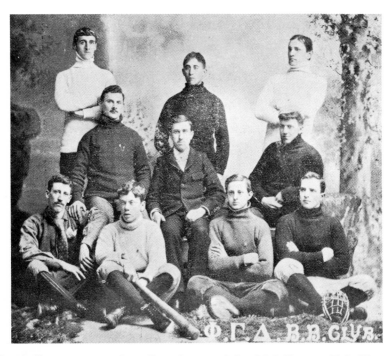

Baseball team, 1894. *Standing, left to right:* V. J. Bauen, F. S. Kuntz, F. W. Wackernagel; *seated, center:* W. O. Laub, W. J. Snyder, C. J. Gable; *seated, front:* O. R. B. Leidy, S. B. Anewalt, W. B. Brobst, N. T. Miller

Muhlenberg vs. Indians, 1906

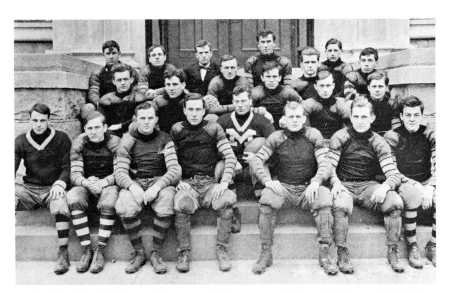

Varsity football squad, 1908. *First row:* Allen W. Butz, Karl L. Reisner, Clarence M. Snyder, James H. S. Bossard, John S. Albert (Captain), Curtis A. Miller, Paul M. Reed, Walter K. Hauser. *Second row:* Peter N. Wohlsen, William B. Shelly, Langhorne W. Fink, Albert C. H. Fasig. *Third row:* Charles Coleman, Roy F. Shupp, Edgar V. Nonamaker (Manager), John M. Aberly, Paul Putra, Warren M. Beidler, Edward M. Keck, Vincent L. Bennett, Harry P. C. Cressman

Muhlenberg College,

REV. T. L. SEIP, D.D., PRESIDENT.

Allentown, Pa., *December 18*, 190*3*,

DEAR SIR :

THIS IS TO CERTIFY, THAT *C. Ettinger*

of the FRESHMAN CLASS has received the appended notations in the several studies to which he attended, during the Session ending *to-day*.

The highest number given is 100 ; the lowest that will enable the student to continue with his class is 75. An average of 75 in each, Latin, Greek and Mathematics, is required for promotion to the Sophomore Class.

There is no report of conduct, unless the student has been guilty of some impropriety, known to the officers of the institution.

Absence from recitations, excepting on account of protracted illness, reduces the notation, unless such recitations are subsequently made up.

A report of absences is annexed.

LIST OF STUDIES.	NOTATIONS.	GENERAL REMARKS.		
Latin	90.2			
Greek	86.1			
German	95			
Algebra	63.4			
Geometry	72.5			
General Biology				
Zoology				
Physiology	83			
Physical Culture				
English *Grammar*	90			
Rhetoric *Literature*	88			
Essays	85			
Declamation	80			
Biblical History	90	**ABSENT FROM**	Excused.	Unexcused.
Universal History	90	Church		
		Prayers		
		Recitation . . .	4	

BY ORDER OF THE FACULTY,

Wm. Wackernagel, PRESIDENT, *pro tem.*

☞ The next Session will begin *January 5,* 190*4*,

Report card, 1903

The German Recitation Room

Euterpia Hall

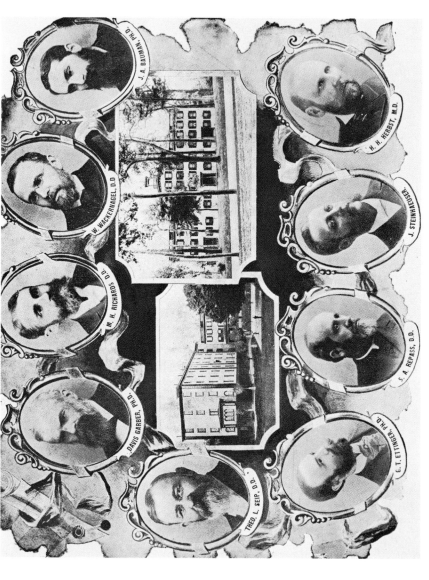

College buildings at Fourth and Walnut Streets and some of the faculty

did an outstanding promotional job in a ready market. Soon there were more students enrolled in the Extension School than in the regular College, with centers located in Hazleton, Slatington, Lehighton, Palmerton, Reading, and Quakertown. Perhaps no one phase of development expanded Muhlenberg College influence further and beyond its original intent than the Extension School. Also, it was a service to teachers caught in the dilemma of being technically unprepared for positions they already held, some with possible loss of status. In addition, there were financial gains for the College, although not as great as might be expected, and for the faculty, which was underpaid. One professor found the monetary reward for teaching in the Extension School so prosperous that he applied for sabbatical leave to devote full time in that field. It was not granted. The Extension School made it possible for women to attend Muhlenberg College; a degree was granted in 1920.

A darker side of the picture must be mentioned. Some faculty members benefited, but not all. Some did not teach popular courses and payment was made on the basis of enrollment. Also, additional duties were involved; several taught two evenings a week and Saturday mornings. The heavy teaching load—fifteen to eighteen hours in regular College and six hours in Extension—hindered effective teaching. Strong arguments persisted that the caliber of teaching and student response were far below College standards. Obviously, there were exceptions, but for both faculty and students extension work added to a heavy full-time job and made sacrifice, somewhere along the line, inescapable. Dr. Haas, in the annual message to the Board of Trustees (1929), lamented that Muhlenberg seemed to be developing into a teacher training institution.

Organized and intercollege competition in athletics provided one of the most controversial of all issues. There was widespread opposition, in the beginning, to all now well-established practices. Church-related colleges demonstrated a desire to remain aloof to athletics, as beneath the dignity of and dangerous and unbecoming to the gentleman and scholar. The spirit they planned and nurtured was steeped with pietism—mind over matter; the aesthetic over the worldly. Self-denial, frugality, and other-worldliness were so

47

firmly entrenched that opposition to change appeared insurmountable. Could the church-related college have survived under such conditions? However, gradual recognition of the need for change came slowly and, at first, unofficially. The brawny athlete eventually was accepted and, along with him, something new was added to the college program.

The old order either ignored or overlooked the fact it was dealing with youth, possessed with a competitive spirit. Some smarted under accusations of being sissy, secluded, and pampered. Physical education and gymnastics, under German influence, gained administrative and theoretical support, but were never popular among American students. To a growing element in twentieth century society, the College was too monastic, too secluded, and too impractical to be a positive drawing card.

The first catalog of Muhlenberg College announced impulsively: "It is our constant aim to combine study and recreation, mental labor and physical exercise, as not only to preserve but improve the health of the student, and harmoniously develop all the powers of both mind and body. For this purpose, a large playground has been set apart for outdoor exercise, and a gymnasium with suitable apparatus for recreation and amusement." A slight exaggeration of both content and purpose.

Financial allowance and equipment were far from satisfactory in most institutions. Haverford College, progressive in most respects, took this stand: "Exercise should be under direct jurisdiction of trustees—one hour set aside for breakfast and exercise." The Muhlenberg College catalog (1898) urged students to take advantage of recreational facilities. The curriculum (1899) contained a somewhat meaningless statement on physical education. The fact remains that gymnastics were unpopular—almost abhorred. They may have been good therapy but were bitter medicine—regarded as a physical task, job routine, or manual labor, they were performed without enthusiasm. Intramural sports, without supervision and poorly supported, had to await acceptance for another generation.

Intercollegiate contests were arranged without authorization and supervision and in disregard of rules and regulations. Students planned for contests played, as a rule, off campus, and when enough players were not available, solicitation for outsiders was a common resort. Just the same, these makeshift arrangements attracted larger audiences than other college functions. Princeton and Rutgers Universities played the first officially scheduled American college football game in 1869—others followed hesitatingly. The press began to take notice and gave more space to games than other college activities. Student publications urged more support and offered suggestions to Boards of Trustees—a grass-roots pressure was beginning.

Colleges were badly in need of students and financial support. Physical plants were expanded, better trained teachers were secured, and changes were made in the curriculum to meet new demands. Important as they were, there was still something lacking: student life was not inviting, alumni loyalty was almost nonexistent, and going to college was not considered a key to success.

In a strange and unpredictable way, organized athletics played an important role in promoting interest in colleges. Something new was on the move in the American scene. The Spanish-American war made the United States a world power. Technology and an accompanying materialistic point of view were forces in social well-being, and a powerful middle class arose, capable of giving financial support to institutions in a free society that promised acceptable benefits.

There was positive proof that colleges could not grow on existing resources. Athletics was not wholly responsible but did contribute and, in a real sense, rose to an importance that almost got out of control. President Theodore Roosevelt came to the rescue. An advocate of the vigorous life, soldier hero, big game hunter, and wielder of the "Big Stick" in diplomacy, he gave White House consent (1905) to college athletics, summoned coaches from Ivy League colleges and offered a blessing to their profession in a much publicized tribute to the "strenuous life."

Acceptance of athletics as a part of the college program caught on to an extent that not only surprised college authorities but also caught them off guard. Inherent and orthodox resistance faded. Athletics contributed a form of rugged competitive individualism generally in harmony with other trends. Ivy halls provided a haven for the athlete, a physical hero who could and did defy admission requirements, class assignments, and lack of funds but became a strange and welcome companion for the serious student. A factor too often overlooked was the athlete with brains as well as brawn— a solace for skeptics and a tribute to a good element in education.

Organized athletics did have a wholesome influence when properly administered. Good coaches insisted on standards which included scholarship, curtailment of rowdyness, drinking, and smoking. They demanded cooperativeness and loyalty which was not the general rule but still important.

The "founding fathers" gave lip service to physical training but were tardy in making proper provisions for it. As late as 1904, the athletic field consisted of two tennis courts and an open space, on which football and baseball players were allowed to practice. Competitive athletics was tolerated, when any opinion was expressed, rather than encouraged. In the early 1890's, without approbation of authorities, Muhlenberg College had fine all-college football teams which attracted much outside attention. Baseball players were encouraged by the Allentown Atlantic League and were coached by the famous Mike "Slide Kelly Slide." Yet the College Board of Trustees refused students permission to organize a baseball club "if said Club was to enter collegiate contests." The reason given was: "danger of too much emphasis on a few who made the teams, and the college amateur might be superseded by the professional." Some lived long enough to retort: "I told you so."

Pressure for favorable action came from many sources: students, alumni, faculty, and the press. The Board of Trustees received numerous student petitions. Stalling for time was obvious, but eventually, on October 23, 1900, in answer to an urgent petition signed by a large percentage of the student body and a few faculty members, it was voted "to allow engagements in intercollegiate athletics under regulation as observed by institutions of our grade." Professor William Reese was asked to be faculty advisor and to head a committee to draw up rules and regulations.

Results were not immediately encouraging. As late as 1903 there were insufficient students interested to form a team. Also the College earned a bad reputation in recruiting too many "ringers." One outstanding player showed up only on Saturdays to participate in games. A student reported that in order to meet requirements the player took occasion to enter the front door of the College building, cross the corridor and exit to the rear, with the remark: "If the question comes up I can truthfully say I went through Muhlenberg."

The new campus location made an athletic field possible, with gridiron layout, baseball diamond, and cinder track. Coaching was limited to volunteers and some were very successful. J. Walter Singmaster, a Gettysburg graduate, with the Reverend Charles M. Jacobs, Pastor of Christ Lutheran Church, as assistant, produced respectable all-college teams.

Dr. Haas did not take a positive stand—at least, none is recorded. However, he did recommend (1907) the appointment of a physical education director but he "was not to be a football coach. . . . No athletic coach be employed nor annually be re-employed by the Athletic Association, without approval of the faculty and endorsed by the Executive Committee." At the same time, basketball was given official recognition and the Assembly Hall in the basement of the Administration building was turned into a "basketball room." It was recorded in the Minutes: "Mr. FonDersmith generously paid for necessary paraphernalia which amounts to $184." He was given a rising vote of thanks. A full-time instructor was authorized with a salary of $125 per annum.

Expansion moved more rapidly and along lines which many, including Dr. Haas, did not approve. What amounted to a hands-off policy came close to disgrace and disaster. Trouble increased as gate receipts grew and popular approval and support exceeded all expectations. The will to win at any price and the rewards of victory were so great that temptation to get players went beyond restrictions.

The coach became one of the better known figures on the campus. This was acceptable if the proper type was procurable, but temptation was too great and tenure of office too precarious for proper controls. Problems seemed to multiply when salaries were attached. A few became first class liabilities: one was dismissed summarily during a school year. The Board of Trustees' action was embodied in a cryptic remark: "shall be relieved immediately but salary will be paid for rest of the year."

Board records do not shed much light on its attitude. There was considerable frustration as to proper action, since there was so much at stake. Not until June, 1911, when a set of regulations was voted, was positive administrative action taken. A student was declared "ineligible if deficient or conditioned in more than one subject." Ineligibility was to continue during the succeeding year. At the same time, an athletic fee of $5 was levied on each student.

Dr. Haas protested from time to time, but enthusiasm demonstrated at games and failure to take positive action were interpreted as support. He published in *School and Society*, which had a wide circulation, a statement against abuses in athletics. "I am honestly in favor of a college crusade against dishonesty and hypocrisy." A retort from an outsider was: "Why don't you begin housecleaning at home?" Dr. Haas did help to organize, and served as chairman of, a committee of college presidents, including Penn State, Haverford, Gettysburg, and Pittsburgh, to consider problems arising from intercollegiate sports. No reports or recommendations were made known. The general situation did improve at Muhlenberg, but for many years it was far from satisfactory.

Financial difficulties were ever present and never ending. The physical plant was inadequate, without a library, science building, gymnasium, or chapel. Dr. Haas knew additional funds were needed and was well aware of his own limitations and the magnitude of the task ahead. The businessman's language was foreign to him; sermons from the pulpit and scholarly books on theology were not enough. However, he remained on the job—refusing an invitation to become President of Chicago Theological Seminary (1915).

The first major campaign for $500,000 began (1915), after planning and pondering for ten years. The endowment fund at the time was only $180,000 and the physical plant was valued at

$187,000. Enough was raised to provide temporary relief. Salaries were increased,* the Commons was constructed (largely through aid from the Athletic Association), the powerhouse was enlarged, and dormitory facilities were expanded.

The Alumni Association functioned in only a limited fashion and on a volunteer basis. In 1911 an appeal was made to the Board of Trustees: "In view of the fact that the College has neglected its most valuable asset, the alumni, we strongly recommend that the Board of Trustees shall at once proceed to make such arrangements that a registrar can devote time to a systematic card index of every man who has attended Muhlenberg College and further attend to the task of regaining and restoring a sentiment of loyalty and true college spirit."

It should be noted the student body took active and wholesome interest in inaugurating and supporting ideas for college betterment. Mention was made of work done by literary societies in promoting dignified extracurricular affairs and in providing library facilities when the College had little to offer. Not until 1911 did the Board vote "to secure a competent Librarian" and that "he be empowered to expend a reasonable sum of money to provide a library for use of students." Professor Simpson was appointed Librarian at $75 per month as extra salary.

Fraternities played an important role on the campus—generally good but sometimes not laudatory. They provided a homelike spirit and relief from commonplace dormitory life. An exclusiveness was provided for kindred souls to find companionship. There were difficulties. Competition sometimes caused friction in the student body and lack of adult supervision, at intervals, resulted in

* The following table reflects the salary situation:

	1911	1916
George T. Ettinger	$1,500	$1,600
William Wackernagel	1,400	1,500
John A. Bauman	1,400	1,500
Robert C. Horn	1.500	1,700
Robert R. Fritsch	1,300	1,400
Harry D. Bailey	1,400	1,800
Stephen G. Simpson	1,000	1,300
James H. S. Bossard	900	1,300

laxity. An unhealthy relationship between fraternity and non-fraternity groups, or, as some considered it, between the "haves" and "have nots," produced rivalries and dissensions. By and large, however, fraternities did serve to add a sense of pleasantness to a few in the student body, which dormitory residents and commuters did not have.

Public demonstrations, other than athletic contests, were not conducive to outside interest. Commencement exercises, for example, were local and provincial. They were, from necessity, because of lack in facilities, held off campus: at St. John's Lutheran Church, the Lyric Theatre (posters advertising forthcoming burlesque shows were much in evidence), and the High School Auditorium. The 1908 Commencement included eight student speakers. Among these were: Latin salutatory, philosophical oration, speech in German, and the valedictory in Latin. Festivities began with the baccalaureate sermon on Sunday; after that came the President's reception for the senior class on Monday; the freshman class play on Tuesday; the junior oratorical contest on Wednesday; and Commencement on Thursday.

From time to time, various functions were held but they were limited in appeal to the general public. The two hundredth anniversary of Henry Melchior Muhlenberg's birth was on October 11, 1911. It was a matter of prime importance to Lutherans, but the College celebration was not enthusiastically planned or received. There was considerable uncertainty over what should be done. Finally it was resolved to use Muhlenberg descendants as key figures in the program: Dr. William F. Muhlenberg, son of the first President, brought family greetings; Dr. Henry Melchior Muhlenberg Richards represented the Pennsylvania German Society; and Dr. Haas paid tribute to the illustrious family and eulogized liberal arts education. The Board of Trustees voted to award honorary degrees to Emperor William II of Germany; Baron von Stamberg, German Ambassador to the United States; the Rector Magnificus of the University of Tübingen; Ex-President Theodore Roosevelt; Governor Woodrow Wilson of New Jersey; Ex-Governor Samuel K. Pennypacker of Pennsylvania; and Dr. William F. Muhlenberg.

Generally, discussion within the Board on granting honorary degrees consumed much time. It was not unusual to have twelve to fifteen likely candidates. Some designated for the honor did not appear. In 1914, William Jennings Bryan was chosen, but with the proviso he appear to receive the honor. He did not appear. At the time, precautionary measures were taken: "Unless at a celebration of peculiar and exceptional character, the number of honorary degrees at any regular Commencement shall, as a rule, be limited to five, other than honorary degrees of A.M. and M.S."

Muhlenberg College became a name spoken with reverence but it symbolizes cornerstones, not buildings; it represents ideas of the past, not always in conformity with the present. Few can identify Muhlenberg portraits if names are not attached. Part of the College celebration for the two hundredth anniversary of Henry Melchior Muhlenberg's arrival in America (May 28, 1942) was the dedication of a statue in memory of the flamboyant General Peter Muhlenberg, while patriarch, scientist, statesman, and even the first President were not so immortalized.

Such is typical of what history records: generals, wars, and victories or defeats. What the Muhlenbergs did for the College remains an illusive quality which is a part of the institution but only the physical substance is now obvious. The history of the College was not confined to one man, or even to a group of men. The "reign of Dr. Haas" was conspicuously altered before the end of his term. He belonged to the "old school" but made notable contributions. It is difficult to imagine anyone having done better, but times were changing. His last years in office substantiate this judgment.

6

The Charted Course Has Difficulties

THE twentieth century, although only slightly more than half-spent, has earned a reputation of wide contrasts: high hopes and utter despondency; prospects for lasting peace and prosperity but the reality of war and depression; high ideals seemingly about to be realized but marred by crime, obscenity, and anti-intellectualism. Liberalism began to challenge a long-enduring conservatism but what form was it to take and where might it lead?

Peace, in the minds of most Americans, was assured: a war affecting the United States was out of reason. Henry Adams wrote: "For the first time in 1500 years a true *Pax Romana* is in sight." World War I came as a shock: another piece of folly in which we would have no part. America would stay out; the Monroe Doctrine assured that privilege. President Wilson's election appeal for his second term included such slogans as: "Too proud to fight" and "He kept us out of war." But the war came and the impact on colleges and universities was immediate and desperate. Their clientele were the soldiers to be and campuses could become deserted. Young men, in and outside colleges, accepted the responsibility—they had no choice; duty called. Historically, older men are responsible for conditions that make war inevitable and sign treaties when fighting stops. Business has a chance to reap profits in a war economy and patriots have an opportunity to parade, yet it is the young men who must risk their lives.

The situation at Muhlenberg was not unusual. A quick response met the request for cooperation from the federal government. Faculty members expressed fear that the College would become a military barracks, which it did, but there was no alternative, short of closing shop. The Student Army Training Corps was initiated by decree and the campus was a military camp with a mobilized student body. Buglers announced the time to arise, eat meals, and go to bed. Administration and faculty, as well as students, took orders from army officers. Student offenders were court-martialed and class instruction was supervised. Aid to the war effort was appreciable but education suffered. Orders for the S.A.T.C. to abandon camp brought a deep sigh of relief. The Reserve Officers Training Corps, which followed, received slight response at Muhlenberg and was soon abandoned.

The hoped-for return to normalcy fell far short of expectations. For soldiers fortunate enough to return, disillusionment was general rather than exceptional. Many had been killed. The Unknown Soldier in Arlington Cemetery was a fitting memorial but a constant reminder of the futility of the cause for which he gave his life. Getting home and trying to forget the weird thing called war were uppermost, but home was different; the country had changed and normalcy was as much an unrealized dream as lasting peace.

President Woodrow Wilson tried desperately to establish an enduring peace but the Senate refused to ratify the Treaty of Versailles which contained the League of Nations Covenant. His words, in face of defeat, were prophetic: "I can predict with absolute certainty that within another generation there will be another world war, if the nations of the world do not concert the method by which to prevent it. What the Germans used were toys compared with what would be used in the next war."

The age, however, was not dominated by politics. Socially it is classified as "the roaring twenties"; a decade of laxity, organized crime, and moral degeneracy. Prohibition came and went—a futile effort in trying to moralize through legislation. The famous Wickersham Report (1931) contained words of desperation: "prohibition is unenforceable but should be enforced, a failure but should be retained." There were over one-half million arrests made in trying to enforce it.

Anti-intellectualism appeared in many forms but it had a particular relevance to colleges and universities. President Coolidge called them "hotbeds of sedition" and Upton Sinclair referred to them as "literary annexes to Wall Street." The college professor came to be known as an impractical "egg head."

The "roaring twenties" were not entirely demoralizing. In many respects the decade was a by-product rather than the real thing. Henry Ford's Model T, assembly line production, and a five-dollar-a-day minimum wage were earmarks of a continuing Industrial Revolution. Merchandising giants were introduced in The Great Atlantic and Pacific Tea Company and Woolworth's five-and-ten-cent stores. Aviation received a boost in World War I when Americans joined the ranks of "Aces," and later Colonel Lindbergh made a solo flight across the Atlantic Ocean and Admiral Byrd soared across the North Pole. American scholarship came of age, supported by various foundations. In 1923, Americans won Nobel prizes in astronomy, physics, and medicine.

Sports and athletics—collegiate and professional—were enthusiastically sponsored and accepted. Knute Rockne pioneered a high pressure "semiprofessional" practice on the campus at Notre Dame Universtiy which became the widespread envy and adoration of other institutions. The President of Texas Christian University admitted: "We had to go out and buy a football team. Otherwise, we could get no money for scholastic programs out of rich oil men." Heroes in sports catapulted to fame: in football, Red Grange and The Four Horsemen; in boxing, Jack Dempsey; in baseball, Babe Ruth; and in tennis, Bill Tilden. "Man-of-War" represented the animal kingdom.

Muhlenberg College, with Dr. Haas still serving as President, also struggled to return to normalcy and, like others, failed to see that it was neither preferable nor possible. In many respects, it was a turning point in Haas's career; he was older, less energetic, more determined, and not so alive to changing conditions. He did accomplish much along certain lines, perhaps more than expected, but other things that needed attention were neglected.

The need for more adequate facilities became imperative. The buildings originally erected on the new campus, to those with

58

vision, were never considered more than a beginning. Dr. Haas was assured the building program would continue; it was expressed as an urgent necessity in his letter of acceptance. Possibilities of expansion, with a chapel high in priority, were intriguing to the point of obsession.

Additional funds were a necessity. Accrediting agencies were critical of lack in facilities and endowment. The Education Department of the State of New York asked, as a prelude to recognition, for a library, gymnasium, and science building (a chapel was not included). The Ministerium increased its yearly subscription by $5,000 and the Rockefeller Foundation agreed to pay the same amount annually for two years. A campaign for $500,000 was set for 1919. The goal was not reached but a further effort for $1,000,000 was planned for four years later: $600,000 for a library, science building, and gymnasium; $400,000 for the endowment fund. The science building and library were completed, but at the cost of $820,000, far beyond the estimate and without a gymnasium. The total indebtedness of the College stood at $412,000.

Meanwhile, hope for a chapel grew with a gift of $125,000 from Mrs. G. W. Hartzell. Plans were drawn for a $375,000 edifice which was completed in 1931. The College Corporation sold $500,000 in bonds to cover the shortage. One year later, total obligations amounted to $628,000. The seriousness of this was crystal clear and overshadowed progress made in other fields. The student body continued to improve and grow; the faculty increased and was better trained; much needed buildings—library, science building, and chapel were realities—even though the price was high; recognition was accorded by leading accrediting institutions and Muhlenberg graduates were well received in institutions of higher learning.

Muhlenberg's financial difficulties were not unique among colleges; in fact, they were depressingly typical. It was not the first crisis, and although larger, was comparatively no more serious than others. Records of the Ministerium and the Board of Trustees show careful consideration and full support of an earnest desire to promote the best interests of the College. Earlier efforts were acclaimed because they succeeded and the risks were forgotten. Here was what appeared to be a logical and necessary sequence that came dangerously near wrecking the College and was not easily dismissed.

The Great Depression of 1929 was a most important factor in the crisis. A depression is never welcome and there is no desirable time for one to occur, but from the College point of view it could not have come more inopportunely—just when a large amount of money was needed. With indebtedness at a peak and sources of income and contributions drastically curtailed, it was necessary to halt all construction, cut salaries from 5 to 15 per cent, neglect repairs, and reduce scholarship aid.

There were bright spots on the horizon: the Depression did not last forever. Some worthwhile things were retarded but later reactivated. Important additions were made in the Administration. Dr. Horn served as Assistant to the President and when Dr. Ettinger retired became Dean. Professor Albert C. H. Fasig, in addition to teaching, was Alumni Secretary and general good-will ambassador. Gurney F. Afflerbach was Field Secretary (1921), Campaign Secretary (1925), Assistant to the President in charge of athletics, and later director of intercollegiate competition. The Reverend J. C. Rausch was made full-time Superintendent of Buildings and Grounds.

Alterations in the curriculum came slowly and electives were allowed cautiously. The number of required courses for science majors was reduced, providing opportunity for electives: geology and biology were made separate departments. Classics majors were given more freedom in choice of subjects. Further allowance was provided in the Bachelor of Philosophy degree (1909). However, as late as 1924, one-third of the freshmen class chose classics for a major.

The 1924 College catalog redefined the aims of a college education: "to lay a broad foundation in the subjects considered essential for a successful career in business or the various professions, while imparting the knowledge, the culture, and the training necessary for the solution of current problems in economics and business, as well as for the full and satisfactory performance of the duties of intelligent citizenship." Certainly this was a broadened concept of liberal arts.

History, for a long time, was given only minor recognition in the curriculum. History of religion, political economy, and philosophy instructors used it sparingly. Columbia University pioneered "The New History" in a Contemporary Civilization course, justified on the grounds that: "There is a certain minimum of . . . intellectual and spiritual traditions that a man must experience and understand if he is to be called educated."

A department of history was organized at Muhlenberg (1887), which included political science, sociology, and economics. There was overlapping in subject matter and instructors were called upon to give courses in many fields—obviously without adequate preparation. Not until after World War I were courses in history and political sciences raised to their deserved stature—principally the work of Dr. Henry R. Mueller, war veteran and Ph.D. from Columbia University. A History of Civilization course was introduced in 1927. A text in the subject was prepared and published by a member of the Muhlenberg staff; it was adopted by over thirty colleges and universities and is now translated into Hebrew, Arabic, and Hindustani.

The status of a church-related college and the extent to which non-Lutherans would be welcome were not clearly interpreted. It was fortunate for the future of the College that this was so. However, an early intent was to prepare men for the Lutheran Seminary in Philadelphia. Young men from other denominations were not attracted and the response of Lutherans came largely from the Ministerium of Pennsylvania area. In 1892, there were 296 graduates, of whom 172 were ordained ministers or in training. Need for a broader appeal became increasingly urgent for curriculum changes and faculty improvement.

The desire to keep Muhlenberg College church-related remained consistent, but not sufficiently strict to defy changing trends. Transformation of the curriculum from one dominated with religion courses, compulsory chapel, and strict observance of many practices purely denominational in character to a more liberal program gradually unfolded.

Religious affiliations were not listed as admission requirements. The catalog (1891) stated: "All students admitted must be of good moral character." There were, however, restraining influences and variable practices in the admissions office. Nevertheless, in 1925, Lutherans constituted only 50.75 per cent of the student body.

Dr. Haas's annual message to the Board (1928) demonstrated confusion bordering on desperation. He suggested that fewer Jews and Roman Catholics be admitted, "without creating any prejudice." He was clearly annoyed at articles published in the *Weekly* asking for fewer required religion courses and a lessening of conformity in religious practices.

Compulsory chapel was a particular target. Protests took the form of disorderly conduct during services: reading newspapers, carrying on audible conversations, forging names on attendance slips, and (somewhat infrequently) studying. Dr. Haas expressed the belief that much of the responsibility came from lack of proper religious influence at home. In a surprise move, compulsory attendance was abandoned (1925); almost complete abstinence from chapel services was the result. Required attendance was restored the following year, without comment.

Dr. Haas hoped that a new chapel building would solve all social problems. Meanwhile, the program in religion deteriorated. There was sporadic and grudging relaxation in requirements; watered down courses; and a disgusted indifference on the part of those in authority. The new chapel did not materially alter the situation: a great disappointment. Among other things, failure to get a promised gymnasium was blamed on the chapel, which was not in the budgeted building program.

Something that was long in taking shape, and a sign of progress when it came, was a student body organization. Little consideration was given to student opinion and responsibility for self-discipline. Student organizations, including early literary societies, even the *Muhlenberg Weekly*, were carefully supervised. The prevailing philosophy of those in authority was: students are in college to be taught. Sometimes student petitions were submitted to the faculty and Administration. A few were considered in faculty meetings, but as a rule they were filed without discussion, referred to committees, or ignored. If consideration was given, it came in statements from Dr. Haas, often printed in *The Weekly*. Gradually, after World War I, a change was noticeable—the requests increased and some were granted. A petition was accepted to allow each section of the dormitories to elect a representative to assist the Senior Proctor (appointed by the faculty). Request for an honor system (1905) was permitted, only to be rescinded at student request the following year.

A plan for student government was implemented by the faculty (1910), after a student petition. A Council was to advise the student body and interpret the constitution, but only on matters of discipline. Dr. Haas analyzed its function: "There are two directions in which the student body shall be called upon to consider in advance. One is for modification of the new rules in student government and for change in the authority of Student Council as to affect a greater sense of independence in moral issues, and a greater fearlessness in combating evils in student life. . . . The other direction in which advance must come, whatever may be the method, is a larger and more constant appreciation of the sense of honor in the student's individual work and in his stand for the college." The College catalog (1920), in a section labeled "government," had one sentence: "The Student Council, chosen by the student body, maintains good order in the College and dormitories, enforces proper conduct among the students, and disciplines any student who refuses to obey regulations." The *Cardinal and Gray Annual* (1921–22) added that "a special duty of the Council is to see that the faculty is informed of matters originating in the Student Body."

Extracurricular activities were encouraged, and, to the extent the physical plant provided, were supported by student body and faculty.

Debating, allied with public speaking, was organized (1922), and much to the credit of Muhlenberg, expanded rapidly to include intercollege competition. The Junior oratorical contest continued to be a major attraction. Specialized groups promoted cultural and social influences outside the classroom. *Deutscher Verein*, the handiwork of Drs. Barba and Reichard, was outstanding as a combination of fun and culture. *Phi Sigma Iota* represented the Romance Languages and was sponsored by Dr. Corbiere. The Pre-Medical Club with Dr. Shankweiler and the John Marshall Club with Dr. Mueller as leaders, encouraged students in medicine and law. *Phi Alpha Theta*, a national honor history society, elected Donald Hoffman of the local chapter National Treasurer, a position he still occupies with remarkable success. The Mathematics Club; *Tau Kappa Alpha*, oratory; *Eta Sigma Phi*, classical languages; *Alpha Kappa Alpha*, philosophy; and *Kappa Phi Kappa*, education, were active. The Mask and Dagger, Glee Club, College Choir, Mandolin Club and College Band were important in shaping student life and providing wholesome entertainment.

Two significant gifts other than general contributions to the general endowment fund, were made. The Florence T. Saeger grant of $50,000 to endow an English Literature Professorship was received and Dr. John D. M. Brown was the first recipient. The Reverend Dr. W. N. Rehrig's gift of $12,000 provided funds to bring prominent theologians as speakers to the campus.

Dr. Haas grappled with coeducation as he did with every problem, good or evil. There is little doubt he considered it unworthy, if not evil; he acted accordingly. Powerful influences, including tradition, the Chairman of the Board of Trustees, and the top echelon in the Ministerium, joined in his support.

Equality of the sexes is an age-old controversy. Next to voting rights for women, coeducation was one of the oldest and hardest fought issues in the battle of the sexes. Barriers to coeducation were not overcome easily but the trend was in its favor. Harvard, by 1890, allowed distaff graduate students to enter its halls of learning. Women were permitted to witness the Yale-Princeton football game in 1885. Oberlin College granted bachelor degrees to women in 1841. Antioch opened its doors in 1852, with coeducation fully accepted. Horace Mann, a "golden voice" in American education, at the opening ceremonies, had this to say: "Such separation is obviously unnatural and if it be necessary for the preservation of sexual purity, it is time the whole community should take alarm and hasten to devise a less monstrous system."

Reasons for change were not wholly sentimental. Women

proved themselves equal, and often superior, in various forms of intellectual aptitudes. Cautious experiments in annexes, often taught by the same faculty, were tried successfully at Harvard's Radcliffe, Columbia's Barnard, and Brown's Pembroke. Furthermore, co-education was taken for granted in the state schools. Finally, there was the little matter of finances and competition for good students that clinched the argument.

Stubborn resistance, tardy retreat, and ultimate surrender, not without protest, tell the story at Muhlenberg College. Dr. Haas believed the "gentlemen's agreement" with Cedar Crest College prevented Muhlenberg accepting women. It is true that Allentown Female College, later Cedar Crest, had been established ostensibly to take care of girls unable to enter Muhlenberg. Allentown Seminary was coeducational, at least in name. Actually it gave birth to two segregated institutions—one Lutheran, the other Reformed.

The Extension School, as previously indicated, provided opportunity for women to attend Muhlenberg; 415 received degrees by 1947. An attempt to found a Lutheran College for Women (1921) was supported by the Lutheran Church. One hundred and eighty-nine acres of ground, near Washington, D.C., were purchased and plans made to open a college by 1930, with an estimated enrollment of 1,000 students. A $1,000,000 campaign for buildings and $500,000 for endowment was announced. The Depression spoiled all hopes, except for a very few and the property was sold (1945) for $49,912.21. The funds were labeled for coeducation promotion, to be administered by the United Lutheran Church.

Numerous events, some comic, others tragic, came as preludes to final adoption at Muhlenberg. One, with elements of both, was the case of a young lady preparing to enter medical school and unable to get certain needed courses in the Extension Department. Arrangements were made to allow her to attend regular classes; allegedly, the first female regular student in the history of the College. While working in the chemistry laboratory, still located in the powerhouse, she was accosted by a fellow student with amorous intent. Charges against the culprit were made. The dilemma lay not only in the crime but also in the admission that a female student was enrolled in regular classes. Her status as a special student was revoked, ostensibly to protect her from further molestation. However, she was given credit for the course and granted a degree. Eyebrows were raised by those in the know and no doubt they felt further fortified against coeducation.

A formal plan to admit women was presented (1933) to the 186th Convention of the Lutheran Ministerium of Pennsylvania. "In view of growing demands on the part of women students who take Saturday and other Extension courses at Muhlenberg College to be privileged to enroll in the regular courses of the College, and also in consideration of our Lutheran constituents of Eastern Pennsylvania for a standard college for their daughters in close proximity to their homes; we hereby petition the Ministerium of Pennsylvania to request the Board of Trustees of Muhlenberg College to open their regular sessions to women students." Thirty ministers and laymen signed the petition.

Dr. Haas was adamant. He admitted need for a girls' school but declared Muhlenberg was not the answer, because of finances, the failure to instill loyalty even among men, and the "gentlemen's agreement" with Reformed churches in Allentown never to admit women. His powerful influence in the Ministerium was clearly demonstrated. Evidence in abundance shows that in 1934 there was little interest among those in authority to act on coeducation at Muhlenberg.

A lengthy refusal was prepared and adopted by the Ministerium. Conspicuous errors in judgment were shown, as was later demonstrated. A few can be mentioned here. "Our experience with boys of Lutheran faith over our own territory does not encourage us to believe there is enough intense loyalty toward Lutheran institutions among many of our people to warrant starting a coeducational policy to meet Lutheran needs. . . . Experience in other colleges has taught us that when a college has long existed for boys alone, the introduction of girls has not proved successful. . . . The present approved standard of Muhlenberg College might be endangered in the eyes of standardizing agencies. . . . Many of our alumni have quietly expressed their disapproval of any coeducational policy."

The Depression, always a convenient omnibus for objectors and joy killers, also was active. Financial resources of the Ministerium were drained to an alarming degree and education expansion logically could not be given priority over what were considered things more important. The soothing hand of time and a succession of changes in personnel and principles during two decades reactivated the issue, this time successfully.

A great tragedy in human endeavor is the inability to know when to retire. Obviously, age is not a dependable gauge, but it is the most convenient—exceptions to it are troublemakers. A notable commentator once observed: "Greatness depends pretty much on when you die." These extremes do not specifically apply to Dr. Haas, but his last few years as administrator dim his greatness. The College, spirit of the time, and personnel, all changed beyond his grasp of understanding.

He continued to serve the College well but progressively less effectively and with increased effort. The College grew but did not prosper. His brilliance resisted time and students and associates continued to appreciate his qualities. A well-earned sabbatical leave was granted (1929–30), which he spent in Germany. An impressive tribute was given (1937) by Muhlenberg College, the community, and the Ministerium. The alumni established a scholarship fund ($5,000) in his honor. He was given an honorary degree with the following citation: "He is a churchman and administrator, a distinguished author, philosopher, an earnest and powerful speaker and preacher, and above all, a successful and distinguished college president. It is particularly for his long and successful service as college president that we wish to honor him. Under his administration Muhlenberg College has grown and prospered: in size, scholarship, prestige, and honor."

His excellent collection of books, specializing in theology and philosophy, was given to the Library. Mrs. Haas gave a bequest of $50,000, the income from which was to be used to encourage worship in the Chapel.

In 1929, Teachers College at Columbia University was authorized to make a study of thirteen Lutheran institutions, later published in three volumes entitled *Survey of Higher Education for*

67

the United Lutheran Church in America. It expounds at length on questionable theories, but, at the same time, there are worthwhile comments. Muhlenberg fared rather badly compared with other colleges. In fact, all institutions covered do not make an impressive picture. A few remarks relative to Muhlenberg follow: "The operation of the College is virtually in the hands of the president, the treasurer, and superintendent of buildings and grounds. There is need for complete administration reorganization, new administrative offices, and redefinition of functions and responsibilities. . . . Muhlenberg has no administrative council."

The following suggestions were made: a full-time registrar; full-time business manager and one assistant; full-time director of health, physical education, and recreation; part-time dean of men; part-time director of research; and part-time physician should be added. "Permanent forms are lacking up to sixty-five per cent of items declared essential by the American Association of Collegiate Registrars. Muhlenberg has an improvised room which is being used as a gym. Since it has none of the attributes of a gym, the limitations are many. The most pressing problem on the campus is a new gym which will care for the entire student body. . . . Recommendations concerning the intercollegiate athletic situation cannot be made because adequate data were not supplied."

The report was presented to the College Board of Trustees with little comment and no immediate action. Copies were purchased by the Library, but little more was said or done. Dr. Horn, not given to adverse criticism in any form, wrote: "In my opinion we never made as much of it as it deserved."

Most of the problems, constantly increasing in number and magnitude, were inherited by later administrations. The successful way in which they were handled eventually is part of a fitting climax in the history of Muhlenberg College.

7

Growing Pains and Financial Burdens

THE most convenient and, in some respects, the most acceptable
way to write the story of an educational institution is to organize it on the basis of administrations. Presidents are given, for
convenience sake, credit or discredit, and there is no denying much
responsibility rests on their shoulders. The sunset of Dr. Haas's
career exposed needs for a new approach, as was the case when
he came on the scene. There was a change in command and a
significant one: from Dr. John A. W. Haas, scholar, theologian,
teacher, and idealist, but grown old in service, to Dr. Levering
Tyson, layman, not a renowned scholar and with little experience
in the whole college complex. Yet he had what was needed and
what Dr. Haas did not have—broad shoulders and a steady hand
to cope with temptations of artificial prosperity and another World
War. He knew the language and philosophy of businessmen and
marine sergeants. Although inexperienced in classroom and pulpit,
he knew how to handle administrative emergencies.

Changes, in the making before Dr. Tyson assumed responsibilities as President of Muhlenberg College, had to be confronted. The
laissez-faire concept of government was shaken and the welfare
state was on the rise. Great Britain went off the gold standard;
The Bank of the United States failed. President Hoover (1930)
assured the nation: "Business and industry have turned the corner,"
but an angry and depressed people went to the polls and elected
Franklin D. Roosevelt President of the United States.

As if the Depression had not been enough, storm clouds of war gathered in Europe only two decades after President Wilson gave warning. Hitler tore up the Treaty of Versailles and occupied the Rhineland. Mussolini invaded Ethiopia and defied the League of Nations. Franco brought the Republic of Spain to an inglorious end. Hemingway's *For Whom the Bell Tolls* could apply to Austria, Czechoslovakia, and Poland as well as to Spain. An uneasy world faced the future and Muhlenberg College was no exception.

Dr. Haas demonstrated his concern over college welfare and suggested to the Board of Trustees some recommendations concerning a successor: "My hope and prayer is you will secure a stronger man than I was, one with a larger preparatory knowledge and training in the specific problems of education, and one who is a thorough and convinced Lutheran churchman. He ought to win the Ministerium of Pennsylvania to his Administration, and at the same time he ought to be sufficiently broad to retain the good favor of the City of Allentown, and to be the able leader of the faculty in his scholarship, and a loving friend of the students."

The search was long and diligent before Dr. Levering Tyson was chosen. He was the first layman to hold the office but was an active participant in church affairs. A graduate of Gettysburg College and Master of Arts from Columbia University, serving the latter as Alumni Secretary, he was editor of *Alumni News* and organizer of home study work in the Extension Division. He was active in radio broadcasting, and had served as President of the Middle States Association of Colleges and Secondary Schools.

The inauguration ceremonies included a symposium on "What the Professions expect of the small Liberal Arts College." The chairman was Dr. Walter Jessup, President of the Carnegie Foundation for the Advancement of Teaching, and the program was broadcast over a nationwide network.

The speakers did not agree on a definition of liberal arts but joined in chorus that it was better than a technical training for any profession. Participants were principally from endowed organizations—Rockefeller, Carnegie, and Ford; only a few had teaching experience in a small college.

Dr. Tyson's expressions were cautious. "Today the liberal arts college is as important in the scheme of things as it ever was." There was no indication of desire to purge the principles but a wish was expressed that Muhlenberg develop a curriculum "to keep step with the world and inject into each student a spirit of inquiry to inspire him to seek new facts in the world about him." Such generalizations were orthodox and had been stated many times before: implementation was the immediate need.

Next to liberal arts, the role of the College as a denominational church-related institution was of prime importance. Here again a new spirit was in the air. Dr. Tyson's position was not defined clearly; however, he promised to support an educational policy to "meet onslaughts of propaganda machines and mundane principles of religious training, as a cardinal principle." "I am," he declared, "and always will be, a strong advocate of the denominational college and I do not object to the requirement of instruction in religion in all four years. But I maintain that in this particular period in world history it is important for a college graduate to have instruction in the fundamentals of economics and government. I believe we can affect the balance in the same way, retaining, of course, the religious instruction for which the College strives irrevocably, and at the same time, provide for instruction in the principles of economics for all students."

Everybody was in for new experiences: Dr. Tyson, the Ministerium, Board of Trustees, faculty, student body, and the Allentown community. No one could deny the theoretical need for such an experience but no one knew exactly what to expect.

The curriculum came in for immediate attention. One of the most persistent vestiges of the past was emphasis on the classics. Retreat began much earlier, and it gradually gained momentum. A decade before Dr. Tyson's arrival, one-third of the students were majoring in classics, but in 1937, only a very few, and two years later the classics were abandoned as a requirement. Greek and Latin were still available as electives for interested students. There were a few mourners but the change was welcomed by faculty and students, since most schools had taken such action a half century earlier.

A substitute for modernization had previously been made in the degree of Bachelor of Philosophy (Ph.B.), which did not require Latin and Greek but otherwise had the same requirements as A.B. in most colleges. At one time, the Ph.B. degree was awarded in several institutions, but it had long since been abandoned practically everywhere but at Muhlenberg. Finally, it was dropped altogether (1940). Dr. Tyson was pleased and considered it a major forward step.

The new curriculum emphasized two fields: B.S. and A.B., with wider range of choice in courses. Science moved forward from the mediocre to the excellent, aided and abetted by the new Science Building. Physics, chemistry, and biology constituted special fields to which photography and genetics were added. Special display rooms and museums, exceptional and extensive, were made available.

Liberal arts continued to be the central theme in which sciences played an important part. Social sciences taught included history, economics, political science, and sociology. Psychology, languages, art, and music were expanded with specialty fields to accommodate a variety of interests. The new Library building with an efficient Librarian and helpers added appreciably to the functioning of the College. It was chosen as a depository of government documents for the Ninth Congressional District.

College personnel was increased, more office space was made available, and clerical assistance was provided. Mr. LeRoi Snyder was made Business Manager and assistant to the much overworked Mr. Bernheim. A Health Service was organized with Dr. Thomas H. Weaber, Jr., in charge. Mr. Gordon Fister of the *Call-Chronicle* newspapers was made Director of Public Relations. The old Preparatory School was turned into a Freshmen Dormitory (1939) and Mr. Harry A. Benfer became Dean of Freshmen.

The Allentown Preparatory School existed as a separate institution from Muhlenberg College but was administered by the same Board of Trustees. When the student body dwindled and deficits increased, it was decided to close the school (1939). In several respects it had served the College well. Many faculty members had received teaching experience there, and in the end the College fell heir to a valuable tract of land, more than fifteen acres, that now is included in the College campus. The modern building that had served as a freshmen dormitory was later transformed into a home for the first coeds. The land was originally purchased (1915) for $13,525.44 through a grant contributed by Mr. Charles Mosser, a close friend of Dr. Haas and a loyal alumnus of the College. Without this building and especially without the land, the College campus would be severely cramped.

Amazing weaknesses of the College persisted and grew in intensity. While the endowment remained intact during the lean years, income decreased, because rents and interest on mortgages declined. Twenty-seven per cent of the endowment was invested in real estate. Dr. Tyson presented to the Board of Trustees (January, 1938) a "twenty-five year program for a 'Greater Muhlenberg'" calling for a $3,000,000 campaign. Tuition was increased to $300 and the Ministerium, after heated debate, voted (1938) to make a $500,000 appeal—half for Muhlenberg and half for Philadelphia Seminary. It netted enough to cover current expenses and to retire $59,000 on the indebtedness. A balanced budget was attained for 1941–42, but a report to the Ministerium (summer, 1942) listed total indebtedness of the College at $671,500. The picture became dark indeed as war added to the gloom. The V5 and V12 military units saved the College from dire distress. Sailors and marines were welcomed with flowers and open arms, for more reasons than one.

The war in Europe struck Americans as being unfortunate, but again they hoped, by some miracle, to avoid participation. They might have had a chance in 1914, but there was no prospect in 1941: Pearl Harbor took care of that.

A last gesture before submergence in war was the commemoration (1942) of the 200th anniversary of Henry Melchior Muhlenberg's arrival in America. The Congress of the United States took notice in a joint resolution which established a Commemorative Commission with President Roosevelt as Honorary Chairman. Guests for the occasion included Mrs. Franklin D. Roosevelt, the Honorable Sam Rayburn, Speaker of the House, Governor Prentice Cooper of Tennessee, and the Reverend Dr. Frederick H. Knubel, President of the United Lutheran Church in America.

Professor John D. M. Brown prepared the script for a pageant entitled "Missionary in America," which was presented many times by a large cast. There were eight episodes: the first depicted the visit of Henry Melchior Muhlenberg at Francke's house in Halle, and the last contained Muhlenberg's prayer for the future of his church: "At the close of my forty-four years of laborious pilgrimage in this western world, this is the desire of my heart, this is my humble prayer: May The Almighty, Gracious, and Merciful Lord build, extend, and preserve His Kingdom of Grace in this part of the world in order that present and future winds, floods, and storms of tribulations may not prevail against it. To this end may He ever prepare and send faithful laborers, and grant them His Spirit and Power so that His Glorious and Holy Name may be known, and His Holy Will be done on earth as it is in Heaven."

Honorary degrees were conferred on Mrs. Roosevelt and Congressman Rayburn at a special convocation. Commencement exercises closed the impressive occasion with a baccalaureate sermon by Dr. Paul E. Scherer and a commencement address by Sir Angus Fletcher, English scholar and statesman.

The war created abnormalities and upheavals in all facets of national existence. The great bulk of the population continued in its routine patterns of money making and amusements, helping at the same time with the war effort. Key industries worked to capacity and shortages and inconveniences occurred. Concern about the progress of the war, especially for those with relatives in the service, was apparent. The time was opportune for racketeers, chiselers, and criminals. However, in no segment of society was there greater disruption than in colleges and institutions of higher learning. The student, watching and waiting for his turn to serve, experienced frustrations, along with a genuine desire for adventure and service. In general, college students conformed and contributed —some to the fullest extent.

The school suffered: faculty and student body were depleted, income decreased, and expenses mounted. The student body numbered 525 in 1939; two years later only 140 remained. Various improvisations were tried. Exceptional high school pupils were admitted without completing four years' preparation. A voluntary training program, first of its kind in Pennsylvania, was set up for those likely to be called into service. Participants were excused from gym. Drill was held on Monday evenings, under the direction of commanding officers of the Pennsylvania Reserve Defense Corps at the Allentown armory. All students were required to take first aid and disaster relief training under the premedical faculty; physical education was directed by gym teachers and the campus physician. A local adult education program, set up by the federal government and under the direction of Professor Truman Koehler, operated during the entire war period.

Muhlenberg was approved (1940) by the Civil Aeronautics Authority as a training center for aviation cadets. A Civil Pilots Training Program superseded it in 1942. One hundred and thirty navy and marine trainees were registered. An outstanding work in local administration was done by Donald G. Carpenter, who was largely instrumental in the College's being selected for a V12 unit. Muhlenberg was one of about a hundred colleges chosen. It was a real honor and high recognition since basic requirements such as a gymnasium and swimming pool were lacking.

Fortunately, the government learned and took to heart lessons from the Student Army Training Corps in World War I. Every effort was expended to keep as much of the regular College program intact as possible. In the words of Rear Admiral Jacobs, in general charge of the program: "We desire insofar as possible, to preserve the normal pattern of college life. . . . We desire our students to have the benefit of faculty counseling, of extracurricular activities—in short, the best undergraduate education colleges can offer."

The entire force at Muhlenberg College took the job seriously. Dr. Tyson was a dynamo of energy: supervising, helping, and inspiring. Gordon Fister handled the publicity and a reception for the soldiers was planned. At 8:00 A.M. Monday, July 5, 1943, 460 officer candidates, 260 bluejackets, and 200 marines, forming a V12 unit, arrived on schedule.

The impact on the Muhlenberg campus was sensational but not revolutionary, impressive but not shocking, and successful but not perfect. There were obvious transformations. The Lambda Chi

Alpha fraternity house was labeled "Sick Bay" and the commons "Mess Hall." Security guards were on duty and bugle calls announced the time to retire and when to arise for trainees and the neighborhood. A navy décor in the best tradition was adopted. The marines were instructed: "to be gentlemen of liberal education, refined manners, punctilious courtesy, and have the nicest sense of personal honor. Slouchiness, loitering, and boisterousness are decidedly unmilitary and therefore intolerable." Shoes had to be kept polished with a special brand of polish. The Cooperative Store responded with military precision: it ordered the brand by telegram from St. Louis, Missouri. Within a week, the mission was accomplished.

The complete confusion in classifying students, as in the S.A.T.C. in World War I, was avoided. College officials studied the scholastic record of each trainee and classified him as beginner or upperclassman. The latter were allowed to complete work already begun and were given diplomas when completed. Most of the teaching was done by the regular faculty with the help of commanding officers and by local architects in engineering drawing. Preparatory courses were given for 129 found lacking in proper background preparation.

A degree of normal college activity was possible. Trainees were elected to the Student Council and served on the staff of *The Muhlenberg Weekly*. They played in the College band and orchestra and sang in the glee club. They participated on athletic teams and rated an invitation to the national invitational basketball tournament in New York City. "Muhlenberg College" appeared in neon over the entrance to Madison Square Garden.

Estimates of the program naturally vary. Contribution to the war effort was evident—beyond that, however, there was room for skepticism. It was a time of crisis and had to be considered as abnormal, but certainly no irreparable damage was done. Liberal arts ideas suffered: the approach was more technological, preconceived according to patterns, and with less room for individual freethinking.

Early in the war, President Tyson visualized problems in the postwar period: "It seemed to me there was every indication that, serious as would be the effects of war upon the colleges, the biggest problem of all would emerge in the period of adjustment after the cessation of hostilities. . . . I am convinced we must make up our minds now that adjustments will be necessary. The world after the war just simply will not be like it was before. . . . If we stubbornly set our minds now against change in the mistaken belief that all we have to do is study and return to a *status quo ante*, we will wake suddenly one day to find ourselves in difficult straits."

Regardless of principles, ideals, exaltations, and lamentations, the big item was financial assistance that came from the government. During 1943–44, there were 445 servicemen in a total of 576 students enrolled. For that year the government check was $426,107.36; the total budget was $671,121.55. It tapered off gradually but was augmented for another year by a Navy academic refresher unit transferred from Monmouth College, Illinois. The reward was a welcome check (September, 1945) for $164,793.29 —over one-third of the total income for the year.

The customary attempt to get back to normalcy following a war had the usual disappointments. However, generally speaking, they were not noticeably severe. For example, the nationwide depression and widespread unemployment that generally followed wars were expected as a matter of course, but did not come. There were pious resolutions and restatement of orthodox principles. The Board of Trustees of Muhlenberg College, well aware that for two years the federal government had paid the bills, expressed an opinion (1949) without dissent: "Against federal aid to non-tax-supported institutions of higher learning." Nonetheless, the welfare state idea was here to stay, and education, along with many other things, would not and could not refuse to share. The mass return of students to college erased the plague of depopulation but it also carried problems.

President Tyson, as early as 1946, had premonitions of what was to come. To the Board of Trustees he advised: "The College will have to surrender part of its heritage of personal influence in favor of such techniques of mass education as use of tests and measurements." The chairman of the United States advisory committee on education pronounced a truism. "The first and greatest responsibility for keeping our universities free and self-reliant rests with the universities themselves. . . . What they do not defend, others will not find easy to understand."

The flood of 1355 students to the Muhlenberg campus (1948) brought near havoc, worse in many respects than war experiences. Mass education, if it could be called that, buried many cherished principles. The free and easy admissions policy of allowing all former students to return, regardless of qualifications, was unfortunate.

Finances continued to dominate the picture. Again the federal government came to the rescue with the G.I. Bill of Rights. It included for each veteran an allotment of $500 a year for educational purposes, to continue for an equal period of time spent in the service. In 1946, 412 of the 719 students at Muhlenberg were on G.I. support; in 1948 there were 935 out of 1355. In addition, temporary dormitory space for 162 men and 37 student families, plus a recreational building, a navy discard, were furnished.

The bulging student body did not pay all expense of operation nor did it lessen the large prewar indebtedness. A $90,000 deficit faced the college in 1946. Costs per student rose appreciably and income from endowment declined from 4½ to 4 per cent. A further complication was the disastrous Administration Building fire (May, 1947). The cost for replacement and modernizing was $250,000 more than insurance coverage.

A College-and-Ministerium-sponsored fire damage campaign for $1,150,000 got underway with encouraging prospects. A buy-a-bond campaign to reduce the outstanding obligation of $671,500 realized almost $100,000. The Christian Higher Education Year appeal, conducted by the United Lutheran Church in America (1949–50), netted $780,000. The Woman's Auxiliary contributed $5,000 to improve campus lighting facilities.

The Administration Building was restored and many improvements were made. Part of the changes were necessitated by state safety requirements—fireproof stairways, one at each end of the building and another in the center. The third floor was made more usable with side walls raised to eliminate dormer windows. Classrooms and offices were modernized. All in all, the building was

Statue of Peter Muhlenberg in the College grounds is
desecrated in a protest against coeducation, 1957

Faculty play *The Boor* given May 17, 1935. Directed by Dr. J. D. M. Brown. *Players*: Mrs. J. E. Swain, Dr. H. H. Reichard, and Dr. J. E. Swain

Undefeated tennis team, 1942. *Left to right:* Walter W. Weller, Jr.,
Robert R. Ranken, Ray Moats, Jack P. Schantz, Jack T. Minogue,
Edward W. Klink, Robert Minogue, Dr. Shankweiler (Coach)

The College basketball team plays Long Island University at Madison Square Garden, 1947

John A. Haas

Levering Tyson

J. Conrad Seegers

Seegers Union

Interior, Seegers Union

The interior of the Chapel

Navy V 12 Unit in front of the Chapel

First Women's Dormitory Council

Three Presidents. *Left to right:* Dr. Jensen, Dr. Tyson, Dr. Seegers

like new and a worthy addition to the physical plant, but at considerable expense.

Finances were far from sound. Remains of the old indebtedness were burdensome and, while student enrollment was high, it meant added expenses: annual deficits continued. The Korean War added further woes. It came just as plans for expansion were underway, partly to redeem promises—for a swimming pool, gymnasium, student union—that had been made in former campaigns.

Because of the decline in G.I. funds, a sudden decrease in enrollment came with an impact: less than a decade earlier students and prospective students had been knocking at every door. The cold war in Korea became hot, and students, some for a second time, were given a chance to serve their country. The College deficit (1951–52) was $100,000; it followed one, a year earlier, of $78,760. Obviously, something had to be done. Dr. Tyson made desperate efforts to arouse interest and support. Appeals were made to congregations and to the Board of Trustees (October 23, 1950). To the latter he made a detailed long-range plan of operation: "increase in student body and tuition is not the answer," was his conclusion.

Fortunately, better things happened. In spite of trials and tribulations, the College did more than just exist. It must be remembered, in fairness to Dr. Tyson, that before Dr. Haas's retirement the indebtedness was close to a crisis stage. But there were new buildings to show for it. The old Administration Building, sections of a dormitory, a President's home, and a powerhouse did not make a college. More had to be added along with growing needs. Yet ghosts of a gymnasium, swimming pool, and student center were not just skeletons in the closet; they were out in the open.

In spite of war and shortages, the faculty was improved, salaries increased, and additional teaching facilities provided. In a very real sense service to G.I. students and the V12 Navy program increased the stature of Muhlenberg. A wider clientele was needed badly. Students came from every part of the country and many became loyal alumni: some are sending their children as students. Favorable attention came from Washington, D.C., from Allentown, and from other institutions of learning. Much was intangible and did not counterbalance the struggles to maintain financial status.

Burdens fell heavily on the Administration but there were turns of despair and sacrifice for faculty members also, who willingly and continuously supported worthy causes. Members of the Board of Trustees, student body, and alumni rose to the occasion. If it had not been for this legion—actually only a handful—the struggle would have been futile and victory empty.

Celebrations of conspicuous events in the life of an institution are worthy events. Anticipation sometimes confuses birthdays. The beginnings of Muhlenberg College were conceived in the minds of great men, beginning with Henry Melchior Muhlenberg. But the goal was not attained until a century later and then through the efforts of many others. Actually, it is a far cry from Allentown Seminary to Muhlenberg College. The year 1848 marked the beginning of physical efforts to produce a college. The great seal of Muhlenberg College indicates: *Instit, 1848—Reconstit, 1867* (literally translated—Founded and Refounded). The refounding marks the beginning of Muhlenberg College as we know it, without changing name or losing continuity. The anniversary date 1967 is correctly termed, without question, the "Centennial of the naming of Muhlenberg College."

The 1948 Centennial celebration, under the direction of the Reverend Dr. Corson C. Snyder, was planned in three stages. A happy coincidence was that the bicentennial anniversary of the Ministerium of Pennsylvania came the same year. Appropriate meetings were held in many places and the founding of Muhlenberg College was given wide recognition.

The College Commencement, June 3-7, 1948, was international in scope. The baccalaureate sermon was preached by the Reverend Dr. John Baillie of the University of Edinburgh. Dr. George W. McClelland, President of the University of Pennsylvania, gave the commencement address, and honorary degrees were given Bishop Hans Lilje of Hanover, Germany; Senator Homer Ferguson of Michigan; the Reverend Dr. Emil E. Fischer, President of the Ministerium; and the Reverend Charles K. Fegley, the Reverend John R. Hauser, and the Reverend Earl F. Rahn.

The community phase (September, 1948) began with an academic procession from Trout Hall, the site of the old College, to the Lyric Theatre, where so many College functions were held. Superior Court Judge Claude T. Reno gave the principal address. Dignitaries attending were: Mayor Donald V. Hock, President Dale H. Moore of Cedar Crest College, and officials of Muhlenberg College. Honorary degrees were conferred on Judge Claude T. Reno, Judge Ethan Allen Gearhart, Major Frederick E. Uhl, Mrs. Hannah Durham, Mr. William Swallow, Mr. Donald Voorhees, and Mr. Charles Seidel.

The third part of the celebration, held on October 16, 1948, was a College affair. Honorary degrees were conferred on Dr. Ira F. Zartman, Dr. Sherman Oberly, Dr. James H. S. Bossard, the Reverend Harvey C. Snyder, Professor John D. M. Brown, Mr. William E. Brandt, and Mr. Percy B. Ruhe. The beautiful Athanasian window in the Chapel was dedicated in memory of Professor Clement A. Marks. A centennial hymn written by Professor John D. M. Brown and set to music by Professor Harold K. Marks was rendered. Dr. Robert C. Horn prepared a Centennial History of the College.

The role of a student body in governing themselves and participating in the affairs of the College was long a controversial subject, at first and for many years uneventful. Dr. Haas's attitude was paternalistic and there was little resentment or opposition expressed. Semisecret "bull sessions" and a few articles in *The Muhlenberg Weekly* were evident and a very limited number of requests were sent to the faculty.

Requests for recognition increased appreciably after World War I. Dr. Tyson was the first President to encourage student action and the response was immediate; the Student Council, so long a rubber stamp, went into action. A committee was appointed (1938) to revise the constitution. The main complaint was factionalism and undemocratic procedure. The following analysis was printed in the *M. Book* (1939–40): "In previous years and to a degree at present, certain minority groups on the campus, through connivance and uncertain action, placed into the numerous student affairs members of their own groups for the purpose of self-glorification, choosing their students blindly from their own faction quite regardless of their competence, and heedless of merits of students of other groups, and even entirely forgetful of the welfare of the College of which these minority groups were only a part . . . a disgrace to our Alma Mater and a gross injustice to the majority of students."

The net result was a complete revision of the constitution and method of elections. George Howatt (1940) worked out a system of proportional representation with various and sundry devices, which did reduce, but did not eliminate political maneuvers. It was so complicated that critics maintained that Howatt was the only one who understood it, and later some changes were made. Howatt pursued his specialty and made a name for himself and the College as consultant to governments at home and abroad. Presently, he is a government consultant in Australia.

The fact that the students began their campaign for recognition by putting their own house in order is praiseworthy. It attracted attention and support in the faculty and Administration—Dr. Tyson gave full approbation. Reorganization of domitory supervision was a starting point. The old system under the Student Council administration had proved a failure—partly because it had limited authority. The new Dormitory Council had assurance from Dr. Tyson and Dean Horn that they would be supported, with punishment for offenders to include "indefinite suspension and even expulsion, if necessary." This was a real test in student government responsibility that set an important precedent. Another early effort, at least partly successful, was a strongly worded petition for a change in Chapel regulations. The physical education program, the system of scheduling examinations and term papers, and the Commons were criticized and changes recommended. World War II retarded the program: a duration constitution was adopted in 1943.

Following the war, and with a full house of students, including many G.I.'s with more maturity and experience than average students, the campaign was renewed. By faculty action, a joint student-faculty committee was established to act as a tribunal and sounding board, with the Dean of Students and President of the Student Council acting as co-chairmen. The constitution, with some Howatt principles still intact, was revised to include presidents of each class in the Council. In addition, it was empowered to act on all violations of student ethics except academic dishonesty.

A further innovation was the inclusion of student representatives to serve, without vote, on various faculty committees, including the following: religious interests, buildings and grounds, health and refectory, academic standards, athletics, library, curriculum, catalog, admissions, and academic standings.

There was widespread belief that the latter practice went entirely too far. In fact, students were not too welcome and were admitted only at the discretion of the chairmen of the various committees. But there was much favorable publicity. Dr. Tyson quoted Roger Baldwin of the American Civil Liberties Union as saying that the "Muhlenberg Constitution is a model for college campuses."

On paper, student government at Muhlenberg College reached an impressive degree of maturity and more recent events attest to its merit. There were eternal problems and opinions on the extent of freedom that should be given the inexperienced, although well-intentioned, students in matters of administration. In practice too, the principle of applied democracy was more theoretical than real. Dr. Tyson seemed to get what he wanted, even to choosing student officers through carefully concealed intervention. This, of course, is widely accepted administrative technique.

As previously indicated, the question of coeducation, with little organized support, bogged down. However, sentiment did not die —rather a grass-roots agitation gained ground. Those in authority remained skeptical, if not hostile. A possible working agreement with Cedar Crest College again was presented to the Board of Trustees but met with silence. The American Council on Education was engaged (1946) to make a survey. A questionnaire, worded to get possible alternate plans, including the institution of coeducation at Muhlenberg, was widely circulated. The result showed a preference to unite with Cedar Crest; the second choice was to send girls to Susquehanna University, already a coeducational institution; and the third choice was Muhlenberg. Since Cedar Crest and Susquehanna were never given serious consideration, it was with Muhlenberg College that the final solution rested.

A new emphasis was advanced in a Christian education appeal (1951) which emphasized the importance of providing doctrinal training for women under the aegis of the Augsburg Confession, to enable them to serve the church to better advantage. A year later a further religious motivation was expressed that equality in Christ should mean equality in education. A new and refreshing breeze stirred. The deciding factor—to be explained later—was economic. Financial troubles, the Korean War, and Dr. Tyson's resignation momentarily overshadowed everything else.

The background of Dr. Tyson's resignation (March 27, 1951) was cluttered with a variety of conditions, personal and general. Certainly, he had troubles that may be classified as unavoidable: an inherited indebtedness; World War II; the postwar burden in heavy registrations; an Administration Building fire; decline in student enrollment and income; and the Korean War. There were strong differences of opinion among Ministerium, Administration, faculty, alumni, Board of Trustees, students, and community, which often resulted in grudges and a lack of cooperation. Dr. Tyson made a noble effort but did not succeed; won battles but lost the war; and was in many ways a good President but not a magician. His resignation brought sighs of relief, expressions of concern, but more significant than either, indifference. There was a low ebb in morale; a crisis to overshadow all former crises.

The Trustees were shocked and startled. They refused to accept the resignation and appointed a committee to iron out the differences. Dr. Tyson replied: "It is in the best interests of the College that I withdraw as of June 30, 1951."

The customary whereases and wherefores followed. The Board of Trustees voted, after some delay, to accept the resignation. The Ministerium, by rising vote, expressed to "Dr. and Mrs. Tyson our enduring thanks and appreciation." A member of the Board of Trustees stated: "I might say that Dr. Tyson brought to Muhlenberg a polish and urbanity which it had not evidenced prior to his administration. Indeed, I would say that he found Muhlenberg a 'hick' school and left it a far more advanced and sophisticated institution. By this comment I do not mean to indicate that the College prior to this was lacking in academic accomplishment; I am merely commenting on a social aspect. I shall also say that he had a delightful personality which appealed to many people and he was most instrumental in making the College more widely known."

8

Darkness Before Dawn

No analysis of an important local problem can be complete without considering its broader implications. The Depression of 1929 was worldwide, World War I spread beyond Europe, and World War II was all-inclusive. The fact that the United States was separated from troublesome Europe and imponderable Asia by miles of ocean remained a source of satisfaction and complacency. Participation in two world wars and in Korea and Vietnam exposed this fallacy, but without appreciable effect.

The result of all this on the thinking and acting of Americans was slow in realization and resisted with a persistence in clinging to a fast disappearing order. The desire to be left alone, apart from and aloof to what was going on in the rest of the world, rendered the idea of making the world safe for democracy in World War I, of saving Western ideas from the ravages of Fascism and Nazism in World War II, and, more recently, of Communism and the cold war, repulsive to Americans. Each participation deepened the bewilderment and broadened the disillusionment.

The result was a lack of understanding of aims and objectives and a failure to realize what really was taking place at home as well as abroad. The great tragedies in leadership and the failure of popular discrimination in a functioning democracy faded into history without remedial treatment. Woodrow Wilson, Herbert Hoover, Franklin D. Roosevelt, and Dwight D. Eisenhower represented top-level failures to prepare the people adequately for a dangerous future.

Meanwhile, foreign complications and American commitments became more involved. Militarily, World War II was won with Communist Russia as copartner, but Communism remained a major peacetime threat, ready and willing to continue a world revolution. In the United States, using the words of General Marshall, "demobilization became a rout." Russia increased her armies and stepped up armaments production. Winston Churchill, facing problems of his own, pointedly remarked: "Allies could hardly wait, after the war, to get back to doing again, with increased fervor, the very things that caused the war in the first place."

What role could education play in this dilemma? Obviously, careful study and intelligent action were necessary in preparation for the citizens of the future. If we were moving in the right direction, what could be done to promote this course? If the course was improper, what was the solution? The role of science and technology was well established. The influence of social science and cultural liberal arts generally was not so well entrenched. Could the institutions of higher learning continue business as usual? The welfare state promoted democratization of education—higher education for the few went the way of *laissez faire* politics. The greatest manifestation of this was in the G.I. Bill of Rights. The ex-soldier returned to college older, more mature, and with changed objectives. However, there were more problems for the college than just absorbing numbers.

Faced with complexities, colleges hesitatingly met the future. Not all the challenges were new, but much of the traditional procedure needed changing. The situation was not desperate enough to require a revolution, but serious enough for caution. Particular emphasis was placed on the small liberal arts, church-related college dedicated to a quality education, with particular emphasis in planning for the future. The preservation of revered ideals in the "new society" was the big challenge. Muhlenberg College met this after several anxious moments that appeared insurmountable. This chapter in its history is one of the darkest, but in the end, one of the most inspiring.

The impact of Dr. Tyson's resignation (1951) was accompanied with the equally important, but less sensational, termination of the services of Dr. Reuben J. Butz, member of the Board of Trustees since 1900 and President of the Board since 1913, and Dr. Robert C. Horn, with forty-seven years as teacher, Vice-President, acting President, and Dean. Who would not be impressed by and grateful for the work of these men, but, by the same token, who would not logically conclude that a change would be beneficial?

The vacuum created was ominous, but vacuums tend to attract and are temporary. A five-man committee took charge (July 1, 1951). It included Attorney George B. Balmer (recently elected to succeed Dr. Butz as President of the Board), Treasurer Howard M. MacGregor, and Dean Sherwood Mercer—the three elected by the Board—and Professors Morris Greth and Luther J. Deck, chosen by the faculty. It was suggested, not entirely in jest, that there should have been six, so that, if necessary, they could serve as pallbearers for a dead institution.

In periods of crisis great leaders often rise to the occasion, and the crisis at Muhlenberg was no exception. With some credit to others, the real honor goes to Attorney Balmer, who deserves to rank with a very select few in the College history. In a manner of modesty, self-sacrifice, and devotion, he undertook and performed a notable task.

There were two general emergencies of major importance: to keep the College functioning, under the most adverse conditions, and to select a President. The "Quinity" lasted only until June 1, 1952, when, through Board action, Professor Greth was chosen Acting President. He did everything humanly possible, and Attorney Balmer would be the first, as indeed he was, to praise him. But the job was thankless; little could be done but to mark time.

The search for a President was urgent. The position was neither promising nor lucrative enough to attract the type of leadership needed. Rumors of bankruptcy, dissension, and inevitable ruin were in circulation. Several contacts and offers were made and refused—one only a few weeks before formal announcement of acceptance was to be made. But genuine loyalty and a sense of duty came to the rescue in the person of Dr. J. Conrad Seegers. With

87

an ideal combination of qualities and experience, which surpassed the fondest hopes of those searching and of those in a state of great expectancy, Muhlenberg College received a new President. He was elected September 27, 1952, and inaugurated May 2, 1953, having assumed duties in February. Attorney Balmer conducted the inauguration ceremony with obvious pride and relief.

From the point of view of a specialized education and experience, Dr. Seegers was well qualified: he was a graduate of Muhlenberg, with an M.A. from Columbia and a Ph.D. from the University of Pennsylvania. He had taught at Allentown Preparatory School, Lenoir-Rhyne College, and Temple University. His experience as a public school administrator in North Carolina, as Dean of Men and head of Teachers College at Temple and, for many years, as a member of the Board of Trustees of Muhlenberg were impressive credentials.

Dr. Seegers knew the condition of the College—so he was not surprised when figures were presented. The deficit for 1952–53 was $126,594; the total outstanding debt $600,000; tuition income dropped $75,000 in one year; and expenses were rising. He summarized the needs: "a gymnasium, more funds for scholarships, additional dormitory space, a swimming pool, a student center, 800 students, and a balanced budget."

A special appeal was made to the Ministerium. The grant for 1952–53 was increased by $35,000 and a committee was appointed to study the entire problem. The initial report made much of aid already given and that building had exceeded sufficient funds—all well-known facts. The real shock was notice from Allentown banks that only $250,000 additional credit would be available in the foreseeable future. That would cover the College expenses only to April, 1954.

A special meeting of the Ministerium and Board of Trustees was held in the College Chapel (December 11, 1953). This was, in every sense of the word, a crisis; a matter of life or death for the College. After prolonged and serious discussion, it was agreed that the Ministerium would sponsor a campaign for $1,500,000.

The true colors of those interested in and responsible for the College came into focus. The Ministerium made clear its responsibility and determination to act. Dr. Seegers expressed his feeling in a statement which he read to the Ministerium in 1954: "The importance of the campaign of the Ministerium for a greater Muhlenberg cannot be estimated. It will not only ensure the perpetuation of an institution which has served the church with distinction for over a century and which has developed many of its most distinguished lay and clerical leaders, it will demonstrate the faith of the church in the cause of Christian higher education, in the independent college, and in the identity of the college as a church institution. It is no exaggeration to say that the eyes of thousands of Lutherans outside the Ministerium as well as in it, and of independent colleges in general will be fixed upon it. Its success will demonstrate that we Lutherans mean business."

The use to be made of funds collected was clearly stated: $300,-000 for emergency needs and anticipated deficits; $650,000 to clear the indebtedness; and $450,000 for new dormitories, with $100,000 designated to inaugurate coeducation. The latter was considered by some as a stab in the back, by others with enthusiasm. It strengthened the appeal and made coeducation a reality.

The Reverend Luther F. Schlenker was named Director and the Reverend Dr. William L. Katz Assistant Director to conduct the campaign. Without delay, it got underway, fortified with the slogan, "Muhlenberg of Tomorrow." Enough was raised in advance gifts to avert the threatened April bank crisis. In 1955, Dr. Seegers was able to report to the Ministerium that the Middle Atlantic States Association praised the College for financial and academic improvement. There had been a question of whether accreditation would be continued. Refusal would have been a blow to prestige and would have required much time and effort to get reinstated.

Things began to happen: the student body increased, tuition was raised from $570 to $700; grants of more than a million dollars came from the U.S. Steel Foundation, General Foods, and the Ford Foundation; church congregation contributions increased by $30,-000 in one year; and other gifts equaled that amount. The annual deficit in 1954–55 was reduced to $36,345, and the year following there was a surplus of $340.62. The confidence of the church was restored and the year 1955 was designated as an "Era of Good

Feeling." President James Monroe had nothing on Muhlenberg College.

Memorial Hall, a health center, Martin Luther dormitory, Hagan Field, new tennis courts, and major renovations for West Hall were completed or underway, at an estimated cost of $1,600,000. Faculty salaries were raised, facilities improved, and student scholarships increased.

After a long wait and seemingly impossible opposition, coeducation inauspiciously came into its own. In the final and decisive stage, those who vigorously opposed it were out of the picture. Dr. Haas had done everything possible to oppose it, including asserting influence in the Ministerium. Treasurer Oscar Bernheim and Chairman of the Board of Trustees Reuben J. Butz were no longer on the scene. Dr. Tyson personally favored it, but was too deeply involved with finances to get results. Dr. Seegers was strong in support and carried through the final implementation. The real and immediate victory came with Ministerium insistence that provision be made for coeducation in the campaign that was to save the College. When $850,000 in cash was raised, instructions were given to proceed with building plans necessary to house the coeds.

The sum of $550,000 was allocated for new buildings and renovation of old, which was tied in with the preparations for coeducation. A new dormitory, Martin Luther Hall, was provided to house the freshmen quartered in West Hall, which was completely modernized and refurbished.

Transformation of the physical plant was a small task compared with needed psychological changes. Die-hards thought the campus would be dominated by women. An opinion poll revealed that 126 male students were convinced coeducation would be a misfortune; 181 thought it would be beneficial. Comments in the *Weekly* were not enthusiastic: "Muhlenberg, after 100 years as a men's college, will finally fall prey to the frays of modern education." The alumni were generally critical. Their reunions and meetings sent up a chorus of sarcasm. However, reality gradually melted opposition: beggars, after all, could not be choosers.

Everybody, Dr. Seegers more than anyone, knew there would be problems. He cautioned: "Our purpose is to remain a liberal arts college with a minimum emphasis on vocationalism. The women will be educated in the same academic fashion as the men."

Application for admission to the first class (limited to one hundred females, because of dormitory limitations) poured in and the Admissions Office had the unusual experience of an excess in the number of good students. Real effort was expended to be fair and considerate. Barbara Fretz, the first coed to be so honored, was given one of the coveted $2,000 scholarships. But many were disappointed and lamentations were numerous.

In many respects, the year 1957–58 was memorable in Muhlenberg history. Financially, the College operated on a balanced budget, the physical plant took on a new look, and girls were among the students to take up residence on the campus. *Life* Magazine ran an article entitled: "Sounds of Girlish Voices Strike a New Note at Muhlenberg." All reports indicated a saneness and tolerance that did credit to the College and promoted the possibilities of success for coeducation at a school that had existed for 109 years (by the old count) without girls. In 1957–58 the College population included 122 women (some transferees) with 103 coed freshmen.

Dr. Seegers' opening address was enthusiastic. "I am personally glad to welcome our first class of girls. They have much to contribute to campus activities and I hope the necessary coordination will be smooth and rapid as they take their places in organizations as well as classrooms."

The very difficult post of Dean of Women was accepted by Miss Heimtraut Dietrich, former Dean at Syracuse University and Wagner College. She had to chart a course of integration that would be both acceptable and workable. For example, one thing among many, was the announcement that women would not be subject to "hazing" by upperclassmen—only by the Student Council and Tribunal. Both sides protested, indicating that they regarded it with anticipation. A spokesman for the girls declared it would "cause a gap and general dissatisfaction"—they wanted the experience. Males expressed concern that Dean Dietrich had such "a low opinion of Muhlenberg men."

Another occasion when boys and girls met on equal terms was

at meal time. Here, in the dining hall, a feminine touch had long been needed. The new Dean moved faster than was acceptable, although she had support of the Dean of Men. Dress requirements were: heels and sweaters or their equivalent for girls and white shirts and coats for boys. A girl was to act as hostess for each table—a big task, arbitrarily and summarily imposed. One coed complained that at her table football players consumed all the food before she had a chance to eat. The transformation was not immediate or complete but ultimately a noticeable change for the better took place.

Protests, not necessarily against the girls but more often against the rules and regulations imposed by Dean Dietrich, were numerous. Some fraternities formed "anticoed" pacts and announced refusal to date Muhlenberg coeds—they preferred Cedar Crest girls, because they were more "sophisticated." But this, and similar complaints, evaporated. The well-worn path across the valley to Cedar Crest College gradually disappeared because of lack of use.

Dean Dietrich was a casualty to the rigors of the task. After little more than a year she resigned. "I have tried," she wrote, "to establish women's education on a male campus and have tried to integrate them. . . . It has been a tremendous experience. . . . Because lines of authority and responsibility have not been clearly defined and understood, it seems impossible to carry out the tremendous task that has to be done." She was succeeded by Miss Anne Nugent, Professor of Education at Temple University. She could and did profit from the experience of her predecessor. "I plan to go slowly in deciding what is important and what is not important." This is exactly what she did with marked success.

Much credit for favorable acceptance of coeducation rested upon leadership. Dean Dietrich made a notable contribution in taking unpopular but necessary steps. Dean Nugent and her co-workers, Dean of Men Claude E. Dierolf and Dean Kendig before him, with guidance and support from Dr. Seegers, are due credit for an undertaking that has come to mean much to the College. Others joined in support, including the entire College personnel. To Miss Jean Hecht should go honorable mention for her work incidental to her assignment as physical education instructor.

Progress in acceptance continued. Local newspapers were complimentary and encouraging. "In these few short weeks we have seen the beginning of a new and greater Muhlenberg. The faculty felt that a great improvement scholastically was evident and the community would be benefited." Even the Alumni Association had a good word in the *Muhlenberg News* (1957): "Like concentric circles, coeducation enlarges the scope of the college, broadens her influence, while providing more pleasant surroundings, a more active social life and greater scholastic spirit."

Proof of thoroughgoing integration was abundantly evident. Girls served on *Weekly* and *Ciarla* staffs, sang in the choir, were elected to the Student Council, attained scholastical honors (in 1962 both valedictorian and salutatorian and eight of eleven students graduated with high honors were females). A Women's Council was organized and accepted (1959) by the Student Council. The Women's Honor Society *Lambda Epsilon Delta* was organized to correspond with *Omicron Delta Kappa* for the men. In the third year of coeducation, two Muhlenberg girls were chosen for *Who's Who in American Colleges and Universities.*

Women became an important element, not only in administration but also in the faculty. Miss Funk, Assistant Librarian, was the only woman with faculty status for some time. Later Dr. Bertha Paulssen became (1942) Professor of Sociology, Dr. Joanne Stafford (later Mrs. Charles Mortimer) and Dr. Katherine S. Van Eerde were elected to the Department of History and Political Science, and Miss Aurelia Arre and Dr. Adelaide Kreinheder joined the modern language and education departments respectively. Another innovation was the election of Sister Anna Ebert to the Board of Trustees. An issue of the *Ciarla* was dedicated to women.

Prosser Hall (begun in 1959), made possible by a gift of $150,000 from Dr. and Mrs. Harrison Prosser, supplemented by a federal government self-liquidating loan of $250,000, provided much needed dormitory space for women.

Dr. Seegers made an evaluation of coeducation: "There is something unique about the Class of 1961. It includes the first full class of women to be graduated from Muhlenberg College. We are cer-

93

tainly looking forward to the years ahead as the women graduates of Muhlenberg make outstanding achievements in their fields of endeavor, just as our present alumni have done for many years."

Student participation in college administration began comparatively late at Muhlenberg. Not until 1950 did it attain sufficient maturity to be generally recognized. The *Annual Bulletin* of that year records: "Under certain basic limitations the students have jurisdiction over the management of their own activities. The Student Council is a body of elected representatives who meet weekly to form and administer policies on student affairs. This organization is given a great deal of authority and responsibility and is looked upon by students, faculty and trustees as being of central importance to the well-being and progress of the College. To the degree that they perform these functions wisely, they are taken into the councils of the College in matters that go beyond the bounds of what is ordinarily considered to be undergraduate responsibility. It is interesting to note with what frequency their judgments are sound and how helpful their opinions are when questions of general College policy arise."

Dean Henry M. M. Richards took active interest in aiding and promoting student government. He supported a Student Honors Court to try students accused of cheating. The *Weekly* was enthusiastic: "the administration has great faith in the student body and in its ability to think maturely and render sensible decisions. . . . Through this court the seeds for a workable honor system have been sown and need only a little encouragement to sprout." In 1959, a proposal was submitted to the students for a new Supreme Court to supplant the Honor Court. It provided a better distribution of power among Interfraternity Council, Men's Dormitory Council, and the newly organized Women's Council. The Student Council would try no more disciplinary cases; they were to be referred to the Court. The proposed changes were ratified by the student body and approved unanimously by the faculty and slated to become operative in September, 1961.

Dr. John Reed, a very active participant in student affairs, spoke to the incoming Freshmen class (1961): "All this is the result of a genuine grass-roots movement. The idea of an honor system has arisen from the students of Muhlenberg College. It is, too, another example of something for which we can be proud, the fact that we do indeed have a democratic student government here at Muhlenberg."

Since the avowed purpose of an institution of higher learning is to educate, the faculty is of prime importance. It must perform the major share of the actual guidance of students. Work in the classroom, through dispensing knowledge, arousing interest and curiosity, setting the example of a trained scholar, and exploring fields of learning, constitutes a major part of an education. Everything else—property, buildings, equipment, administration, and Board of Trustees—would be functionless without teachers. Also, faculty members have duties and responsibilities other than presiding over classes: sharing part of the responsibility of administration, performing community services to promote proper public relations, and continuing their own education through constant awareness of what is going on in their own fields of specialty. Individual research for publication is often a necessity for promotion and increase in salary. Fortunately, this has not been true at Muhlenberg.

The status of a faculty in a college or university naturally is a very important measuring stick for evaluation, not only by accrediting institutions but also by prospective students and parents. It is a well-known fact that consideration and reward for faculty members are sometimes neglected for the more obvious social centers, gymnasiums, athletic fields, chapels, dormitories, and Administration.

Muhlenberg College, by the middle of the twentieth century, reached a stature in which an evaluation of its faculty is worthy of consideration. The status of a liberal arts and a church-related institution, with facilities to render public service in line with modern needs, puts a particular emphasis on the curriculum and those responsible for its implementation. Liberal arts carries the broad implication of general knowledge, while church-related might require a particular denominational approach. It is a point of pride that Muhlenberg has attained notable success along these lines. Certainly by the time of Dr. Haas and with continued increased emphasis the College was committed to liberal arts, church-related status, and awareness of the general needs and qualities of an education.

The growth in importance of the faculty both in quality and responsibilities was constant. Academic freedom at Muhlenberg has never been an issue of grave importance. Preference in matters of religion, politics, and race has been prevalent in the choice of faculty and admission of students, but even this has ceased to be a matter of concern. The very important matter of freedom of action in the classroom has been inviolate.

An interesting expression of student opinion was given in the *Weekly* (March 4, 1936): "A professor should not advocate any great social change, he should only discuss it to evaluate its merits and to understand it, not advocate it." In regard to religion, the Ministerium (May, 1947) went on record— "(1) that all professors at the College should be affiliated with some Christian church and participate in its work, and should also encourage, by their attendance and participation in, chapel services at the College. (2) The underlying philosophy of the College and of all its teaching should be positively Christian, and the speculative interpretation of all facts should be in harmony with the Christian outlook on truth and life."

The College came through both World Wars without disturbances of particular importance. The postwar furor over "Un-Americanism" and McCarthyism had an impact which required the utmost caution. A textbook written by a Muhlenberg faculty member containing the statement, "Russia has made some progress under her system of government," was reported to Washington, D.C., as evidence of subversion, but no action was taken.

One of the few incidents that came out in the open at Muhlenberg was the showing of a Charlie Chaplin film (1955), as part of a general program entitled "Great Films of Yesterday and Today." The public was invited. The local American Legion post adopted a resolution condemning Chaplin as Un-American and protested to the College against showing his picture. Dr. Seegers announced it would not be shown to the public, but would be to the student body and faculty, if they so desired. The Student Council adopted a resolution of protest claiming the action as censorship. This was not taken seriously, and quiet was resumed.

Academic freedom is variable and nebulous. Like all forms of freedom, it can be neglected or abused, but between these extremes there is common ground for practical application. The American Association of University Professors *Bulletin* (1949) codified a somewhat pragmatic definition of academic freedom which included: possibilities for research; freedom in the classroom; and freedom to speak on issues as a citizen in the community. "The common good depends upon the free search for truth and in its free expression." Muhlenberg's rating under these standards is good.

The general idea of academic freedom was stated in nineteenth-century Germany and widely quoted in the United States. The German *Wissenschaft* refers to knowledge in the most exalted sense—the methodical search for truth wholly irrespective of utilitarian uses. *Lehrfreiheit* insists the teacher may teach what he chooses, as he chooses, and it gives the same freedom to students. Those who conceived a Muhlenberg College, with the German background, took these things seriously. The ideals may not have been fulfilled to the letter, but it is clear that none was seriously violated in the later history of the College. This is to the credit of the Ministerium, Board of Trustees, Administration, faculty, and students.

The changing role of the faculty at Muhlenberg College plays an interesting and important part of its history. The Administration, acting through the authority and direction of the Board of Trustees—which according to Dr. Fetter, Chairman of the Board, "does not run the College but sees to it that it runs"—is responsible for the over-all management of the institution. The faculty's role, beyond departments and classrooms, is not well defined and varies with each administration or change in general conditions.

Muhlenberg developed a pattern of administrative procedure with a few variations in technique and timing. For about half a century, the President, without benefit of a dean, had close personal contacts with Board and Ministerium. Actually neither Dean

97

Ettinger nor Dean Horn did much policy making, advising students, or guiding the faculty. The 1934 amendment to the By-laws defined the Muhlenberg faculty as: "the president, professors, assistant professors, and anyone so designated by the Board of Trustees. . . . Each professor shall have charge of the instruction and discipline in his department and will be held responsible therefor. He shall give advice on any subject connected with his department when required to do so by the president. He shall make no change in the schedule of studies, after its adoption by the faculty, without its consent. . . . Each professor shall confine himself to his own department and the branches that may have been assigned to him, and in all ways strive to maintain due professional courtesy towards and uphold his associates."

The development of faculty role in administration cannot be judged solely on the basis of rules and regulations. There are numerous instances, mostly unrecorded, of the influence of faculty members taken into the confidence of the President. The general faculty meeting, which is as old as the institution, asserted a considerable amount of influence. Curriculum and requirements for admission of students were topics for long discussions. Supervision of the catalog and degree requirements, including a rule to require all applicants to take the college entrance examination (and before graduation, the graduate record test), were decided in faculty meetings.

Faculty committees gradually became an extensive and important part in administering the College. The Academic Regulations and Standards Committee was one of the more important. It was to "inspect the curriculum, look into the teaching load of professors and inquire into their efficiency." In 1951, it began a policy of examining the program of the College with a view of the future. "It is expected that out of the deliberations will come significant suggestions to strengthen even more the College's academic program." The Executive Committee of the Faculty, or, as sometimes designated, the Committee on Educational Policy, and later the Faculty Senate, was designated to "determine where and when we can increase the effectiveness of teaching in the College; how best we can add to the attractiveness of our curriculum; and in general, what can be done to maintain the high academic rating of the College?"

A complete listing of all committees and activities is too long to enumerate. Some will be referred to later. In general, the number and scope indicate the growing influence of the faculty. Of particular importance were instances when members of the faculty and the Board of Trustees worked together on athletics, planning for the future, and academic regulations and standards.

A summarization of the responsibilities and organization of the faculty was made in an amendment to the Bylaws (1959): "There shall be a Faculty Senate composed of the President, the Dean of the College, and the heads and acting heads of all departments of instruction. The Faculty Senate shall meet whenever necessary to handle routine matters under faculty regulation and to act in emergencies.

"Each member of the faculty shall contribute to the general welfare of the College by supporting the fundamental principles upon which it was founded and is being maintained, by promoting its religious life; by sharing in the general activities and attending the public exercises and formal functions of the institution; by aiding other college officers to uphold discipline and to eliminate academic and other delinquencies; and by promoting through precept and practice, a healthy and normal community life for the College."

Dr. Seegers did not neglect internal administration. His intimate knowledge of the workings of the Board of Trustees, many contacts with the Ministerium, friends and former associates in Administration and faculty, and a natural and effective way of dealing with people, provided excellent working conditions. His own comments on the role of the faculty are revealing. "I would say, in general, that the faculty, especially during Dr. Tyson's administration and mine, assumed more importance and gradually received more authority."

During the Seegers administration the Faculty Senate became moribund and a more personalized procedure was adopted. "I suppose one could say my administration was pretty much person to person." He further described his position: "I met frequently with most of the committees in addition to meeting with chairmen, as did the dean. . . . Final action on new appointees required consent of the department, the dean, and me. Budget requests were handled by the treasurer, later the assistant treasurer, and me, then were sent to the Board. Department heads were appointed by me, after consultations, subject to Board approval. . . . The faculty and students had unlimited access to me and other college administrators."

Dr. Seegers announced his resignation on December 1, 1959, to take effect the following June. It surprised no one, but was widely regretted. He gave eight years of auspicious service, having accepted a challenge to rescue an institution in dire distress, and left it, not only in a state of recovery, but also on the march.

His accomplishments were many and varied: financial recovery —a difference between life and death for the institution; coeducation, a long-cherished dream; restoration and continuation of a building program—Memorial Hall, dormitories, the health center; acquisition and remodeling of Millerheim, Alumni House, Bernheim House, and Faculty House; admission standards raised, faculty salaries increased; and a "sane athletic program" instituted. The Seegers Union is a monument of respect, utility, and beauty. In typical fashion, Dr. Seegers summarized his service: "The greatest burden was that of financial responsibility. The greatest reward was in seeing students grow and develop and to see general progress in the College from year to year."

His community and extracurricular activities consumed time and energy. He was always in demand and willingly responsive as a speaker and became a symbol of Muhlenberg wherever he went. Dr. Seegers' other responsibilities included membership of the Board of Directors of the Art Museum and work with the Community Council, the Redevelopment Authority, Swain School, and with the church. He also participated in activities of The Association of American Colleges and Middle Atlantic States and Maryland.

Faculty and students expressed their appreciation for his dedicated services in two very unusual farewell parties. They were memorable and very much appreciated.

9

In the First Stages of Maturity

THE administration of John F. Kennedy had repercussions, for better or for worse, which were in the direction of what has come to be known as "the Welfare State." He was youthful, charming, sincere, wealthy, a Roman Catholic, a war hero, and he had an attractive wife. He instilled vigor and enthusiasm as well as consternation and foreboding. During his term of office the White House was transformed into a dignified social center and a museum of Americana. Nobel prize winners were invited to dinner. In words of welcome to the distinguished guests, the host observed: "This is the most extraordinary talent ever assembled at the White House—with the possible exception of when Thomas Jefferson dined alone."

"New Frontier," the name chosen for the Kennedy program, was defined in his inaugural address: "We dare not forget today that we are heirs of that first revolution. Let the word go forth from this time and place, to friend and foe alike, that the torch has been passed to a new generation of Americans—born in this century, tempered by war, disciplined by a hard and bitter peace, proud of our ancient heritage and unwilling to witness or permit the slow undoing of human rights, to which this nation has always been committed and to which we are committed today at home and around the world."

He faced many difficulties. Nevertheless, he seemed to gain

CARL A. RUDISILL LIBRARY
LENOIR RHYNE COLLEGE

prestige with each crisis. He sensed the difficulties ahead but eagerly faced the challenge. In his last speech, the day before his assassination, he spoke: "This is a dangerous and uncertain world. . . . No one expects our lives to be easy—not in this decade, not in this century."

When Lyndon Johnson became President, his first message to Congress proclaimed: "Let us continue." When the Federal Education Act was passed he announced: "But now, at last, in the year of our Lord 1965, we have quit talking and started acting." Over two billion dollars was made available for scholarships, loans, work opportunities for students, and for grant-in-aid subsidies for equipment and facilities.

Government support of education and the great demand for trained men and women in all areas afford opportunities and challenges to the entire system of education. In President Franklin D. Roosevelt's administration, college-trained experts were frowned upon and labeled "eggheads," but President Kennedy appointed, with wide approval, so many Harvard professors to government positions that the question arose, "Who is left there to teach?"

The effect was immediate and far-reaching. Fifty years ago only 5 per cent of Americans between eighteen and twenty-one years of age went to college. In a short time, the number rose to 40 per cent and apparently will continue to climb. What was a luxury is now considered a necessity: "a college education is a good thing for everybody." It became a must for job opportunities and a necessity for good citizenship. As a result, colleges suddenly were faced with more students than they could accommodate. Only a few years ago the Carnegie Foundation predicted the demise of a number of colleges—particularly the liberal arts and church-related ones. Now they are flooded with applications and out of success another kind of crisis is born.

With the new order, a broad frontal attack is made to improve society generally: a new youth, a changed middle age, and a secure old age. Youth is promised freedom, education, employment, leisure time, health insurance, and, when the time arrives, old age retirement and protection. The challenge is: can it be done? Obviously more is required than legislation and finances. Training, leadership, and cooperation are needed if we are to escape becoming a bureaucratic and authoritarian society. In order to achieve this goal, a broad educational base, which must include more than technology, material well-being, and contented conformity, is required. A revolution must come in responsibility, willingness, and moral fortitude that includes knowledge, appreciation, and willingness to help. The liberal arts church-related college, dedicated to excellence in all fields, now may have its greatest opportunity for service.

Dr. Seegers withdrew as Muhlenberg's President with ease and grace, having given invaluable service. The College moved forward with brighter prospects than ever before. This did not mean that victory was complete or that effort and sacrifice were no longer needed. "God's in his heaven: all's right with the world" could not be logically applied to Muhlenberg College.

Making a change in leadership is not only important, but also difficult and soul-searching. Board President George Balmer established a precedent in asking a faculty member (Dr. Victor L. Johnson) and an alumnus (Mr. Harry Oxenreider) to serve with Board members John Repass, the Reverend Dr. William Moyer, the Reverend Dr. Lester Fetter, Attorney William S. Hudders, and Mr. Russell Fulford (chairman) to secure a new President. Their instructions were direct and matter of fact: "Get the right man."

They accepted the charge and proceeded, perhaps conscious of the old adage that a college president should be "a magician with a strong stomach and free of neuroses. He must be for and against unions, both Republican and Democrat, yet have no political bias at all." Preliminary requirements were agreed upon: he should be a layman; have close Lutheran connections; an earned Ph.D.; and distinguished in at least one special field. Russia's Sputnik brought to the fore the desirability of a scientist; preferably a physicist.

Dr. Erling N. Jensen filled the requirements admirably; he accepted and came to Muhlenberg on February 1, 1961. He was born in Iowa. His earned degrees are: B.A., Drake University (1932); M.A., Columbia University (1933); and Ph.D., Iowa State University (1947). His teaching career began at Grand View College, continued as Professor of Physics at Iowa State University, and as Senior Physicist at the Iowa State University Institute for Atomic Research—a position of prominence in one of the leading centers for the promotion of this important work. Meanwhile, he served on the Board of Trustees at Grand View College, for ten years as chairman. He is an active Lutheran, having served the church in many capacities.

A Trustee summarized reasons for what he called an admirable choice: "Dr. Jensen was chosen President of the College because he could bring the scientific background which would be helpful in this age to the further development of a liberal arts institution. In view of the merger of various Lutheran Churches, it was thought advisable to bring to the College a president from another synod. The Committee firmly decided that a new president would have to be a man whose career is in the academic field and a layman."

Judge James F. Henninger had this to say: "Specifically his masterly analysis of the colleges in the constituent churches of the Lutheran Church in America and his program for their financial support brought him to the favorable attention of the committee, as a master college administrator."

In his inaugural address (October 6, 1961), Dr. Jensen stated his convictions. "I have every confidence that, with the cooperation and assistance of its various constituencies, Muhlenberg College will be able to meet the problems of the present and the future, and emerge as a stronger and more effective institution of higher education. It is with a deep sense of humility and responsibility that I accept the position of President of Muhlenberg College, an institution that has been, and will continue to be of service to the Church, the community, the nation, and mankind." In a few well-chosen words, he stated what is widely accepted as the ultimate goal: "Muhlenberg should strive for nothing less than to become the best Christian liberal arts college dedicated to excellence in all areas."

The new President proposed the following three principal fields of endeavor, each with several subdivisions: reorganization and expansion of the Administration to meet greatly increased responsibilities; an increase in funds to expand the physical plant, facilities, scholarships, and personnel; and curriculum revision in keeping with modern trends.

Increase in the size of the College, the changed environment in which it operated, and an anticipated future, heralded a new era— part and parcel of growth and progress. One, among many things, was a centralization in administration and policy planning which was in line with the training of a scientifically oriented President.

The Eastern Pennsylvania and the Slovak-Zion Synods, as organized (1963), are the basic contacts between the Lutheran Church in America and Muhlenberg College that realistically makes it a church-related institution. Without this association the College would have difficulties. Realistically, the Ministerium served, and the Eastern Pennsylvania and the Slovak-Zion Synods are serving two major functions: financial assistance and an ever- present, although unobtrusive, religious guidance and inspiration.

The College Board of Trustees, as stipulated, has authority "to act for the corporation in the exercise of all rights, privileges, and powers." Thirty-one of the thirty-four active members are elected for three-year terms. Eighteen are chosen by the Eastern Pennsyl- vania Synod of the Lutheran Church in America (by Synod regu- lation these are divided equally between lay and clergy); one from the Slovak-Zion Synod; nine by the Board; and three by the Alumni Association. Presidents of the College and the Eastern Pennsylvania and Slovak-Zion Synods are ex-officio members.

An annual report by Muhlenberg College is presented to the Synods. Discussion is open but there is no direct intervention in college affairs. The religious life and policy are not interfered with. Contacts are channeled through the committee on religious interests in the Board of Trustees and are not authoritative in character. A closer college-church relationship came about when Muhlenberg established the position of Director of Church Rela- tions. The Reverend George F. Eichorn, Jr., was appointed to this post.

In various ways, church-college relations have benefited both parties. College indebtedness to the church is widely apparent— financially and otherwise. Faculty members and administrators provide services other than those at the College. Dr. Morris Greth, then chairman of the Sociology Department, made an extensive survey of inner missions, and Professor David E. Thomas, of the same department, did a study of "Lutherans in Allentown." Dr. Henry M. M. Richards of the economics department is aiding in research for a history of the Ministerium. Faculty members often serve as supply pastors and speakers for various church organizations.

The Executive Committee of the Board of Trustees has nine members: the Chairman of the Board, the President of the College, and seven elected by the Board. Duties as summarized are: It "shall possess and exercise all the supervisory powers of the Board of Trustees in the intervals of the meetings of the Board, but subject to its regulations and such instructions as may from time to time be given by the Board." In practice, monthly meetings are held to decide matters that cannot await Board action, or that may be handled more advantageously than by the Board. It is specifically understood that the Executive Committee decisions are not an infringement on the authority of the Board of Trustees.

A Committee for Future Planning was supported by both Dr. Tyson and Dr. Seegers. Such a group was formed in 1959. Later (1961) a Long-Range Planning Committee, consisting of members of the Board of Trustees, Administration, and faculty, drew up a program for the College needs over a ten-year period. The program was adopted by the Board (1963). A central plan was to arrange for fund raising, consisting of goals and a method of procedure. To facilitate matters, the Board Committee on Development was made responsible. The whole program amounted to $14.5 million; $8.5 for buildings and $6 million for endowment.

Currently the Board of Associates is actively engaged in organizing business, professional, and civic leaders of the community, whether alumni or not, to serve as a public relations arm of the College. George W. Gibbs is Director of Development.

It should be noted that while the Board of Trustees takes an active part in College affairs, it remains aloof from direct internal administration. Finances, in particular, and general overseeing are fields of particular activity. Effective operation is due, to a large degree, to the type of leadership in the Board. Dr. Reuben J. Butz, Attorney George B. Balmer, and the Reverend Dr. Lester E. Fetter cover an unbroken record for more than half a century. However, members of the Board do maintain keen interest and personal contact, individually and collectively, with faculty and Administration. Frequent joint conferences are held and the Faculty Club reciprocates modestly with an annual luncheon at Faculty House.

Duties of the President are defined in the Bylaws (1966) as: "The medium of communication between the administration and faculty and the Board, and also between the students and the Board; the President shall be the chief executive officer of the College and shall have the direction of the discipline, instruction, and worship of the College." Details of administration, organization, and procedure are determined by the incumbent, which, in turn, are largely affected by the personality and convictions of the President himself. While the College was small, it was possible for him to keep direct contact and make decisions without procedural routine, but the College is no longer small.

When Dr. Jensen became President the College had a faculty of 85, a student body of over a thousand, an operating budget of about 2 million dollars, a physical plant valued at 10.7 million dollars, and an endowment of 2.7 million dollars. This happened gradually and changes began in earlier administrations, but clearly pace was not kept with the aggregate growth of the institution.

"The job is to show leadership in all areas of the College, including academic," Dr. Jensen observed. "It involves, in practice, a complex relationship with Board of Trustees, students, alumni, faculty, church, administration, and community." A consultant was employed to survey the existing administrative setup and make recommendations. Many of these gradually were adopted, as time and occasion prescribed.

The President's administrative authority is guaranteed in the permanent nature of his position. He has full power of voice and vote in the Board of Trustees and in the standing committees of Board and faculty. He presides at all faculty meetings, and has close contact with student body organizations, the Woman's Auxiliary, and the alumni associations. It is a highly complex and extensive role. The College must take a place in the community as a large and flourishing corporation. Since the College is not tax supported and depends largely on gifts, more or less by freewill offering, it must be properly and efficiently operated.

Changing organizational procedure from direct personal contact, top to bottom, with the chief presiding officer, to a highly organized and centralized hierarchy of authority, came as somewhat of a shock. There is much to be said in favor of the former system, but we are living in a different age and with an institution that has grown and progressed in every way. Methods in administration had to change too. The big test is: can we maintain the basic characteristics of a Christian liberal arts college with excellence in education? If these are lost, all will be lost.

10

Growth: Spiritual, Intellectual, and Physical

For the historian, the present as a challenge is second only to that of the future. Ever present are grave dangers of omission and commission, difficulty in determining values of things untried, and in doing injustice to men still in service. Also, there is personal risk for the chronicler. Almost four centuries ago Sir Walter Raleigh warned: "Whosoever, in writing modern history, shall follow truth too near the heels, it may haply strike out his teeth."

The effect of things that may seem important today may turn out to be wholly insignificant tomorrow. Yet it is the present in which most people are interested: tomorrow is another day, come what will. However, to ignore the present, in spite of lack of proper perspective, would be shirking a responsibility. The future is elusive and posing as a prophet is presumptuous, yet the importance of the past is reflected in the present, and provides the only available clue in planning for the future.

The extent to which the morrow will be understood and prepared for is among the demands made on education. Never in the history of human society has a definite group had the power to do so much. Unfortunately, it may be for evil rather than good. Dr. Albert Schweitzer must have had this in mind while writing: "We are living in a most dangerous age because man has learned to control the forces of nature without first learning to control himself." The poet Goethe underscored the same thought when he recorded: "There is nothing so frightening as ignorance in action."

When over-all needs are considered, science and technology are not enough and economics is only a part in providing solutions. Nor are the long-cherished humanism, romanticism, and religious practices altogether promising. The approach that can produce desirable results will be most welcome.

Absence of careful planning followed by a too cautious procedure impedes progress. It has been a quality of youth to aspire and old age to conserve. Middle age should be the ideal but it is short-lived and is constantly bombarded from both sides. The early period in the history of Muhlenberg College lacked planning in material things but was blessed with an abundance of faith, hope, and dreams. Dr. Haas was possessed with visions of grandeur, but Dr. Tyson was the first President to emphasize sufficiently plans involving economic and physical planning to substantiate dreams. They were carried on with evident results and acceleration by Dr. Seegers and Dr. Jensen.

The Future of the College Committee (1959), with both faculty and Board of Trustees participating, was an auspicious beginning. A meeting was held at Buck Hill Falls and Dr. Seegers was elected chairman. He was supported by three Board members: Attorney George B. Balmer, the Reverend Dr. Richard C. Klick, and Dr. Clifford H. Trexler, and by seven faculty members: Dr. Robert A. Boyer, Dr. David H. Bremer, Dean Claude E. Dierolf, Dr. Thomas Lohr, Dr. Charles E. Mortimer, Dr. Harold L. Stenger, Jr., and Mr. Raymond J. Whispell.

The spirit that produced and continued to accompany the work of this unusually capable committee is noteworthy, because it initiated things that later developed into a full-scale program, now (1966) in the initial stage of operation. Important as the specific recommendations were, the criteria agreed upon were just as significant. It expressed a hope that the College Administration systematically and continuously study and review the program. This happened and, in retrospect, demonstrates a most encouraging modern trend, in light of rapidly changing conditions.

Four objectives were summarized: (1) That Muhlenberg College should strive for nothing less than "to become the best possible Christian liberal arts college, dedicated to excellence in all areas." (2) "Muhlenberg should make the Christian understanding of life the unifying center of its total educational program . . . relating knowledge and skills to worthy ends and values." (3) Students should be given experience to "acquire an understanding of themselves, the world in which they live, and the society of which they are a part . . ." (4) Hope is expressed that cooperation and understanding among students, faculty, administration, and Board are bound together in a common endeavor. "Within this community there must be a maximum of freedom for expression, growth, and self-realization of all its members."

Most of these recommendations were previously stated and will need repeating, but it is difficult to imagine a more skillful, convincing and inclusive presentation. The challenge was summarized by Professor Lohr: "The question of how these things are to be accomplished is the real problem and the really difficult problem facing Muhlenberg College. It requires something special in the way of an administration, a board of trustees, a student body and especially a faculty. It requires a soul-searching examination of curriculum and extracurriculum. It involves controversy and risk."

A complete analysis of the work of the committee is inappropriate because so many things introduced are being carried out and will be discussed later. However, a few samplings will show the continuity of thought and action and provide evidence that while some are idealistic and impractical dreams, others are on the high road to realization.

For example, it was stated that a full-scale curriculum study be undertaken as soon as possible; that weaknesses in the admissions policy, in the athletic program, student recruitment, and physical plant be investigated. Suggestions also were made concerning faculty and student organizations.

In two areas in particular steps were taken in plans for administration of the College and public relations; both of which are receiving much attention and substantial progress is being made. The organizational structure of the College was one of the first endeavors of Dr. Jensen.

The change in administrations led to acceleration along many lines but the business of teaching, administering, and extracurricular functioning continued. Alterations in certain instances were sudden, although principally along mechanical lines, where drastic interruptions were made without alteration of general policy. Consistently and continuously there was alertness to maintaining traditional fundamental concepts.

Long-Range Planning was not just a committee; neither a temporary nor an immediate incident. It was a culmination of past effort and commitment for the future that was not limited to one phase but to the entirety of the College program. Certainly, leadership was needed and particular assignments were made, but the heart of the project was a spirit of progress which permeated the entire effort.

Dr. Jensen's first official report to the Board of Trustees (December, 1961) expressed this desire: "It is hoped that a study of the long-range plan of Muhlenberg may be instituted in the near future, headed by a committee consisting of Board, Faculty, and Administration. It seems to me that this is a very important project, since it would furnish a sound foundation for future plans of Muhlenberg for the next ten to twenty years."

The basis for action within the College was a complete reorganization of the Administration which was put into effect in the fall of 1962. There are five specified areas: academic, under the Dean of the College; student affairs, under the Dean of Students; financial and physical plant, under the Treasurer; development, under the Director of Development; and religious program, under the Chaplain. With the President as chairman, they form the Executive Council; the policy-making body.

In order to broaden the base of contacts, the Executive Council together with six faculty members and six students, with the College President as Chairman, form the College Council, which meets once a month to discuss and consider college problems. The six faculty members are from the six standing committees of the faculty while the six students include the president of the Student Council, the president of the Women's Council, and the editor of the *Muhlenberg Weekly*.

A definite step forward was taken at a Board-faculty retreat at Buck Hill Falls (fall, 1962) where particular attention was given to curriculum and long-range planning. After eighteen months of study, the Long-Range Planning Committee, under the chairmanship of Mr. Frank Martin, presented (fall, 1963) a plan which was adopted by the Board of Trustees. It called for an $8.5 million expansion program—nine new buildings and additions: a women's dormitory, women's gymnasium, auditorium, science building, library addition, swimming pool, two men's dormitories, and a fine arts building. Two months later it was agreed to increase the endowment fund by $6 million, making a total of $14.5 million for the long-range program. The program also took into consideration the anticipated new curriculum which was passed by the faculty and approved by the Board of Trustees (spring, 1964).

The Office of Development became the center for promotional purposes. This was something comparatively new in college administration. Until a short time ago, principally the Ivy League Universities used it; now only a few colleges are without something similar. Fund raising, church and community relations, alumni affairs, and publicity are coordinated in this office. Formerly the responsibility for all these rested directly on the President's shoulders.

Time will be needed to put the intricate machinery into operation but the core framework is functioning and capable assistants are being trained to supervise details. The change produced in the over-all picture of College operation is far-reaching, and to some, schooled in the older philosophy, somewhat extreme.

The principal *raison d'être* of an educational institution is the promotion of learning. The heart of learning is subject matter, which is the teacher's job to present. Coordination and statement of principles must be agreed upon or ultimate objectives will not be realized. This should be done without damaging restrictions on the teacher and with a minimum of rules and requirements. Experience has shown that all available regulations placed on a poor teacher will not create a good one; conversely, unwarranted restrictions imposed on a good teacher can be detrimental.

Curriculum making is one of the most delicate operations in the administration of a college. Someone said truthfully that changing a curriculum is as difficult as moving a graveyard. Degrees of consistency and permanency are desirable but too much can breed stagnation. An outdated curriculum can be a real obstacle but unwarranted and radical mutilation can spell disaster.

Curriculum committees at Muhlenberg labored over a long period of time but without tangible results. Demands from students, accrediting agencies, foundations, state requirements, and better preparation of high school students made further change necessary. In 1960 a Curriculum Committee, after a recommendation was refused by the faculty, asked for consideration of a survey by an outside expert. The Board of Trustees agreed and appropriated (fall, 1961) $25,000 for such a study. Action began: the curriculum was no longer sacred, inviolate, and untouchable. It became the subject of a rational analysis.

Dr. Earl J. McGrath, then executive officer in the Institute of Higher Education at Teachers College, Columbia University, was retained to make the study. He was well qualified, versed in educational theories and with a wide variety of experiences. His findings were presented in an impressive sixty-one-page mimeographed report (fall, 1962). Like most such reports there were characteristics that surveys make unavoidable; at least an excellent start was made. It was never considered a command performance by faculty or Administration and they did not resort to rank obstructionism, but accepted it as a desirable shock treatment, conducive to action.

Background for understanding the report is included in a quotation from Dr. McGrath's definition of a liberal education. "The introduction of the student to the basic facts, principle, theories and recent developments in the three major branches of study customarily included among the liberal arts and sciences, namely the natural sciences, the social sciences, and the humanities, and fine arts. The cultivation of the processes of reasoning and communication which characterizes the tutored mind. The nurturing of a reasoned philosophy of life, including the stable traits of personality and character that normally accompany a relative permanent set of values."

The report cannot be summarized sufficiently to show the many points investigated and described. The following selections are among the more important: A greater flexibility in course requirements; added courses in geology and astronomy; possible year-round operation; increase in the teaching week, to provide more space for classes; a combination of small group discussions and lectures; and an honors program.

Most of these were discussed previously and favorably in several faculty committees but were not accepted by the majority. The added prestige of McGrath's recommendations gave renewed hope. Meetings were held, including a faculty-Board retreat at Buck Hill Falls. A year was spent in profitable contemplation and, while the report provided a basis, many things were added through discussions by faculty and Administration. Faculty approval of the curriculum came (April, 1964) and the Board of Trustees acquiesced at the spring meeting.

The "new" curriculum is not revolutionary or even entirely new. All of the recommendations were considered, some were discarded, and all were altered, in one way or another. Changes were made that were not in the report—actually, the result bore the distinct imprint of Muhlenberg College and not the dictates of an outside expert or a small clique in the faculty.

Greater flexibility was allowed in various options for required courses except in English composition, religion, and history of civilization. Also required were one year of mathematics and/or philosophy; and one year of foreign language above an elementary course, depending upon pre-college preparation. Two years of physical education were required and a proper distribution of specific requirements in sciences, humanities, and social science. Advanced standing could be arranged, "upon demonstration of required level of competence and achievement in particular subject concerned."

Enrichment courses were provided in geology, art, and music. One of the most important innovations was an "honors program." This, of course, was an adaptation of the tutorial system, long in vogue at Oxford and Cambridge Universities. It provides particular inducement and opportunity for outstanding students. Five departments and ten students were accepted in the fall term of 1966. Hopefully, it will grow to include a considerable percentage of upperclassmen. There are problems in getting sufficiently high caliber students, teaching staff, and funds for operation. The total cost for five years is estimated at $432,250. An initial gift of $72,-000 came from the Board of College Education and Church Vocations of the Lutheran Church in America.

Much credit must go to those responsible for the program. Particularly noteworthy is the belief that it is only a beginning and will be kept constantly activated. Dr. Jensen reported to the Board of Trustees (December 16, 1964): "The new curriculum will permit the student to better explore his possible fields of interest at an earlier time in his collegiate career, and will assure a broad liberal education in the three divisions, while giving the opportunity for specialization in a chosen field of interest."

However, all that is included in a program of study is not found in committee reports, course listings, requirements for admission and graduation, and in codified rules and regulations. The full impact of the education process does not appear in written form. If that were not true, it would be a mere mechanical process—perhaps it still is too much that way. Going to classes, passing tests, getting an accumulation of credit hours and quality points, and graduation are obvious student concerns. For the faculty, using the same logic, punching the clock for fifty-minute class periods twelve times a week, abbreviated office hours for consultation, ten months' work, and the pay check are common motivations. The percentage of the whole thus consummated cannot be determined and is certainly a variable factor.

In addition and, in direct opposition, there are other contributing situations which help to constitute the curriculum as a whole—generally speaking this occurs outside the classroom. It includes: informal associations between faculty and students; meetings of clubs and honor societies; such things as Professor Simpson's rendezvous in the old Library; informal student gatherings—before coeducation they were called bull sessions; and classes such as the History of Ideas.

The History of Ideas (History 71) originated in a small group of the faculty with strong convictions about liberal arts and a belief that common association of outstanding students from various disciplines would be both profitable and enjoyable. The course is unique in that the material covered and class procedure is determined by the students with faculty participation, if invited. Recognition of effectiveness was demonstrated at Commencement time (1966), the tenth anniversary, when a course reunion was held. The response was most encouraging.

The Psychology and Sociology Departments are successful in special projects assigned to small groups of students. Independent research is required in the sciences, in History and in English Departments. Humanities majors are required to participate in a Seminar in the senior year. A new course, "history of science," taught jointly by an historian and scientist, is planned for fall, 1967.

The teacher holds a unique place in human progress. Christ, the greatest of them all, set a standard for the Christian world. Socrates prided himself in explaining the facts of life to those sufficiently interested to listen. The Age of Enlightenment set a new stage in raising the dignity of the individual and put a premium on learning. The teacher characterized in "Hoosier Schoolmaster" and the college professor branded as "Egghead" were not all-inclusive points of view, but they were widespread. Such observations as "If you can't do anything else you teach—if you can't teach, you teach others how to teach," were not uncommon. Part of the problem was insufficient compensation and limited standards of living. This was answered by an offhand remark—"one-third are underpaid; one-third are paid what they are worth; and one-third get too much."

Such attitudes, in varying degrees, were more pronounced in America than in western Europe. There the title professor carried a genuine mark of distinction; and still does. It came as a surprise to the Western world when Lenin, in Communist Russia, put teachers in a preferred occupational rating.

Not all teachers properly trained and accredited measure up to the ideal. There is no agreement on standard or type. Even experts, students, alumni, and general public do not agree. A student remark emphasized that "you should have at least one 'lousy' teacher in order to appreciate the good ones." Quoting the Danforth report: "there seems always to be a nucleus of able dedicated teachers who will stay with the institution through time of adversity as well as prosperity. This is perhaps the greatest asset of the small college."

The early faculty at Muhlenberg should not be underrated. It was outstanding in classical languages, mathematics, philosophy, and theology and, in addition, professors taught in unrelated fields, with a teaching load that now appears unbearable. Praise from successful men trained in this environment is legion.

Judge James F. Henninger (1912), one of Muhlenberg's most distinguished alumni, had this to say about his undergraduate training: "It [Muhlenberg] was the best not because of imposing size, luxurious surroundings, famous faculty, or distance from home. . . . My best college didn't have all the equipment it needed to make it a first class institution, but it had a faculty whose members knew their subjects, knew how to teach them, and were interested in their students. . . . Most important it was Christian. As our minds opened to scientific truth, that truth was related to Christian teaching. Students emerged with the faith of their fathers intact; buttressed by reason. Probably the greatest benefit from Christian education was the realization that one's talents, developed by higher education, were to be dedicated not to selfish gain but to the common good. . . .

"The leadership of tomorrow will be provided by college graduates and it is important to you that that leadership be Christian. For that end, Christian Higher Education is the concern of *every* Christian."

The emphasis shifted—classics, theology, and philosophy are still taught but other fields of specialization dominate. There is doubt whether there still exists the cross-fertilization among the various subjects that might be considered desirable and that was prevalent in the early period.

Faculty meetings are scheduled three times a semester and special sessions held when needed. Duties other than teaching are numerous, serving in various assignments, including six major and numerous *ad hoc* committees. Some of these take a great deal of time: Academic Policy and Personnel, in particular. In addition, there are many general fields of activity in which all are expected to participate: "to guard fundamental principles of the College, to participate in general activities, and to maintain proper discipline through precept and practice."

The Future of the College Committee made this observation (1959): "In summary, it appears that to provide a quality education a faculty must develop a community of purpose and strive for excellence in teaching. The College for its part, must provide recognition for good work and adequate compensation for a teaching load which permits time for the faculty personnel to strive toward equality."

Currently (fall 1966), there are 112 teaching faculty members; 95 are full-time. In addition there are seven other staff members who are members of the faculty, making a total of 119. Ninety-two per cent of professors and 80 per cent of associate professors hold Ph.D.s or equivalents. They are graduates of Columbia, Pennsylvania, Cornell, Harvard, Yale, Chicago, Purdue, Freiburg, Hamburg, Oxford, and others. A variety of religious faiths are represented, fourteen in all. Lutheran and Presbyterian (48 and 13 respectively) are the most numerous but others include Roman Catholic, Jewish, and Hindu. This inclusiveness is recent—exclusion of several faiths did exist. Presently, a most liberal attitude prevails, to the point of including non-Christians and an occasional agnostic.

Salaries have undergone marked increases beginning in 1958–59 and reaching a point where Muhlenberg rates with other similar institutions. Plans are underway to continue the upgrading.

Benefits other than salaries are favorable, when compared with other colleges. Working conditions have improved: the Library and office space has been expanded and there are now special funds for supplies and equipment. On the average, fringe benefits amount to 15 per cent of the salary and include a retirement program, major medical plan, life insurance, and tuition refund. Inducements for research and study, and recognition for outstanding teaching are liberal, including sabbatical leaves, funds for advanced research projects, expenses for professional meetings, and grants for research in humanities and social science.

Muhlenberg officials encourage publication, but do not insist on

—"publish or perish." The general feeling is that it is conducive to good teaching but not a necessity. Several works of importance have been published by the faculty and grants for research have come from outside sources. Community service has been generous: speaking, working in social agencies, service clubs, and in supporting various projects.

A college or university campus, buildings, endowment, administration, alumni, curriculum, and faculty would be meaningless without students. They are grist for the mill—citizens of the future, for which the college assumes much responsibility.

A phenomenon of the age is a change in attitude toward a college education. Once a luxury, except for a few professions, now it is considered a necessity. A startling phase is the rise in demands of Negroes for higher education. The ratio in numbers of whites to blacks is twenty to one, but in 1965 there were over 234,000 Negroes in American colleges and universities. The increase is as it should be, but still short of an idealistic goal. Expanding enrollments have created problems for schools, students, and parents. For the schools it is how to provide room and facilities; for the student great pressure to get into college and to stay there, once accepted; and for parents financial strain and other responsibilities. The pressure on students is manifold. The necessity for good grades is conducive to cheating. A survey of ninety-nine colleges reveals that more than half of the students admittedly cheat in some form. This answer came from a student, without apparent remorse: "Business and graduate schools use your grade as a measuring stick." Pressure and concern over grades often cause mental disturbances. Another challenge to the tradition that college years are the best years of one's life is the number of students that suffer confusion, misery, and frustration. At the University of Pennsylvania, 20 per cent require aid from mental health services during the college years. At Harvard, 25 per cent of undergraduates seek guidance from psychiatrists or social workers. Use of the University of Washington psychiatric clinic rises faster than enrollments and there is an alarming growth of "serious" mental illness. A poll of 600 psychiatrists in various colleges indicates about

15 per cent of students require assistance. There is the extreme example of an honor student in architecture at the University of Texas who took seventeen lives, including those of his wife and mother, with no sign of alcoholism or barbituates.

But there are broader and more generalized considerations. "Students are bright but also cynical, deceitful, and arrogant," commented one professor. On the other hand, the President of a large Midwestern university expostulated: "The more I get to know today's students, the better I like them. I think they are superior to any group which has ever been here."

Students are not hesitant to state their case. They have few doubts about the future, but do show concern on how to fit into an age of cyberneticists and astrophysicists. The attitude of elders, teachers, and politicians bothers them. The Carleton College student paper retorted: "What's bugging them? Adults are the troubled generation."

Students do look at things differently, seemingly conscious of changes in store. More and better training is indicated by the choice of 52 per cent to attend graduate school; 36 per cent to teach, and 21 per cent to make a career of science or engineering. A questionnaire prepared by *Newsweek* in answer to what may be considered a key controversial question brought astonishing results: 98 per cent believe Negroes and whites should be allowed to eat at the same place; 93 per cent approve of using the same dormitories; 85 per cent believe social clubs should be open without racial discrimination; 47 per cent believe in unrestricted dating; and 36 per cent approve intermarriage.

Many practice what they preach. Nine hundred students at Harvard volunteered to teach underprivileged children. North Carolina University had 100 students offer to tutor Negroes in city slums. More than 70,000, across the country, from all types of schools, volunteered similar services. Response to the Peace Corps' appeal is surprising and revealing.

A *U.S. News and World Report* survey indicates a decline in old time "rah rah" college spirit and more support for intramural and individual sports that could be followed after graduation. "Panty" raids, fish swallowing, and pole sitting have lost allurement.

Art and music courses are more popular for cultural reasons, not just easy credit. More students are interested in world affairs and politics, but seldom have radical views. Fewer are interested in going into business for themselves and plan to seek employment in established industries and corporations.

The great influx of applicants for admission to college places a heavy burden on officers in charge. The policy set up as a guide is indicated in the following statement: "Muhlenberg College accepts applications for admission from students in the college preparatory course of accredited secondary schools and selects students who will profit from the opportunity afforded in the academic community on the basis of ability to do college work at Muhlenberg and the capacity to make constructive contributions to student life on the campus, maintaining standards of conduct in conformance with the honor code in all areas of college life."

The Admissions Office has taken steps to meet the challenge, not only of the great number of applicants but also to attract students from a wider geographical area. Furthermore, a changed athletic recruitment policy and coeducation necessarily have altered previous practices. College Board scores, high school class ratings, and I.Q.'s are used, but not to the exclusion of other qualities and characteristics. This, to the credit of Muhlenberg College, is contrary to an observation of common practice reported by the Danforth Foundation: "In general, colleges are simply raising the aptitude test score for acceptance of students and are not giving sufficient attention in the selective process to other factors that are important in matching students with colleges."

A number of recent improvements have made Muhlenberg a more inviting place for students, in addition to the educational program. The Honor System, inaugurated and administered largely by students, has given a dignified atmosphere, clearly noticeable. A health center, recently enlarged and modernized, is considered a real asset. Dormitories now accommodate most of the student body with facilities both functional and comfortable. Two new fraternity houses were added on the very attractive site south of Chew Street. Perhaps the greatest asset, from many points of view, is the Seegers Union, opened January 27, 1963, and dedicated February

8. Actually, it made a seven-day week college, because the custom had been for students to go home for weekends, as a result of the five-day board plan. The seven-day board plan (1962), and the extension of library hours, helped to further the cause. Recreational and social facilities are available. The College campus is no longer depopulated on weekends.

Activities of the student body brought favorable comment from the Evaluating Committee of the Middle States Association. "The students at Muhlenberg College enjoy and exercise a degree of freedom and initiative that is found on few campuses in the United States. . . . Today's student leaders at Muhlenberg show a lively concern and interest in the basic problems of education; the makeup of the faculty, the development of the curriculum, the content of courses, degree requirements and related questions. They share with the faculty and administration a desire to see Muhlenberg College advance in its pursuit of excellence."

Student government is one of the most conspicuous activities in the College over-all picture. It is well organized, capably led, and has an awareness of duties and responsibilities. The Council has jurisdiction affecting all areas of campus affairs: supervision of student organizations, campus functions, including assembly programs, lecture series, and social functions. Campus politics are active and well organized—rivalry among factions such as fraternity and non-fraternity, resident and commuting students, and between sexes is no longer crucial. The *Weekly, Ciarla, Arcade* and radio station WMUH operates without faculty censorship.

Generally, organized student support is cooperative but not without frequent expression of disagreement. Particular concern was expressed over the growing centralization of power in the Administration. The President of the Student Council (1964) expressed this opinion: "The Administration has undertaken to coordinate all activities on the campus, thus exerting almost total control over the manner in which the College as a whole will strive toward making its program. . . . This is the problem of Muhlenberg College." Similar concern was expressed (spring, 1966) over the new setup for faculty committees.

Feelings ran high and bitter words were spoken. It should be pointed out, however, that this is a very mild and dignified expression of democratic action and freedom of speech when compared with occurrences in many college communities. The Middle States again comment pointedly: "The primary need regarding students who react vigorously to their environment is to channel their desire for participation in decision making into useful and constructive projects. Well-used student criticism can lead to new insights into the educational process and can have a beneficial effect on the development of the College. . . . At the moment, the visitors feel, the avenues for the exchange of ideas and information by students, faculty, and administrative personnel are there, but are not used effectively."

Increase in the number of students naturally affects the over-all picture. From 1960 to 1966, regular students increased from 1139 to 1480. This was orderly; in line with availability of physical facilities and promises to continue within limitations as the Greater Muhlenberg program unfolds. A chief concern, recognized by all parties involved, is to maintain a small school character. "Small" is, of course, a relative term which does not remain constant.

Coeducation continues to have a strong influence. It made admissions more selective: 63 per cent of women in the 1966 Freshman class were in the upper tenth of high school graduating classes. Both the valedictorian and the salutatorian (1965), and eight of the eleven receiving *Summa* and *Magna Cum Laude* were women. The number continuing in graduate school and research is equally impressive. They serve as editor-in-chief of the *Weekly, Arcade,* and *Ciarla*. The dormitory council, organized in 1961, is worthy of commendation; participation in the Student Council is effective. It caused some to fear possibilities of a matriarchy; one critic called the intrusion of women "a default on the part of men," and another, more old-fashioned than others, feared "they might not be treated as ladies." There were occasions when combat lines were drawn between men and women: on dress regulations, change in qualifications of the president of Student Council, and discrimination against women. The "weaker sex" does not win on every count, but they give a good account of themselves.

Conduct and morals have been, and will continue, to be a major concern in college communities, as they are in adult society. The use of alcohol is a most challenging problem. Complete abstinence would be preferable but since the Volstead Act failed with adults, there seems little hope of success in college society. The new social code (1963) is a realistic and reasonably successful effort. First, it insists state laws be honored; second, there must be compliance with a clearly stated rule that prohibits the use of alcohol in all campus affairs—Seegers Union and dormitories; third, special permission must be obtained from the Dean of Students for each occasion when alcohol is used off campus; and fourth, a faculty member must be present at the party.

Evidence of scholarship attainment is shown in the number of grants and awards for research and graduate study, including Woodrow Wilson fellowships, Root-Tilden Law School scholarships, Danforth fellowships, National Science Foundation awards, and National Defense Education fellowships. In five years (1961–66) 124 grants, substantial in nature, were awarded.

Student participation in extracurricular activities (1964) presents another interesting sidelight. Those participating in various organizations were: 329 in departmental clubs; 157 in religious groups; 144 in music; 114 in publications; 113 in honorary fraternities; and 113 in science clubs. In the same year, 458 men and 185 women participated in intramural sports.

Some more outstanding recent group activities in which students were responsible, solely or in part, are: Festival of Arts; Foreign Policy Forum on Vietnam (this included Senator Morse of Oregon, Senator Stennis of Mississippi, and a *New York Times* correspondent); Opera Workshop (with students, faculty, and townspeople); Visiting Scholar Program; Faith and Culture Series; and weekly assemblies (with Pearl S. Buck, Norman Thomas, and Philip Roth). In addition, funds were raised to support an Ethiopian student at Muhlenberg; and volunteers, in association with Cedar Crest College students, tutor needy children.

Religion is very important in the training of any student, regardless of some decisions of the United States Supreme Court. More than ever, a greater responsibility rests with church-related institutions. It is all the more important because of a trend which has marked antireligious characteristics.

The oldest and most continuous dispute in the College history, dating back to the first decade, was compulsory chapel. This was one point over which administrations were unrelenting, even though Muhlenberg was not limited to Lutherans. There were charges that this intransigent attitude was due to Ministerium influence; but this is difficult to prove. Indeed, it was later in the century and entirely a matter of internal policy when noticeable changes were made without intervention.

The change was very much a part of other alterations, including curriculum, athletics, and social code. It was part of the new spirit but more belated than most changes. There were a number of contributing factors: the rise in prestige of the College could not tolerate such restrictions; the enlightened and persistent attitude of chaplains; the forward look taken by the religion department; and loyal support, on a wider basis, from Administration, faculty, and students.

Chaplain Bremer's monograph, "History and Purpose of Chapel-Assembly Programs and Attendance Requirements" is a clear presentation of the issues. Another praiseworthy and unique affair was an open forum on the subject of compulsory chapel that included two students, Dr. Staack, Dr. Lohr, the Reverend Dr. Lester Fetter, and Dean Marsh. Dr. Fetter and a student defended existing practice, while Dean Marsh, Dr. Staack, Dr. Lohr, and a student, for a variety of reasons, opposed.

The ruling finally adopted was drawn up by Chaplain Bremer, after serious study and consultation. It included a brief voluntary prayer service—Monday through Friday—a complete chapel service, and an assembly program each week at 10:00 A.M. Eight attendances at assembly and/or chapel programs were required per semester. Voluntary Sunday worship service also was provided. Three denominational organizations are on the campus: Muhlenberg Christian Association (Protestant), Hillel (Jewish), and Newman Club (Roman Catholic). All religious groups support the Institute of Faith, Ecumenical study group, Faith and Culture series of lectures, and the College Concert Choir. Speakers and music are outstanding and all have support much beyond expectation. Recreational programs are planned for Allentown State Hospital and Cedarbrook County Home.

The Middle States committee reported: "Special commendation

is deserved for the significant contribution made to spiritual and intellectual well-being by the office of the Chaplain of the College." The report made by the Danforth Foundation that: "In some denominations there is a feeling that the church college is obliged to provide education for almost all young churchmen, regardless of aptitude or interest," has little validity at Muhlenberg.

Physical education and varsity athletics make strange bedfellows. The Muhlenberg "founding fathers" expressed belief in development of mind and body and declared intentions of providing proper facilities for both, but little was done. Athletic competition with outside teams was strictly forbidden but off-campus contests were held. When once allowed on the campus, they became an attraction for townspeople as well as students and enthusiasts were willing to pay for the entertainment.

Patronage brought pressure for good players and winning teams: the coach became an outstanding staff member of the College and football players were heroes. The pressure to win was so great and income so lucrative that College authorities, although expressing opposition, closed their eyes to what was going on. Intercollegiate athletics became commonplace: educational institutions were known through athletic prowess and buildings, stadiums, and equipment were among the most expensive items in budgets.

Meanwhile physical education was even less regarded than before, although a requirement in most curricula. Gym classes were routine, squeezed between regular classes and taught principally by coaches. Benefits included the building of the school spirit; athletes with ability were helped to go to college; and financial support was drawn from various sources otherwise uninterested. Also, it was a public service providing wholesome entertainment for a growing sports-minded public.

However, there were abuses that caused headaches. While students accepted the star athlete as a hero, they resented the favoritism shown. While collegiate sports aided and abetted growth and provided income, the college policy was dictated too often through motivations for benefit of athletic programs. Alumni groups clamored for winning teams at any cost. Such offenses appeared in well-established and highly respected institutions and in state schools as well as private.

From the beginning, there were attempts at reform. Frequently they came from within the Department of Athletics at Muhlenberg College. Policy-makers at top level approached controls with moderation; they were dealing with a real colossus and knew it. Early protests, the result of wishful thinking, were knowingly ignored. The following is typical: "An athlete must be an amateur, agreed upon by authorities, athletic directors, coaches, and players. Money-making and entertainment are out, and material remuneration expressly forbidden." Obviously, this was not taken seriously.

Ivy League universities published (1954) this statement: "In the total life of the campus, emphasis upon intercollegiate competition must be kept in harmony with essential educational purposes of the institution." Ways of avoidance existed and were pursued vigorously. Improvement did follow, for a variety of reasons, including an increase in enrollment and government support. A good student athlete could enter without necessarily selling himself as an athlete. Basic problems, however, continued. The returning G.I., many trained in sports in the armed services, made college athletics almost professional. Eventually, there was a return to a degree of normalcy by many colleges unable to satisfy pressure for winning teams.

At Muhlenberg an important forward step was in the appointment of a joint Committee on Athletics, including members of the faculty and Board of Trustees. Dr. John Shankweiler and Mr. Harry A. Benfer were decidedly a good influence with cooperation from the coaching staff. The Head of the Athletic Department and associates were made eligible for membership in the faculty.

Various accrediting agencies and consultants supported the need for a basic change; most of them recommended a revitalizing of a physical education program. This had been sadly neglected and was a fundamental cause for criticism. Dr. McGrath recommended: "that two years of physical education be required, involving two periods of two hours per week and emphasis be placed on the physical skills which can be continued throughout adult life." The Middle States Committee took occasion to say: "Physical activities [at Muhlenberg] are unusually well planned, though the pinch of facilities limits the ideal implication of the plans." They did point out what everybody knew, that the women's gymnasium was wholly inadequate.

It should be noted that coeds made a name for themselves without exorbitant expense, athletic scholarships, and any undue favoritism and wrote an important chapter in college athletics. They have had undefeated seasons in hockey and enviable results in other sports, including basketball.

Diligent study and cooperative effort supported constructively by all parties concerned resulted in a new athletic program (1961). It was far-reaching but not revolutionary, included both intercollegiate and intramural sports, and integrated in a program to meet demands in line with outstanding institutions in Muhlenberg's class. It included a complete separation of admissions from financial aid. Beginning in September, 1962, athletes were to be admitted and awarded scholarships and grants-in-aid on the same basis as all other students.

Equally important was the rearranging of schedules to include schools in the same class as Muhlenberg—obviously removing strain of competing with larger schools. In order to facilitate this program the College transferred from the University Division to the Southern College Division of the Middle Atlantic Conference. Success in making the shift exceeded the most optimistic expectations. There are rough spots but there is reason to believe the new athletic program will be an important part of the New Muhlenberg. The following is a statement of policy: "Muhlenberg College recognizes that athletics are of social significance in our national culture . . . and when utilized properly, serve as potential educational media through which the optimum growth—physical, mental, emotional, social, and moral—may be achieved."

Dr. Jensen commented: "We expect this change to benefit all of our students because it evolved from our total education policy. This policy, then, is not a de-emphasis of varsity athletics; it is rather a re-emphasis of athletics as a proper means of realizing our total educational objectives."

Throughout Muhlenberg's first century the financial situation was mainly discouraging. With a lighter heart a discussion of present economy is most welcome. Much of the background of to-day's prominence goes deep into the past when many sterling qualities were born and nurtured in the midst of poverty. An abundance of wherewithal does not necessarily ensure quality—affluent society is beset with undesirable features.

However, it does bear repeating that much of the early weakness was due to lack of foresight and proper planning. A strong bul-wark for the present status is prevalence of both and now indica-tions are that material results are developing to add to many virtues which Muhlenberg previously possessed.

A basic limitation emerged: a tardy transition, due principally to poor public relations, from financial dependence on the church to securing aid from other sources. Protestant churches have not seen fit to give their educational institutions sufficient aid to advance, even to exist. This could be a blessing in disguise if the institution were moribund and limited in service: church-controlled rather than church-related would have prevented the present-day Muhl-enberg.

These things and many more were brought into focus in the Decade of Dedication Campaign: not enough was raised to complete the building program already underway. An additional $550,000 government loan was necessary. Was another episode in deficit financing about to be enacted? Two sets of circumstances indicate otherwise: careful planning on the part of the Board of Trustees for an $8.5 million campaign and preparations within the Administration for future campaigns centered in the Office of Development.

Plans for fund raising were formulated to include an expansion program of physical plant and an increase in endowment to $9 million, making the total sought within a ten-year period $14,500,000. To date (fall, 1966) $3.4 million has been realized in addition to an equivalent endowment fund resulting from increased appropriations from the Eastern Pennsylvania Synod.

Increased costs of operation are shown in the budgets: from $2,106,000 in 1961 to $4,210,000 in 1965. The cost per student continued to rise but Ben Franklin's comment that "an investment in knowledge pays big dividends" still carries weight. What many people thought for a long time was a myth became increasingly evident: namely, that a college cannot operate from tuition alone. Worth noting is the fact that tuition at Muhlenberg in four years (1961–65) increased 39 per cent although the entire budget increased 100 per cent. In the same period, income from the federal government for student loans through the National Defense Education Act increased from $75,000 to $134,000. In 1966 financial aid for 45 per cent of the student body was more than $500,000.

The broadened expanse of financial support is impressive. A complete listing of donors is impossible, but here are some examples: Foundation for Independent Colleges in Pennsylvania; Bethlehem Steel; Pennsylvania Power and Light; Lehigh Portland Cement; Sears Roebuck; Lehigh Structural Steel; *Call-Chronicle* Newspapers; Trexler Estate; National Science Foundation; and National Institute of Health. A very special grant, added to previous generosity, came from the Trexler Foundation. It was for an annual grant of from $20,000 to $25,000 for the Harry C. Trexler visiting professorship, to continue for six years, beginning in fall, 1967. A very substantial amount, increased periodically, comes from the Lutheran Church. The Eastern Pennsylvania Synod contributed $150,517 to the operating budget in 1961; $201,149 in 1964; and $231,135 in 1966; the Slovak-Zion Synod gave $5,000 each year from 1963–65 inclusive, and $6,000 in 1966. The largest gift bequest of $1.1 million came from the Peter S. Trumbower (1899) Estate. Plans are underway to raise additional funds for specific and general purposes. This is proof that church-related is not meaningless terminology.

Individual gifts, from a few dollars to over a million, are substantial and show a healthy increase. Alumni, parents, Woman's Auxiliary, Trustees' Fund, Friends of Muhlenberg, and Board of Associates broaden the base of income.

11

Mirth, Myth, and Miracle *

Escapades, frolics, and mild misdemeanors are teen-age frivolities. Generally, stories about them contain an element of truth but are more often embellished or even imagined. They constitute, for the older generation, much of the College tradition. If they interest the younger generation at all, it is through curiosity: few are envious.

Pranks, generally boisterous and mildly destructive, crude and belittling, and accompanied with an occasional brush with police, seldom if ever, resulted in loss of life or limb. It is doubtful if youngsters in any age—primitive to modern—differ in basic motivations. However, environment, technology, and affluence afford greater opportunities: drag-racing in high-powered sports cars and the more alluring and tempting amusements. Easter vacation assemblies at Fort Lauderdale, Florida, and many other places, were out of the question a few generations ago.

A center of attraction for "Old Grads" was the College personnel, who responded, intentionally or otherwise, magnificently. In observing the College today, alumni lament the absence of characters like Wackernagel, Ettinger, Simpson, Bernheim, and Haas. No one actually wants to return to the "good old days" but they are, for a fading generation, pleasant to recall.

* Material for this chapter was gleaned from a questionnaire sent to alumni chosen by the Alumni Association.

Hopefully, this chapter is for "Old Grads" and for curious youngsters who would like to know what the "old man" is talking about when he spills tales about the "good old days."

Athletics

Athletics contributed to mirth, myth, and miracle because it was one of the first and most widely supported of the organized College extracurricular activities. Much of a genuine spirit generated among Administration, faculty, students, alumni, and outsiders, centered in athletics. Without it, romance, spirit, and much hero worship would be lacking.

The new campus provided a so-called "gymnasium" in the basement of the Administration Building, an athletic field with goal posts, and a cinder track. "Pop" Reese was a chemistry professor, but he was better known as "patron saint of football." He coached the team, engendered a College spirit, and was father confessor to all students. Equipment was meager—some let their hair grow (Beatle type) as a substitute for headgear—and uniforms were a miscellaneous assortment. In spite of limitations, Muhlenberg won fifth place in the Pennsylvania Relays (1905), which was reported in Philadelphia and New York newspapers. A curious item on athletics was included in the student body constitution (1905): "Only bona fide students should be allowed to play on athletic teams."

There followed a disastrous decline—defeats outnumbered victories. Some claimed too much ethics was involved. A yearly drubbing by Franklin and Marshall deepened the gloom: something had to be done. An enthusiastic group of alumni took charge and, without official sanction or opposition, searched for a coach. Coach Alonzo Stagg, in his prime at the University of Chicago, recommended Thomas Kelly, his All-American tackle, and he came.

Coach Kelly—"Ulysses from the West," "Wise man from the West," "Coach Peerless"—was acclaimed immediately. Alumni and Allentown citizens joined in the welcome and showed up in great numbers not only to see the games but also to watch practice. Students idolized him: freshmen stood in awe as they watched the team being whipped into shape. A student commented: "The 'beef' collected on the football field at the end of the first week was appalling. . . . Two hundred pound huskies seemed to be so numerous as to become commonplace, and whenever three or four aforesaid gentlemen get mixed up in a scrimmage, the pile has the appearance of a baby mountain. The qualities of these arrivals, however, were not confined to weight alone, for speed, there was abundance. Lightning, well greased, is the only thing to which some of the men should be compared."

Results were notable: Lafayette was tied, New York University swamped, Carlisle Indian Reserves were overcome, but a Waterloo was bestowed by the Carlisle Indian Varsity. The big game and most resounding victory, however, was over Franklin and Marshall (1911). Gambling was poorly concealed; factionalism between Lutheran and Reformed went beyond Allentown as far as Lancaster. There was a shirt-tailed parade downtown and pep rallies took precedence over attendance in class and Chapel. The chant often repeated was: "March, march on down the field. F and M may fight to the end. but *We Will Win!*"

A player, "Walt" Reisner, described the event: "The day dawned bright and beautiful. The stands were packed and everyone reveled in the entertainment provided by the stirring music of Allentown's famous Klinglers band. . . . When the game got underway, we managed to score first when Henry Wacker grabbed a free ball and raced for a touchdown. I managed to kick the goal after touchdown. . . . The following Monday was declared a holiday by President Haas (who was as enthusiastic as the students), which enabled the students to forage for timber to climax the occasion with a huge bonfire victory celebration."

Such omnipotence that Coach Kelly acquired would seemingly make him a permanent fixture. He built a school spirit which was the envy of many institutions. A student, Henry Snyder (1915), spoke as follows: "During Coach Kelly's term, it was considered a crime to miss any pep rallies or games, at which Freshmen attendance was a strict requirement." The Metropolitan press of New York and Philadelphia explained in glowing terms the "Kelly System" used at Muhlenberg College, and players Reisner, Skean, Coplay, Hubbard, and Barry were described as outstanding.

Glory so often is followed with gloom, and that happened to Kelly. It seems he did not get far enough off campus to practice certain indiscretions. Dr. Haas got word and wielded the axe. The uproar was furious but numbers and complaints did not count; the ultimatum from the good Doctor—"Kelly must go or I will go"— settled the matter beyond appeal. Recovery took some time.

Oratorical Contests

Oratory, long before athletics, was an intercollegiate rivalry and attracted much attention. Senator Henry L. Snyder (1915) writes about one of his experiences as an orator.

"During the years 1912 to 1915, intense rivalry developed on the campus, especially between the ATO Fraternity and Delta Theta, a local organization. Also, the same sort of rivalry existed between the Euterpean and Sophronian Literary Societies. On March 24, 1915, the annual Preliminary Oratorical Contest was held at which Muhlenberg's representative at the Inter-Collegiate Contest was to be selected. Having been chosen to represent Muhlenberg on April 9, 1915, at Lafayette College, intense preparations were made. Dr. John D. M. Brown of the faculty was in charge of all oratorical activities. It was required that the oration be committed to memory and at frequent intervals the manuscript was marked by the doctor for the use of appropriate gestures.

"On or about April 5th, I developed a case of sore throat and laryngitis to a point where Dr. Seiberling came to the dorms and, as he stated, 'penciled' my throat with some horrible tasting liquid and made much ado about my high temperature and put me to bed.

"On April 8th, which happened to be the anniversary of my birth, Professor William H. 'Pop' Reese, of football fame, representing the ATO Fraternity, came to the room informing me that I must get in shape at all costs and went so far as to say that he lacked a bit of confidence in Henry H. Bagger who was being primed as the substitute. He, being the head of the chemistry department and knowing something about the effects of alcohol, told my roommate to go to the Fairgrounds Hotel and purchase two bottles of Rock & Rye, and, as I recall, donated the required funds. Further instructions were to the effect that during the course of the afternoon and the evening, I was to consume one bottle, which I proceeded to do excepting that my roommate helped himself to a portion of it. The final instructions were to leave Muhlenberg for Easton several hours before the opening of the contest and to, by all means, take the second bottle along. My roommate had charge of this and perhaps much too frequently urged me to take a swig or two en route. I can now confess that I rather enjoyed the taste and probably the effects.

"When we landed at Lafayette and walked into old Pardee Hall, several Lafayette students inquired whether the Muhlenberg representative would deliver his oration in English or Pennsylvania Dutch. I have always felt that that remark gave me special impetus.

"On the program I was listed as the sixth and last speaker. The hall was without adequate ventilation and as time wore on, perspiration increased and the gown became heavier by the minute. While the other contestants were putting forth their finest efforts, I tried to review my own oration, and it might be added, the program to me was the longest and most monotonous experience of its kind.

"Finally, it came my turn to speak about 'Peace in Armor.' Under the attending pressure, I fortunately got off to a fairly good start but before I reached midway, I failed to recall the word for word language on the printed page which was clandestinely held by Dr. Brown, who was in the audience. When some lines were forgotten, I can still recall that the color of his complexion changed, all of which had a serious effect upon me. However, I recalled the central thoughts and kept on pounding away for a total of probably fifteen minutes and then sat down completely convinced that the first speaker, representing Swarthmore College, had won the contest.

"When the result was announced there was no room for rejoicing because in my own frame of mind and in a flood of perspiration it was utterly impossible to believe what I had heard. Many of my classmates gathered around me and I recall that Ernest R. 'Mose' Keiter was bent upon finding the Lafayette student who inferred that the Muhlenberg oration would be delivered in Pennsylvania Dutch. It is hardly necessary to add that on the return trip to Muhlenberg the second bottle of Rock & Rye was then emptied in an atmosphere of rejoicing."

A Cadaver Pays an Enforced Visit to Muhlenberg

Preparation for medical school was one part of early training at Muhlenberg. An incident in that worthy endeavor, which remains in the thoughts of early participants, was the acquisition of a cadaver for experimental purposes. Dr. Lear, Professor of Biology, felt that experience in dissection of the human body would be desirable for future medical students. A corpse arrived in the winter of 1906, and the students took advantage of the opportunity for a frolic. Speeches of welcome were given and an honor guard was formed. The very first night, it was removed from the laboratory, taken to the dormitory and put in a freshman's bed. After student enjoyment of the ensuing events, the "stiff" was returned to the biology lab, apparently none the worse for wear.

Dr. Wackernagel's classroom was directly above the science laboratory and fumes penetrated the floor. The Professor objected, declaring: "This is not a medical school." A student protested, "It can hardly be denied that to offend the noses of the entire College in order to accommodate three or four students of human anatomy, shows lack of consideration for the comfort of students not connected with such work."

Shortly before Easter, what was left of the cadaver was put in a final resting place near the Lehigh County Almshouse. However, the 1907 *Ciarla* printed what was reputed to be an autobiography. The last paragraph reads: "I left the institution again before Easter vacation. It really is a wonder any of me remained to leave. If you wish the details or any further information call at my office near the Lehigh County Poor House. All questions answered free of charge."

Old "Grads" Report on High Spots in College Life

Glee Club trips, next to football invasions of other campuses, were highly regarded. Philadelphia, New York, Washington, Lancaster, and Albany were regular stopovers. Students were entertained royally, generally in homes of church members. Particularly fortunate were those assigned where "the host family included one or more attractive daughters." Some were less fortunate. One complained that only outdoor toilets were available.

Stunts that were commonplace included taking a coal wagon apart and carrying it piece by piece to the top floor hall of the dormitory. There it was reassembled, to the consternation of the janitor when he arrived the next morning. Each spring, for a number of years, the Freshman Class held an elaborate ceremony to cremate all Latin texts: Vergil was a favorite. Tickets were sold to Freshmen for the privilege of using radiators in their rooms. It was not unusual for the master electric fuse to blow the night before scheduled examinations. This necessitated going to the power-house, presumably to study, but actually for an unscheduled frolic. The telephone booth in the arcade was a favorite haunt for tricks. One was to place a bucket of water at the top of a partly opened door and then inform the intended victim he was wanted on the phone. A concealed audience enjoyed the show.

The "bowl fight" between Freshmen and Sophomores was so rugged that injuries mounted to the point that Coach Kelly interceded to have them stopped because football players were endangered physically. The tug-of-war took its place. A day and night was set aside for the two lower classes to insult each other with derogatory pictures and slogans. Then came the task of protecting them lest they be torn down or defiled. A night of gang warfare was the result with no apparent damage other than bruises, exhaustion, and unprepared assignments for classes the next day.

Gathering places off campus, remembered with widespread nostalgia, were: Allen Hotel for lunch, beer, dances and alumni gatherings; Tallman's Café for beer parties; Glick's Restaurant for baked beans; and Mealey's Auditorium for dances. Before the Commons was made available, meals were served at private homes. Stories about wonderful meals abound. Those most commonly mentioned were: "Granny's Down the Valley" (the football team ate there), Kistler's at Twenty-third and Gordon Streets, and another, referred to as several blocks down Chew Street (the name did not survive). Cakes, pies, homemade bread, and, in quantities, all the meat and vegetables desired formed the bill of fare. When the Commons appeared and patronage was required there were widespread complaints against the chef, who was the target for half-baked potatoes and anything else considered unedible.

Of course, the scene of greatest activity was in the dorms after study hours. An example of a dormitory escapade was reported by a member of the Class of 1913: "In the cemetery on Chew Street there was a pile of cannon balls between two cannons. . . . It was easy to carry these solid shots to the dorms, and, then in the middle of the night, roll them down the hall. Normal thunder could not compete with this."

Student Opinion of Professors No Longer in a Position to Defend Themselves

Dr. Wackernagel, by popular acclaim, had high priority. He must have been a remarkable man, with allowance for exaggerations, poor memories, and the confession on his part that he "never flunked a student." His father was a Professor of German Literature at the University of Basel; his brother, Professor of Greek Language and Literature at the same institution; and his mother, a sister of a Professor of Political Science at Heidelberg University. Before coming to Muhlenberg, where he was Professor of German and (1903–04) Acting President of the College, eleven years were spent in the Holy Land—for a time he was "Mayor" of Jerusalem.

Former students in chorus refer to him as "most beloved of all." Apparently they could learn, if they so desired. He was devout, scholarly, dignified, and well spoken. However, he enjoyed jokes, pranks, and students' irregularities but never lost their respect. Good students were praised and the not-so-good and lazy were ridiculed. *"Sie sind entweder krank oder verrückt"* (You are either sick or deranged!) was a choice remark.

Year after year, students presented him with a live turkey at Thanksgiving. It was a grand ceremony, held in the classroom or chapel. The gobbler was dressed for the occasion with colorful pants and bedecked with ribbons in school colors. Presentation speeches were made in many languages, prepared after weeks of training, to which Dr. Wackernagel answered in the same tongue.

The gobbler was encouraged to add his voice to the assembly. After the ceremony a parade of the student body delivered the bird to Dr. Wackernagel's home: some were fortunate enough to be invited to share in the feast next day.

The general routine during class was serious and orderly but digression was usual and sometimes riotous. On one occasion, some of Dr. Wackernagel's students decided to hold a revival meeting during a scheduled German class. The Doctor objected mildly but was intrigued, so he consented and slyly locked the doors to keep Dr. Haas out. The energetic students provided sawdust to make the "trail" realistic. Almost the entire class was "converted" with riotous acclamation. On another similar occasion, Dr. Haas did intervene and roundly lectured the offenders. When he departed and the door was closed, a student arose, shook his fist, and condemned "that Old JAW Haas." "Wackie" enjoyed it immensely.

Dr. John Bauman, Professor of Mathematics and anything else where a teacher was needed and no one was available, made a lasting impression. He had a most impressive beard, reputedly never shaved or trimmed. He wore a Prince Albert coat, year in and year out, but needed no necktie because his beard covered the space allotted. He rode to school on a large front and small rear-wheeled bicycle with books and lunch dangling in a green cloth bag from the handle bars.

He was very strict and demanding, but the students, good, bad, and indifferent, met crises as they arose. Late in life, he was nearsighted and hard-of-hearing. Dr. Bauman had a set routine: examinations were put on the board prior to the time scheduled. A good student (apparently they took turns) would sneak into the room, copy the questions, leave the room or drop the solutions out of the window to a preassembled multitude. There was a flurry of activity while copies were being made but eventually everyone appeared, a little late sometimes, but with full confidence that the exam was a cinch.

Dean Ettinger ranks high in the opinion of "Old Grads." He seemed an indispensable part of the institution; possibly everlasting. He was kindly, and easily led astray from assignments.

Universally, the opinion persists that very little Latin was learned but much good wholesome philosophy rubbed off and was painlessly absorbed. He loved to talk politics and was an ardent Republican propagandist. An exposition on politics habitually closed with: "It will help you as much as Latin."

The deanship required little of his time or effort—Dr. Haas did all the work. Dr. Ettinger loved to converse with the boys and chided them for shortcomings. One student read an excellent Latin translation with the help of a "pony" but failed miserably on questions concerning grammar. Dr. Ettinger commented: "How can you be so beautiful in the translation, yet be so weak in grammar?" Another student went to sleep and fell off his chair. After the confusion died down the Dean remarked, with his usual twinkle and wry little smile, "I guess there wasn't much Latin spilt."

Dr. Robert Horn wrote: "Dr. Ettinger taught a philosophy of life that has influenced many Muhlenberg men, who will remember the twinkle in his eye when he used the particular phrase, "Now my young friends." "Georgie," as he was affectionately known, was a thorough scholar and an inspiring teacher.

"Teedy" Simpson had the reputation of being a combination good teacher, rigid disciplinarian, and a real "character."

The following article, contributed by Warren S. Smith (1933), expresses many ideas that summarize Teedy Simpson's many revered qualities:

"Teedy was himself a character in search of an author—perhaps Dickens, though he would have scorned the association since he considered Dickens a sensationalist. I can still see him—he had no thumb on his left hand, and one of his mannerisms was to rub the stump with the thumb of his *right* hand. He might at any moment break into a spirited recitation of 'The Congo.'

"When the time came for the annual Allentown Fair, we used to think—fools that we were—that the Fair might prove more entertaining than Teedy's class. It never did, but it seemed to be an annual gesture for each student to purchase one cigar and place the weeds in a neat pile on the desk in his room at the west end of the Administration Building, before the class began. Teedy

141

would enter and eye the pile suspiciously. 'Do you people have the effrontery,' he would bark, 'to offer me a bribe?' Then he would pick up the cigars one by one and carefully place them in his pockets. 'The class is dismissed,' he would announce drily.

"Teedy never took any grading system very seriously, and it was generally understood that it was practically impossible to fail his courses. This accounted for some strange thirsts that appeared at the font of literature. Nevertheless, when you were in Teedy's room you were in a world of books, and it was a fascinating world even for those who wouldn't think of doing any reading.

"I remember one football hero who regularly fell asleep in Teedy's class promptly at ten minutes past eight every morning. Teedy, without pausing in his lecture, would carefully select the classified page from the Allentown *Morning Call* and gently spread it over the peaceful features of the sleeper. I think the hero got a B for the course. The rest of us got A's.

"Don't suppose that he was an ineffectual teacher. Those who stayed awake found it difficult to resist reading the novels—even the eighteenth century ones—by the time Teedy had spent half an hour imbedding the roots of some character in his listeners' minds. On reflection it seems to me now that he accomplished this by some sort of hypnosis, induced by lifting his eyebrows, sucking in his cheeks, and winking either eye slyly.

"I have one more image of Teedy's class that survives over the years—his dented waste basket. It sat just to the right of his desk, and I used to spend absent-minded moments wondering what it had ever come by that it should have arrived at its present sorry condition. At length I found out.

"Few things got on Teedy's nerves. Daydreaming and general inattentiveness did not. Absences did not. But reading *one* book while he was discussing *another*—that did. One sorry young man had been warned about this once or twice but he evidently persisted. One day Teedy stopped his lecture in the middle of a sentence, and for a half second his temper flared. Up went his right foot, and the waste basket shot with deadly accuracy toward the caitiff's head. When the rumbling had subsided, and the offender had begun to piece together what had happened to him,

Martin Luther Hall

Memorial Hall

Prosser Hall

The President's House

Student Health Center and Infirmary

Walz Hall

Benfer Hall

Teedy finished the sentence and the lecture in the good spirits of a man who has expressed himself vigorously and well.

"That was the only time it happened while I was a student and I considered myself fortunate, since by computing the number of dents, it became clear that the basket was kicked only once in every two or three years. I might easily have missed the show altogether.

"I suppose my recall after all these years means that there must have been something symbolic in the act, and that I myself, like many others, had felt the impact of Teedy's less palpable waste baskets."

A precious remark Teedy made on a theme utilized these words: "It is all right to call a spade a spade, but don't call it a damn dirty shovel."

Oscar Bernheim, known as "Bernie," was not a teacher but he did almost everything else. He served as Secretary to the Board of Trustees, Secretary to the President of the College, Secretary and Treasurer of the College, Bursar, Registrar, bookkeeper, printer, purchasing agent, Manager of Athletics, rental and real estate agent, Alumni Secretary, Superintendent of Buildings and Grounds, and Manager of the Commons. He was an ardent Democrat—arguments with Dr. Haas, an ardent Republican, were the source of much amusement. He was gruff and said "No" more often than any other word in the English language. If more than one word was needed he had them ready. To a young instructor who foolishly pressed a point, Bernie closed the argument with: "Young man, we have run this College a long time without you and I am sure we can continue to do so."

For thirty-nine years Bernie ruled with an iron hand, but there were those who knew how to handle him. Dr. Shankweiler tells the delightful story of an order he submitted for earthworms and cats for use in the laboratory. The answer was "No," that the boys could dig the worms and steal the cats. A few days later the same order was repeated but as *lumbricus terrestris* and *felis domesticus*. It went through without any question in spite of the fact Bernie knew Latin.

Dr. Robert Fritsch (1900) is mentioned frequently by "Old Grads" with mixed emotions but with due respect. He was a

143

stalwart in many ways: thoroughly orthodox and fundamentalist in beliefs, loyal to church, College, and community, and a capable scholar in classical languages and German. He loved etymology; a specialty was Biblical terms. For years he contributed a column to local newspapers entitled "Words in the News." Responsibility for keeping students in line, as he saw it, was taken seriously. A student was chastised soundly for saying *duuner-wedder*. Many took advantage of opportunities to annoy him. They told him stories of what they were taught in other classes, contrary to the Doctor's convictions. A favorite was to quote a young instructor who taught History of Civilization and was liberal in interpretations of the possible origin of man and earth. Finally, in desperation, Dr. Fritsch remarked: "Let the young fellow have his say; then I shall set you straight on what to believe."

Teaching was fortified with miniature tracts and leaflets, which he had for sale (at cost, of course). A story survives that sales were unusually brisk at examination time because purchases seemed to bolster grades. Also, he loved to formulate catchy phrases. "Kiss a girl and smell a camel" and "Midnight on earth is the noonday in hell" are examples.

Coeducation

Fortunately there is no end to a sense of humor. Examples of mirth, myth, and miracle still happen but time is needed for them to mature. Later in the history of Muhlenberg College, however, tradition has grown around the establishment of coeducation that promises to hold its own with older examples. Comments printed in the *Muhlenberg Weekly* are revealing. (November 3, 1953): "I came here for the purpose of getting away from women, now this." (January 14, 1954): "Women are an integral part of life, not a toy to be put away until lessons are finished." "A sizeable number of Muhlenbergers think of women as targets for tonight. . . . Women are nice people and some of you ought to get used to having them around for more than a short date before you marry one." The April Fool issue (1956)—"Flunk me again Heinrich . . . I want to be here when the coeds come."

Lamentations outweighed jubilations by far. The *Muhlenberg*

Weekly quoted a student (September 20, 1956): "East Hall men will be distracted by girls on the tennis courts, Professors will have to 'clean up lectures,' and the campus will be full of Don Juans. . . . But now that the threat is upon us there is nothing we can do about it. Muhlenberg after one hundred years as a men's college will finally fall prey to the fangs of modern education." The day coeds officially arrived on campus the statue of General Peter Muhlenberg was dressed in female clothing.

A student took a stab at poetry which was printed in the *Weekly* (September 26, 1957):

> *What have we here?*
> *A little lass*
> *Sitting in*
> *On physics class?*
> *Off. This is a man's school.*
>
> *And what is this?*
> *A bright pink room*
> *Shining from*
> *A once gray tomb?*
> *Can't be! This is a man's school.*

(Two stanzas of equally inferior poetry are omitted.)

> *Poor Muhlenberg*
> *You've made the room*
> *Now prepare to meet your doom*
> *Oh Well . . . This was a man's school.*

Signed: Mary Hyett (pen name for Marv Hyett).

Most alumni comments are unprintable.

Cedar Crest had something to say. The *Crestiad* carried an editorial arguing for a one-sexed school as the best atmosphere for learning. Fear was expressed that competition between the two schools would be harmful but hoped that "coeducation would pick up 'Berg and give it the spark it needed." One girl did say she planned to transfer to Muhlenberg.

The *Ciarla* (1958) smoothed things over: "Fading smiles were soon replaced with mischievous winks. . . . Traditions begin to disappear. . . . This is the New Muhlenberg." Women are too much a part of the College life to be considered apart from men. They have made their mark at Muhlenberg and are here to stay. Future records of mirth, myth, and miracle will be different. Let us hope they will not disappear entirely.

Each and every alumnus remembers pranks and offbeat experiences, either by giving or receiving. Experience in college means more than book learning or class recitations. Passage of time has left its mark. To the younger generation mirth, myth, and miracle seems dreadfully dull, immature, and commonplace. Today the college experience, although not devoid of relaxation, is a more serious matter: the country club life has lessened. Not to succeed in college is a misfortune and to drop out is a calamity.

12

Retrospect

The Church-related College

A CLOSE relationship between religion and learning and church-related educational institutions goes back many centuries. The Greeks combined philosophy and religion and the Romans used religion as the basis for imperial authority. The Christian Church and the Roman Empire parted company but as the latter declined the former progressed, making use of Roman hierarchial principles in its own organization. In the ensuing "Dark Ages" classical learning in the West was preserved in cathedrals and monasteries. The Renaissance, Reformation, and Enlightenment had religious connotations. A close association between learning and organized religion provided significant forces in the intellectual betterment of mankind.

Ideas about religion and education were brought to the American colonies from Oxford and Cambridge Universities in England and from Halle University in Germany. In both instances, schools and churches were closely related: ministers of the gospel preached and taught rudiments of learning. A prime concern of leaders, Henry Melchior Muhlenberg especially, was to provide proper training for ministers: a strong conviction in Germany. The founding of early colleges and universities, including Muhlenberg, was with this particular purpose in mind. "Muhlenberg College primarily was founded to secure college training of candidates for the ministry in the Lutheran Church without detriment to ancestral faith and religious character."

There was little opposition to or competition with church control of education in the American colonies. Yet there was deep-seated conviction, also transplanted from Europe, that the church supported political tyranny and suppressed freedom of thought and action. So much so, that the first amendment to the American Federal Constitution declared a separation of church and state. Today, the extent this separation has on education is still largely undetermined.

A public school system gradually emerged, first at the lower and secondary school levels, but not until past the middle of the nineteenth century was there concerted national effort to provide college education. Even then most of the states hesitated and avoided responsibility. Pennsylvania did not have a system of education until 1836 and not until thirteen years later could it be called operational. The Morrill Act (1862) provided national support to state institutions of higher learning through land grants. Meanwhile, denominational colleges spread rapidly, mostly in the South and Midwest. Unfortunately, many were inferior; they were poorly supported and some were forced to close.

An issue, a mixture of politics, religion, and general concern, arose over compulsory attendance in public schools. In 1925, the Supreme Court declared unconstitutional a state law which required all children to attend public schools. Legal battles over the status of colleges and universities gradually went in favor of private institutions, but the matter of state financial support added another issue. Legal status for private and church-related schools was assured but they still had to compete with state institutions.

Church-related colleges declined in number, although several leading institutions maintained a church status, often with considerable modifications. Others retained affiliation in name only. In 1965 17 per cent of U.S. college students were enrolled in church-related institutions. However, the United States Office of Education listed (1962) 817 "church-sponsored" schools from a total of 2,200. The real test was, and continues to be, the quality of education. There were encouraging reports. An extensive survey made (1953) by Robert H. Knapp and Joseph J. Greenbaum showed that an impressive percentage of students going for advanced degrees came from liberal arts church-related colleges. The Danforth Foundation report (1965) indicated similar results for graduates continuing in the study of law, medicine, and college teaching. Muhlenberg has an excellent record in all these fields.

Lack of uniformity in quality and prestige among church-related institutions naturally was great. Many were on the verge of collapse when the great influx of students came after World War II. Sixty-nine, of 817 listed, had less than a hundred students and 50 per cent were considered marginal or without accreditation. A number broke from church ties because this relationship was no longer considered an asset.

Also, there were discouraging reports that church schools had not maintained a reputation of quality in religion courses. Here is a Danforth Foundation comment: "It is our considered opinion that religion is not as strong in church-related institutions as one might expect." Furthermore, "Church-related higher education is not much better in helping students face fundamental questions than are other institutions." Still further: "Student religious organizations are weak and struggling on most campuses. In many places they are close to extinction."

Ineffectiveness of many church-related colleges arises from many sources. In no small degree, it stems from basic difficulties which the church faces in handling enormously increased social problems. Lack of unity, even among Christians, makes concerted effort difficult, in face of what should be a common cause. Rank denominationalism and prejudice is illustrated in a statement made by a member of the Indiana Legislature—a Presbyterian. "There is not a Methodist in America with sufficient learning to fill a professor's chair, if it were tendered him." One is reluctant to imagine what he might say about a Roman Catholic.

There is too much local competition among institutions supported by the same church. Examples are: three Methodist colleges in Indiana, five United Presbyterian in Missouri and four in Iowa, and three Roman Catholic colleges for women in Milwaukee. There are cases to the contrary that show promise. The University of Dallas (Roman Catholic) is sponsoring a move to combine neighboring church colleges. Westminster College at Salt Lake City (Protestant) suggests local schools work out a unified plan for economical operation. The National Catholic Educational Association and the Council of Protestant Colleges and Universities are engaged in promoting college cooperation nationally.

From the beginning, finances have been and continue to be an ever-present problem: the cost of learning has risen in similar proportion to the cost of living. Once it was possible to get along with few facilities, meager personnel, and limited income, but that day is past. Tax-supported institutions are luxurious, basking in the bright sunshine of generous government support and acclaimed by an affluent society. There are more than enough students, but tuition alone cannot finance a college. The independent college must also depend upon endowment income, gifts, grants, and government aid. The latter introduces an entirely new set of principles and problems which must be encountered.

Contributions (1963) of churches to their colleges averaged only 12.8 per cent of operating budgets. Appreciable improvement is apparent but the situation is still serious. Increase in current income is a most pressing need. A solution could come from increased government support. The big question is: how will it affect the status of a church-related or independent college?

The Lutheran Church in America, with its eighteen colleges and universities in the United States (not counting junior colleges and seminaries), plays a significant role in education. A strong cultural as well as theological background permeates the program. The early story of Muhlenberg College shows that the great desire of Henry Melchior Muhlenberg to establish a seminary and college in eastern Pennsylvania was realized. Muhlenberg College outgrew the original intent, but in taking on new responsibilities did not entirely eliminate the old. The transition is an important part of the Muhlenberg saga.

Instances of concern were numerous. Ministerium interest in the College ranged from apparent indifference to interest, if it didn't cost anything, then to an eventual acceptance of financial responsibility, not only to rescue an ailing institution but also to give it new life and hope.

Minutes of the 1920 meeting of the United Lutheran Church record that "educational institutions, in order to have moral and financial support" must conform in certain particulars. The Educational Committee (1920) recommended to Muhlenberg College that "a Bible Department should be maintained with a full-time professor or instructor in charge, with three periods a week for at least two years of academic work." Very few such direct suggestions were made but personal contact was not wanting. There are proofs of free exchange of ideas and mutual agreements. The Lutheran Synod of Eastern Pennsylvania does little supervision and rarely intervenes in College policy.

Public recognitions of Ministerium authority were numerous. The comments of Board President Dr. Reuben J. Butz, made at the inauguration of Dr. Levering Tyson, are typical: "We are part of the educational life of the Lutheran church and the child of the Ministerium, and the historic and corporate connection between it and the College must be conserved for our mutual benefit." Every Board Chairman and every President of the College, in substance, has said the same thing.

A chaplain is very important in the proper functioning of a church-related college. He is the personalized center of a religious environment—otherwise church-related would be meaningless. The task is not easy: he cannot be adjudged only a preacher; evangelism is not a primary need; and theology is taught in the religion department. His duties were defined admirably by the late Dr. Emil Fischer: "A chaplain at a church institution is the tangible symbol of a church's conviction that the teaching and personal ministry which she exercises through her pastor is a vital ministry and must never be interrupted when a student leaves his old environment to make his home on the campus of one of her colleges." Muhlenberg College has been fortunate in having outstanding chaplains.

The chapel, a world-wide symbol of a place to worship, provides the physical embodiment of church-relation on the campus: a building, but a very particular building—a thing of beauty and at the same time a sanctuary. It is dispensable but exceedingly desirable.

Late in life, Dr. Haas, with renewed conviction, risked his reputation and the financial security of the College on the remedial and idealistic influence of a chapel. "In fact," he said, "it has the supreme place among buildings. . . . It stands among all the visible things of life, for the invisible. . . . We need a building of beauty to help us to follow realization of worship. . . . Too often the academic life stifles the development of the heart."

Proceeds for his heart's desire were realized, in part, from the bequest of Annie J. Egner Hartzell. The dreams of a building visualized by the donor and Dr. Haas were far beyond available means. The College, at the time, was heavily in debt and operating with a constantly growing deficit. There were reasons for urgency since the will required Trustees of Muhlenberg College to accept the conditions within six months, and if accepted but not carried out in three years the bequest would be revoked. There was to be a set of eleven chimes, weighing 16,000 pounds, the cost not to exceed $6,000. A codicil was added: "If $6,000 will not pay for the chimes, the amount may be added to chapel cost." Obviously, this sum was absorbed without chimes. The total Chapel cost was $375,000; returns from the bequest were $126,810.76. Numerous gifts were received from many sources for windows, pews, and other needs and decorations.

Dr. Haas and all parties concerned were pleased and impressed with the beautiful new building. However, the extent to which it served as a general panacea for college problems was a disappointment. Finances cast a gloom over the entire institution, including the Chapel. Disparaging remarks came from a variety of sources. They deplored money "expended for a chapel that could and should have been used for a swimming pool." All these things, meaningful as they may have been, do not deprive the College of a lovely building to grace the campus. Indeed, it is difficult to imagine Muhlenberg without its impressive presence. The swimming pool will come—then the factions may rejoice in unison.

The Chapel was designed by Frank R. Watson of Philadelphia. The stained glass windows were created by the D'Ascenzo Studios, also in Philadelphia. The exterior length is 194 feet; the total interior width 47 feet. In size, it is miniature compared with the great cathedrals of Europe, but still a gem of Gothic architecture.

The dominant sentiment expressed in symbolism is "progress of Christianity under the inspiration of great leaders; past and present." Figures on the stalls for clergy, president, dean, and sub-dean depict Dr. Haas, Dr. Ettinger, Dr. Seip, Dr. Bauman, Mr. Bernheim, and Professor Simpson.

The great window is flanked by statues of Martin Luther and Henry Melchior Muhlenberg. The Ascended Christ is shown above the middle entrance to the nave, done in Italian marble inlaid with gold leaf mosaics. The monumental altar and tables are made of Tavernelle marble. The reredos above the altar is carved oak, representing figures of the Four Evangelists. *Te Deum*, the Lord receiving the praises of the Church Triumphant and Militant, is illuminated with groups of figures in polychrome and gold. Above these are five lancet windows, pointing to the Gothic lacery beneath the ceiling vault, depicting The Lord's Great Commission to the Disciples. All are accentuated by an embellished Cross.

A crowning glory, typical of Gothic architecture, are the stained glass windows. The four in the sanctuary represent St. Peter, Irenaeus, St. Paul, and Tertullian. The transept windows, on the lower level, present medievalists: Athanasius, Boniface, Augustine, and Wycliffe. The north windows record the story of the Reformation in Europe and those on the south portray leaders of Lutheranism in America: Peter Muhlenberg, Conrad Weiser, Justus Falckner, Charles P. Krauth, William A. Passavant, and John Augustus William Haas. The great west window has the command for Christian service: "Go ye into all the world." Activities at Muhlenberg College are presented in ten windows in the north and south entrance and ambulatories. Six lancets in the sacristy and chaplain's office represent work of the Christian ministry.

Muhlenberg College represents a church-related institution creditably and thereby profits greatly. A further summation as to the future will be made in the last chapter.

Liberal Arts

There is a close and realistic relationship in the basic ideals of liberal arts and church-relationship. An inherent conflict existed when theology and ministerial training dominated the curriculum, but were united when classics and mathematics were adopted as the core of instruction. The union was intensified when scientific and preprofessional, along with a wider diversification of courses, appeared. The classics and liberal arts, as they were then defined, were inseparable but not so closely associated with church-related objectives. This could not continue when motivations for college education changed. Liberal arts remained in nomenclature but it changed in character and content. There is a current possibility that a divergence in church-related concepts, as well as liberal arts, is again bringing them together. It may well be one of the important changes now in process.

Few concepts, including freedom, individualism, and democracy, are considered with so many variations, and with such contrasts of veneration and condemnation, as liberal arts. It is always difficult, perhaps stifling, to confine ideologies to a definite creed or restrict them to a stereotyped *modus operandi*.

There is general agreement that since the working relationship between classics and liberal arts lessened and finally parted company, no working combination was substituted. Yet free from classic influence, liberal arts continued—possibly more talked about by more diversified groups than ever before. A random selection of comments *pro* and *con* will illustrate.

"Nobody is against a liberal education except students, parents, citizens, and most Ph.D.s," wrote Columbia's Professor Jacques Barzun, who predicted the demise of the liberal arts college. Author and scholar Archibald MacLeish says: "We have lived a long time in a climate of abstract principle of high and noble rhetoric. Some consider it old-fashioned and others think our whole educational system is going to the dogs and liberal arts may be the reason."

The other side also has sponsors. Yale's late President Griswold wrote: "The liberal arts have constituted the basic studies from which all phases of the educational process . . . drew nourishment and without which they languish and fail. . . . In all controversies held over educational theories, liberal arts have been the chief casualty." On the same subject, another spokesman said: "[a liberal education] is as enduring as man's love of freedom, for finesse, for fellow men, and for God. . . . It makes people not only acceptable to God, but also approved of by man." Educator Dr. Robert Hutchins followed the same reasoning: "The aim of education is to connect man with man, to connect the present with the past, and to advance the thinking of the race." Dr. James N. Hillman believes: "The influence of a total college program is to liberalize and broaden the souls and ideals of all mankind."

Compromise views and generalities supporting liberal arts have neither ceased nor decreased. "One could not live reasonably without science nor gracefully without arts and letters" is a soul-satisfying idea. Another popular thought: "A well-trained faculty man may teach all concepts of liberal arts regardless of subject matter." Admiral Hyman G. Rickover points out the dangers of technology to the liberal arts idea. "It [technology] is a product of human effort to benefit man, encompassing all interest and needs of man: not an end in itself but a means to an end."

Certain generalizations strongly supporting liberal arts are widespread: encouragement of the individual student to develop inclinations and capacities; skills needed by everyone—reasoning, writing, and speaking; and learning to adjust to new situations. The *Proceedings of a Conference of Academic Deans* (1963) summarizes liberal arts as: "an education in discrimination, in creative imagination, in logical thought, and in political wisdom."

Some of the problems and obstacles likewise are generally recognized. Are such realizations possible in face of specialization, materialism, an affluent society, and the welfare state? Is the democratization of education and large increase in number of students, a detriment? Are the complexities in modern civilization so demanding that such idealistic principles are no longer adaptable?

The story at Muhlenberg College provides an interesting case study.

General commitment to liberal arts is genuine and widespread at Muhlenberg. Every President of the College from Dr. Frederick Augustus Muhlenberg to Dr. Erling N. Jensen has given complete approbation. It is part of all publications covering the College: catalogs, journals, brochures, and in those emanating from the Synod, through the entire Lutheran hierarchy, including students.

The *Self-Evaluation* analysis prepared by the faculty for the

Middle States Association includes this statement: "Muhlenberg holds that a liberal education is the vital agency for freeing the mind from those elements of parochialism and prejudice which normally confine it, and perhaps the only instrument for coping with the complexities of our contemporary world." The over-all objective is summarized by Dr. Thomas F. Lohr, Professor of Psychology: "We believe Muhlenberg College as an independent, church-related liberal arts college should attempt to find and realize its unique role in the service of God and mankind. To perform its special service it cannot rely on a declaration of good intentions but must continually probe to understand the nature of its unique role in specific terms and search for ways to fill that role."

Dr. Earl J. McGrath, a well-recognized spokesman in the field and one whose advice and counsel were sought by Muhlenberg, commented on what he calls a "Liberal Education": 1. The introduction of the student to the basic facts, principles, theories, and recent developments in the three major branches of study customarily included among the liberal arts and sciences, namely the natural sciences, the social sciences, and the humanities, including fine arts. 2. The cultivation of processes of reasoning and communication which characterize the tutored mind. 3. The nurturing of a reasoned philosophy of life, including the stable traits of personality and character that normally accompany a relatively permanent set of values.

There is proof of the serious intent at Muhlenberg to attain these ends. There is wholesome skepticism by some whether the results are commensurate with the effort. However, liberal arts and church affiliation are deeply rooted at the College. If there is a problem, it is to make efforts and objectives sufficiently related to create a tangible objective. Further observations will be made in the next chapter.

The Library

The library, depository for a storehouse of learning in printed form, is, in reality, the nerve center of an educational institution. Textbooks, laboratories, and classrooms are but appendages to the library. The reading room and desks in the stacks provide the proper environment for study and reflection—companionship with records and literary products of the ages. The library should be made as inviting as possible and should have the focus of attention of those responsible for the institution's welfare.

The story of the Library at Muhlenberg College constitutes a measure of progress—a line of development running through the entire history: as the Library was, so was the College. The meagerness of the early collections indicate a frailness while the stature of the present center reflects justifiable prestige.

However, at all the stages of meagerness there were elements of quality. Libraries of the literary societies had well-selected books. Also, activities within the societies ensured that the books available were in constant use. Not until they began to decline did the College Library show signs of growth. When the move was made to the new location in west Allentown, the Library had to find a nook in the Administration Building; there was no other place to go. The second floor was chosen. Three rooms ran the full width of the east end of the building—the Chapel on the first floor and one of the literary societies on the third. Here it remained until the present Library was completed, almost three decades later. Parenthetically, these were lean years for the College.

But the sojourn on the second floor of the Administration Building was not entirely barren. There were book shelves, partly filled, but without an adequate system of cataloguing, two or three small tables intended for students, and extremely poor lighting. The center of attraction, at least in later days, was in the northwest corner of the room where there was a disheveled rickety table and a stool, almost engulfed with papers, books, and magazines. It might have been taken for a waste heap had it not been for the presence of a lovable, devoted, and unusually capable man with a thumbless hand, a bald head, and an ever-present and perpetually half-consumed "stinky" cigar: Stephen G. Simpson, affectionately called "Teedy." There were always students and often some faculty around, running errands, listening to sage remarks, sometimes punctuated with a soliloquy or recitation, like "Face on the barroom floor" and "Mumbo Jumbo." If one were to seek proof positive of a bit of liberal arts education at that time, here would be a likely choice.

In the midst of this organized confusion there were signs of quality: little concentrations here and there of unusual selections, the handiwork of men like President John A. W. Haas and Professors Henry R. Mueller and John D. M. Brown.

After a long period of waiting, the new Library was built and it was regarded with high hopes. Speeches at the dedication referred to its capacity for students and books as more than ample for the foreseeable future. The building aroused some enthusiasm but also detractions. The dome was referred to as resembling a milk cow's inverted udder. At the time, there was space to spare; the third floor was vacant, seminar rooms were used for storage, and empty stacks resembled the interior of an empty cave. Gradually, this all changed; only recently was the Librarian able to get rid of various nonlibrary concentrations to provide much needed space for his own use. Now, in the path of progress, the building is no longer satisfactory. The Middle States Evaluating Committee (1965) made this reference: "The library building, though solid, handsome and attractive, is old and not adaptable to emphasis on study cubicles or economical expansion to present additional stacks."

The evolution of the Library was an integral part of the College growth. Professor Simpson, not a librarian in a technical sense, gave way in course to trained personnel. Mrs. Robert C. Horn made an appreciable start and Mr. Richard L. Brown continued with pioneering skill. The present staff measure up to expectations of faculty, students, and accrediting committees.

The Middle States investigating group did not like the building but praised the contents and management. "Under the highly experienced and competent direction of its librarian and his professional staff, the Library presents a picture of efficient operation and general adequacy for the present student body and programs. . . . The stacks are open, and the visitors found practically no student feeling that they met with anything less than full cooperation in their use of the library. . . . Members of the team were gratified by their spot checks of library holdings in their own academic areas."

The Muhlenberg Library has most of the qualities and characteristics for satisfactory services for a small undergraduate college. The budget for books and periodicals (1967–68) is $40,000. Over 5,000 books are purchased annually which makes 124,000 volumes in the total collection to date. Necessary equipment including a photocopier and a microfilm reader are provided, with proper assistance available when needed. An interlibrary loan service is in operation and the Library is a depository for United States Government publications.

The book collections in Humanities and Social Science (due partly to the Haas collection in philosophy and the Stopp Library) are outstanding. Marked advancements have been made in other fields and there is a well-balanced selection in the collections, as a whole. A noticeable need exists in specialized fields for faculty research and for the Honors Program as it develops. The Pennsylvania German collection is nationally recognized. Other specialties show promise, including the Muhlenberg Collection.

The Woman's Auxiliary

Foremost among the groups that support the College financially and otherwise is the Woman's Auxiliary. For fifty years members have been ready to give helping hands where a feminine touch was needed and where masculine efforts were lacking. The Auxiliary made Muhlenberg coeducational in service, before women students were allowed. Many had no college affiliation but a more loyal and helpful group never existed.

Financial support was noteworthy. In fifty years, they contributed cash, exclusive of work and material assistance, that amounted to $144,657.81. Much of this was provided when the College exchequer was very low. Since their organization in 1915 the ladies have taken part in every campaign for funds. In the Field House Campaign (1916), their team was second highest in the amount collected. Among their most notable gifts are: the Skinner Organ ($19,750); shrubbery and landscaping ($15,000); renovating and equipping the Commons ($7,397); Memorial Hall Lounge ($15,000); tennis courts ($29,000); and Seegers Union ($30,916). Recently, the purchase of a new organ for the Chapel was underwritten.

Money is indispensable but it is not everything; and important as dollars are, the love and service, even just the ladies' presence, are a continued blessing adding to that intangible something that makes the College.

Further proof is given that winning the heart of a man is through his stomach. Long before facilities in Seegers Union were available and the Commons anything like adequate, the faithful Auxiliary was on hand with cookies, cake (homemade very often), tea, coffee, soft drinks, and remarkable hospitality at commencements, College days, receptions, alumni meetings, church gatherings, and campaign meetings. The Navy Program at Muhlenberg in World War II could not have been the same without the Woman's Auxiliary. While the embryonic sailors and marines were addicts to female youth, they were still close enough to mother's apron strings to be grateful to these kind ladies in their maturity. On one auspicious occasion when the dining facilities failed in the Commons for a week, lunches were served by the Woman's Auxiliary. Among their many other activities were: furniture repaired and curtains put up in dormitories; Christmas packages wrapped for boys in service; table linens mended and napkins hemmed; sweaters repaired and socks darned for the football team; an active part in the Muhlenberg Bicentennial celebration; sponsorship of the "Ice Vogues" in Memorial Hall for three years, clearing more than $13,000; the sale of subscriptions to magazines; entertainment of wives of alumni during commencements; and sponsorship of Mask and Dagger plays, organ recitals, lectures, and choir concerts. The first gift of the Woman's Auxiliary to the College, as recorded, was a dozen napkins; cost, $8.46.

This remarkable organization came into being in 1915, largely through the inspiration of Mrs. George K. Mosser, president until her death (1934). The first meeting, as recorded in the minutes, was held at Christ Lutheran Church where lunch was served to a committee planning a campaign for the benefit of Muhlenberg College and Philadelphia Seminary. After lunch was over and dishes washed, an election was held—Mrs. Mosser, president; Mrs. Charles Ziegenfus, secretary; and Mrs. L. Shankweiler, treasurer.

The list of officers reads like an Allentown ladies *Who's Who*.

Mrs. Mosser was followed by her daughter, Mrs. Dewey Fuller (1934–43), Mrs. G. Donald Marks (1943–46), Mrs. Elmer H. Bausch (1946–49), Mrs. William C. Berkemeyer (1949–52), Mrs. Karl B. Gilbert (1952–55), Miss Dorothea Kostenbader (1955–59), Mrs. Harold J. Rickmers (1959–62), Mrs. Richard G. Miller, Sr. (1962–65), and Mrs. Stanley L. Harter (1965——). Other officers, committee chairmen, and willing workers, if space permitted, should be added. There are (1966) more than 5,000 active members; 313 are life members.

It is difficult to give proper credit to such an organization. Members are always present or near at hand who work quietly and unobtrusively. From time to time, credit is given—names on identification plates in various buildings show that. A *Ciarla* was dedicated to them, and in 1965 Mrs. Walter H. Gross, a very successful treasurer, was given an award by the Alumni Association.

The Alumni

The alumni are the finished product of a college. The process itself does not result in financial profit because it costs more than return from tuition. They are not a standardized commodity, since no two are alike. Some show good effects of a college education and are successful in life; others have little of importance to demonstrate, except a diploma that hangs conspicuously on a wall. Loyalty is demonstrated through support, financial and otherwise, but indifference is commonplace. The preferred element fortunately overshadows others and the net result is favorable, indispensable, and well worth all effort expended.

Alumni, like all other aspects of a college, are changing. While Muhlenberg essentially was a training school for the Lutheran ministry and other attractions for attending college were limited, the alumni were few in number and, while loyalty was not wanting, enthusiasm was. Nonacademic allurements at college were limited mainly to pranks, bull sessions, and a few off-campus diversions. Athletics, debating, oratorical contests, and better communications injected a new spirit. Yet, attending college was not considered a must except for preprofessional purposes, and it was regarded as something of a luxury.

A marked change began before the mid-twentieth century. College students and, eventually, the alumni were different. The older generations missed the "good old days." Those who returned after a decade or so were disillusioned. Students were more serious, and for the alumni interests were more varied. Future success depended more and more on a college education—athletics and amusements, in the interim of four years, were no longer so important in their recollections. Loyalty took on different characteristics. College attachments were more widespread: graduate work in other institutions; wife from a different school, and children wandering afield. The old-time *Alma Mater* has competition.

This does not mean all work and no play—the plush Seegers Union disproves any such contention. Comfortable chairs, lounges, game rooms, and refreshment facilities have dignified the environment without affecting a serious student attitude. Coeducation would have many problems without the new and improved surroundings.

The change in student attitude is praiseworthy and a partial transformation of alumni has possibilities. They have a more important role to play than ever. Dr. Edgar M. Carlson, President of Gustavus Adolphus College, puts it this way: "If a college has not succeeded in persuading its students to give after four years of experience on its campus, after having been subjected to the whole education program of the institution, it has failed in its mission. If it trains men to 'get' but fails to train them to 'give,' it really has no good reason for existence."

The alumni association at Muhlenberg has changed from an inadequate group, getting along as best it could, to a systematized and up-to-date organization, thoroughly integrated in an over-all College plan. As late as 1911, the Board of Trustees was petitioned for funds to provide personnel and office setup for the use of alumni affairs. Not until the arrival of the Navy Unit in World War II were suitable arrangements made. More recently changes were made to make the Alumni Office commensurate with the College generally.

The accomplishments are notable. Up-to-date records are kept, publications keep alumni informed, and a medium of contact with the College exists which renders a two-way service. Response to requests for financial assistance is good and improving rapidly. The Loyalty Fund, recently changed to Annual Alumni Fund, provides appreciable results. It started with a few thousand dollars—one year when the Loyalty Fund was earmarked for the Student Loan Fund it was less than $1,200, but it had increased to $55,047 in 1959–60, to $69,076.09 in 1965, and to $91,514.57 in 1966.

A plan to collect $5 annual dues was inaugurated June 1, 1965, in order to raise funds and "to make membership more meaningful." The Minutes of the Alumni Executive Council (October 31, 1964) contain a statement of incentive. "There is room for vast improvement in Muhlenberg College Loyalty. . . . Our thinking and doing demand us to be objective, not subjective, and to move forward constructively now, not compounding our past mistakes. . . . Muhlenberg needs our help to make them [new traditions] purposeful and objective. To do so is the responsibility of all alumni."

The listed objectives are: "to promote good will among alumni and the community for the College. To promote ever-increasing activity of alumni in: Annual Alumni Fund and capital campaigns . . . reunions . . . and assistance in formation of new alumni clubs. . . . In serving as needed or requested in other ways to advance the interests of the College. Assisting in the indoctrination of students from the freshman year on. . . ." It was further recommended that the Alumni Association should function through its Executive Council and Secretary directly to the Director of Development to assure a proper College relationship.

Alumni holding degrees (1966) number 5,639 and others who qualify for membership make a grand total of 7,800. Fifty-five per cent are Pennsylvanians: 15 per cent from the Lehigh Valley. No presidents or vice-presidents of the United States and no Nobel or Pulitzer prize-winners are included, but when it comes to community leaders and those in the upper stratum of many professions the total is substantial. Muhlenberg is basically a middle-class institution, serving the backbone of modern society. The distribution of alumni is impressive: in each category there are important representatives. In 1964, there were 656 active in the ministry and 1,900 in teaching. Medicine has 594 and law 195. Almost half of the total are engaged in business, which speaks well for the varied types of training available.

To choose individuals for special recognition is extremely difficult and most hazardous. Opinions differ in those eligible at the topmost level and marginal cases are numerous. I decided, after long deliberation, not to list names because of unavoidable injustices that would occur both in commission and omission.

Teacher Training and Adult Education

The general commitment of Muhlenberg College to serve the public, whenever feasible, was responsible for establishment of the Extension Department. There is no question that this was a valuable service, especially to teachers in service without a degree and faced with a state ruling that one was necessary to insure tenure. However, many doubts arose as to the general effect on the College program. This was not vital until the College grew beyond all expectation and when possible accreditation became a matter of concern.

The Future of the College Report (1959) summarized the situation: "The Committee believes that the relationship between the regular program of the College and its extension programs in Evening and Summer School courses needs clarification. Many of our present practices are unsatisfactory both to students and faculty. The present unwholesome policy of gearing course offerings and instructors' salaries to registration should be discontinued. In its place, careful survey and planning should precede the establishment of course offerings, and they should then be made on the basis of firm commitment. One of the sources of poor public relations for the College appears to be a misunderstanding attendant upon the college course offering in the evening school and upon the availability of a full degree program in the evening sessions. In the light of present demands it would seem unwise for the College to commit itself to offering full degree programs in evening session."

The Summer School, although under the direction of the Extension School, was also a continuation of the regular College program. There were many annoying irregularities for the Administration admissions policy, for faculty, and for students. The Summer School was established in 1915, and Professor Reese, whose name was associated with so many College innovations, was Director. The idea was good but did not prosper until non-College students were admitted.

The whole matter was given early attention in Dr. Jensen's administration with the cooperation of Dr. William F. French, Head of the Education Department. Dr. McGrath's report (1962) on the curriculum suggested a closer relationship between Summer Session and regular College term either on a trimester or quarter basis. He also recommended a broader service in the Evening School for "citizens who may have completed their formal schooling as well as for those who find it necessary to work for a degree at irregular hours and at a slower pace than is normal."

A revised program was adopted by the faculty (March, 1962) which coordinated the Evening Session with the regular academic program: "students may proceed to the degree entirely on the basis of work done in the Evening Session, if they apply for and are admitted to candidacy for the degree."

A further important innovation was in offering noncredit short courses in evening session on special subjects "to meet the needs of interested adults in the Lehigh Valley who wish professional guidance in the exploration of certain contemporary problems." No College credit is involved. All courses are taught by members of the Muhlenberg College faculty. However, occasional guest lecturers participate.

The following is a sampling of noncredit courses offered: Sociology of Literature, by Dr. Heinrich Meyer; Approach to a Living Philosophy of Religion, by Dr. David A. Reed; Geography of Latin America, by Mr. Peter Sardo; An Approach to Reading the Modern Poets, by Dean Thad Marsh; Demonstration Lectures in Physics, by Dr. Robert Boyer; Esperanto, by Dr. Rodney Ring; Conversational French, by Mr. Martin Kopf; Through the 19th Century with English Poets, by Dr. Minotte Chatfield; Natural History of Vertebrates, by Dr. Carl Oplinger, and Ecumenism, by Dr. Hagen Staack.

Dr. Jensen reported to the Board of Trustees (December 18,

1962): "This is an encourging action and I am sure that it will be of considerable benefit to many individuals in the surrounding community."

In conjunction with the Middle States evaluation, Muhlenberg applied for and received accreditation, both in elementary and secondary fields (September 19, 1965), from the National Council for Accreditation of Teacher Education (NCATE). In April, 1966, the Department of Public Instruction of the Commonwealth of Pennsylvania approved not only the College Department of Education but all other Departments where prospective teachers are trained. Teaching certificates will now be issued to Muhlenberg graduates in Biology, Chemistry, Economics, Elementary Education, Mathematics, Physics, English, French, German, History, Spanish, and Latin.

An interesting sidelight and a praiseworthy demonstration of good that came from a controversial part of the early program is demonstrated in the loyalty and support given by the Muhlenberg College Alumnae Association, which includes those who received degrees in the Extension School. The declared object "is to sustain and promote the interests of Muhlenberg College." The organization was begun in May, 1940, and now has a participating membership of seventy members. They presented the College a $1,000 memorial fund in honor of Dr. Isaac Miles Wright.

13

Prospect

To write an appropriate ending for a story that began with doubts and misgivings and now has bright prospects is difficult. How long this success may continue without damaging interruptions cannot be determined. However, hope that they will not come, in some form, is unrealistic. There would be a sense of futility and irresponsibility not to indicate apparent trends, in spite of the risk involved.

Aims, objectives, and ultimate goals in education increase when greater responsibilities are incurred. As long as a diploma, signed, sealed, and presented is considered the magic key to the future, the educational process is not unusually important. If such was ever true, times have changed.

Public complaint that college graduates, in great number, cannot write, speak, or think clearly are exaggerations, although inexcusable deficiencies do exist. Proficiency in training for a specialty is important, yet preparation for a life fortified with happiness, a willingness to serve in public welfare as a responsible citizen, and having sufficient moral stamina to assure dignity and ethical standards, are recognized desirable qualities.

Liberal arts, fortified with church-related ideals, can, if true to calling, instill these principles. However, the danger continues that they may become stereotyped and meaningless. Slogans are important; they have been effective in winning wars and elections but, as a rule, they are transitory and become ineffective. To get maximum results, the same slogan is seldom repeated. Liberal arts are proudly proclaimed, but with monotonous expressions that are dangerously near clichés. The idea of a "general" education is commonplace, but generalities in an age of specialization are not impressive. The curriculum is described as in line with liberal arts, yet required survey courses are generally unpopular. The appeal lessens with a growing demand for less time to be spent in undergraduate work.

The meaning of liberal arts and church-related have lost some significance in modern usage. "Liberal," once considered the embodiment of moderation, now has an outer fringe of unrespectability, approaching radicalism. "Art" has aesthetic connotations somewhat sentimental in character. "Church" includes institutions widely separated, seething with conflict and somewhat ineffectual in solving problems.

None of these can be taken as inherent weaknesses or as valid claim for radical change. Basic principles have not been altered: rather, they are more pertinent now than ever. Perhaps a more clear-cut description with more meaningful application to present needs would strengthen the cause. Article II of the amended Charter (1966) reaffirms the College Board of Trustees' stand. "The said Corporation is formed for the purpose of providing higher education in the branches of human learning in an atmosphere of Christian culture, thus making real a thorough academic cultural preparation for all avenues of life."

The Muhlenberg curriculum reflects vitality, alertness to change, and a consciousness of sound traditions. There is less rigidity in course requirements and adequate opportunity for specialization. Independent study is not just a catalog entry but is freedom to try new ideas.

Progress aided by science has kept pace in military preparedness, technology, industry, and conquest of outer space and ocean depths. It overcasts the humanities and social sciences, but at the same time, scientists have aided them with notable contributions from Dr. Albert Einstein, Dr. Albert Schweitzer, Dr. James B. Conant, and others.

The possibility of making Muhlenberg a one degree college could narrow the gap that tends to separate and departmentalize, if there is realistic amalgamation. Support of science is widespread. It not only attracts wealth but also a disproportionate number of highly intelligent people. Future plans for Muhlenberg include a new science facility, an auditorium, and a fine arts and humanities center. With customary lamentations, social science is still without a separate house and home. A new and enlarged Library would afford consolation.

Religion at Muhlenberg, including courses and practices, contributes dignity to church-related status. Transition from a curriculum overburdened with religious subjects and denominationalism to a broader scope with rules of conduct relaxed, without losing idealistic and ethical principles, is noteworthy. Dr. Hagen Staack's participation as a delegate-observer at the last session of Ecumenical Council Vatican II and weekly ecumenical chapel services conducted by the Chaplain and a Roman Catholic priest are examples of the new frontier in religion at the College.

English literature and modern foreign languages (except German) were late arrivals at Muhlenberg: for some time ancient languages had preference. Teaching beginning students the rudiments of English grammar as well as elementary courses in foreign languages, a long-standing burden, now shows signs of declining as students are better prepared and as improved methods are introduced.

Social scientists have greater problems and responsibilities than ever, because of basic changes. The economist faces a shift from capitalism to the welfare state. The political scientist confronts decline in individualism and a trend towards authoritarianism. Sociologists meet with new concepts greater than any since the original impacts of the Industrial Revolution. It would be extreme folly to belittle their efforts and accomplishments but responsibilities have broadened and require greater attention.

History enjoys a degree of immunity because of some claim to fame among humanists and scientists. It has many functions; some neglected and dormant, others vigorously pursued. It is functional, inclusive (everything has a history) and, to all intent and purpose, necessary for the welfare of society. A most important function is to preserve records, promote cultural values, and encourage tolerance. There are those who think too much emphasis is put on the cultural: "1492 and all that."

Challenge to teaching is likely to increase because responsibilities multiply. The easy secluded life, without pressure and criticism, if ever true, has all but disappeared. Pay is higher, teaching hours less, and fringe benefits more, but results must be more specific and leadership more positive. Basic qualities that make a great teacher remain the same, yet the degree to which they are encouraged should be a matter of concern.

Training for the Ph.D., a must for prestige and advancement in college teaching, is valuable in itself, but provides little assistance for undergraduate pedagogy. Very often it is a chore and invariably, for practical purposes, overemphasizes research. A change in requirements for training college teachers is advocated and anticipated. This is practically an unexplored field and must have serious consideration.

A successful teacher is always at a premium. Criticisms of the profession are widespread and, while overdone, do carry some validity. Qualities are unique and so often the fortunate who possess them are lured into other fields. A recent magazine article is captioned: "Is there a teacher in the faculty?" A Harvard Fellow views results with skepticism: "A student may sit through lectures and write examinations—and professors may let them do merely that—collecting verbal 'answers' without really thinking through and about any new aspect of his own life in any course." Dr. Harold Howe II, former Director of the Learning Institute of North America and now Commissioner of Education in the Department of Health, Education, and Welfare in Washington, D.C., has produced this criterion defining responsibilities of a teacher: he should not be exempt from carrying a reasonable and agreed-upon teaching load. Senior members of the faculty should spend some time teaching freshmen and sophomores. Effectiveness in teaching should not be based on popularity alone. Teaching and no research often make a faculty member a dull teacher; therefore about one-third of a full-time teaching load should be set aside for research or experimentation of a kind which could lead to publication but primarily for teaching benefits.

The extent to which Muhlenberg approaches these standards is encouraging but not sufficiently assured.

The student of tomorrow is the most unpredictable of the unpredictables. There are signs that something is in store, but as yet, there is no certainty what to expect. What happened at Berkeley, California, in 1966 was a shock with considerably more noise and publicity than deserved, but with ugly repercussions. Students are on the go, and go they must—but which way?

There are signs which hopefully may emerge as acquired characteristics. Students, in the preferred category, see dangers ahead that must be confronted with remedies not readily available. They abhor riots, picket lines, and mass meetings, but realize possible strength in their usage. They seek security in substance and action, not confined to words and wishful thinking: an appreciable number are determined to get at the root of challenges that confront them. Leaders show resourcefulness in purpose and willingness to contribute. They are searching for something—not half-heartedly but with determination—and they may find it. They need help, and education should be the proper place to secure it.

A prospectus of Muhlenberg's future includes wide varieties of opinion seasoned alternately with optimism and pessimism.

Dr. Earl J. McGrath comments on the aim of a church-related college: "Whatever its other aspirations and activities, the dominant purpose of the church-related colleges must be to provide a place in which faith can be nurtured and strengthened. Without this they will inevitably lose their vitality and ultimately disappear. With it they can occupy an enchanted position in American higher education and immensely enhance our common life."

The problems of change and modern teaching attract the attention of Professor Katherine S. Van Eerde. "I believe that while we continue genuinely to honor the freedoms of our western civilization and to make way for some of the values of non-Western peoples, we should not despair of change. I believe further that the transmission of values and attitudes *does* occur, and notably in the besieged liberal arts college (which has already survived depression and wars in this century). Muhlenberg changes, and will change, but the framework of its values remains visible."

Professor G. N. Russell Smart anticipates the impact of Junior Colleges and overexpansion. "One cannot accurately foretell whether a two-year Muhlenberg will be educationally coherent or financially stable. If not, there may be an option. If the educational establishment of the future excludes us from grades 13 and 14, it may also thrust us into grades 17 and 18. A four-year experience could be restored by embracing the existing junior and senior years and the two years of a master's program. An insistent and increasing demand for education beyond the bachelor's level is as certain as anything can be in an uncertain world.

"Let us be clear. This is an analysis, not an advocacy. However, if such changes in collegiate structure are shown to be either necessary or desirable, Muhlenberg should not be the last to respond."

Attorney Jon F. LaFaver, Muhlenberg alumnus, on the other hand, advocates a *status quo*. "Alumni can also do an invaluable service for their alma maters in raising probing questions about changes, including 'Why?' and in attempting to influence the direction of the college toward worthwhile change and progress. They can also remind the faculty, administration, board of trustees, and student body of those few 'old' concepts, traditions, values and standards which may retain some utility and importance even in this fast moving age, and which should be discarded only reluctantly for some reason deeper than merely 'keeping pace.' "

Dr. William D. Reimert, President of the Trustees at Ursinus College, speaks of survival. "In the light of these pessimistic comments, is there room in the future for the independent college? I think there is, providing boards of trustees, administration and faculty are willing to cast aside much of the lethargy of the past in favor of innovations and imagination, a willingness to cooperate on a broad scale with sister institutions and an eagerness to adapt to the insistent demands of today's discriminating and selective students."

There are certain imponderables, forces which because of current involvements cannot be evaluated effectively. At least three crowd into the foreground; the welfare state, democratization of education, and possible change in demands on institutions of learning.

The welfare state, a softened form of regimentation and possible authoritarianism, has two motivations which require use of education. One is to propagandize ideas and make them logically acceptable. The other is to train the masses to be willing participants in the new order. Conceivably, they involve basic threats: an almost inescapable fascist political system and complete government control of education. The extent to which they are accomplished is a matter of grave concern at Muhlenberg and elsewhere.

American philanthropy, on which independent schools must depend, has played an important role in the responsibility for a large percentage of educational institutions, hospitals, museums, foundations for research, churches, and charity. This is idealistic and praiseworthy but there exists a growing feeling that coverage is insufficient, that too many are ignored and neglected, and that the only solution is government control. Some prefer to call it "creeping Socialism."

The extent of declared interest and responsibility of the government is recorded in the National Defense Act (1963). "We must increase our efforts to identify and educate more of the talent of our nation. This requires programs that will give assurance that no student of ability will be denied an opportunity for higher education because of financial necessity; we will correct as rapidly as possible the existing imbalances in our educational program which have led to an insufficient proportion of our population educated in science, mathematics and modern foreign languages and trained in technology."

Thoroughness of investigation and planning in government action does not enjoy high prestige. Lengthy studies of great value made during and after terms in office, by Presidents Hoover, Truman, and Eisenhower were largely ignored. Education could suffer the same fate.

Theoretical validity to expansion of government support is obvious: it is manifest in the entire complex of our democratic society. Recourse is given the capitalistic system. What would happen to free economic enterprise without government orders and subsidies? The crux of the question is the extent to which control follows. Also, the possible dangers of politicians, remote from the scene of action, guiding intricate and complicated processes like a national educational program. Advisability of government interference in public schools is understandable but where do private colleges and universities stand? Even the distribution of funds leaves room for favoritism. In 1965, twenty universities received 75 per cent of federal funds distributed.

A broadened base and an enlarged middle ground, including more intensified specializations for a greatly enlarged student body with wide variations in capabilities, are an integral part of the democratization of an educational program. The American Council on Education has this to say: "It is apparent that a permanent revolution in collegiate patterns has occurred, and that higher education has become and will continue to be the common training ground for American adult life, rather than the province of a select portion of society." A worthy goal and a challenging assignment.

The impact of student population explosion has been discussed. If it continues, expansion and larger group approaches are unavoidable. The diversity of students who appear for learning is appalling, in quantity and in quality. What can a college professor, or any teacher for that matter, do with a large class ranging from those with little background, slight interest, and a below average intelligence to the brilliant student who is not challenged? A middle-ground course may avoid both extremes but limit results to near mediocrity.

What might happen if our belief that a college diploma, or even four years spent on a campus, are not necessarily a key to success? And what if the present population explosion is held in check—what disillusionment to build for enormous numbers and then find fewer customers? In 1965, there were 180 completely new colleges and universities being built or planned. Since 1950, new buildings have cost $15.5 billion.

What will Junior Colleges and vocational schools do to college enrollment? The United States Office of Education estimates that by 1975, one in every two students at the time will attend a two-year college. Dr. Smart discussed this issue. Any other possibility cannot be ignored in planning for the future.

A third imponderable—new demands on educational institutions—may be considered a summation and an outgrowth of all others. Aims and objectives of a new program are clear and theoretically consistent. They include a broadened approach in educational opportunities and provide for a fuller and more beneficial life for everybody, at work or at play, for young and for old, and regardless of color, race, or creed. How to do this or even make an approach is the question. It could conceivably call for an entirely new system; what exists may have too many limitations to meet the demands.

Optimism is warranted because ponderables of high quality overshadow imponderables. At long last, education and those participating in it have come into prominence. Scarcity of wherewithal is no longer a basic problem. How to use abundance without sacrifice of principles is something new and challenging. Progress, always a measure of success, is evident everywhere. An interested public, a willing government, and a responsive student body provide real encouragement for educational institutions.

Muhlenberg College, conscious of the mission ahead, fortified with principles accrued from long experience, stands on solid ground with enough of yesterday to warrant stability and a sufficiency of today to give assurance for tomorrow. The struggle isn't over: a persistent historical tradition remains that progress depends on intermittent crises; that too much uninterrupted success breeds stagnation. The outmoded classical economist believed a depression, every so often, was good for the economy. Warmongers argue that war, in spite of all its devastation, generates advance along all lines. Some time ago Gilbert Murray wrote: "Probably most Christians are inclined to believe that without some failure and sense of failure, without a contrite heart and conviction of sin, man can hardly attain the religious life." Hopefully this is becoming, to the mutual advantage of both, a historical relic through cooperativeness of education and religion.

The establishment on the Muhlenberg campus of a chapter of Phi Beta Kappa, the highest ranking honor society in the country, long has been the desire and aim of those interested in promoting high academic standards. In October, 1964, the Phi Beta Kappa members of the faculty submitted a preliminary report, requesting permission to establish a chapter. Subsequently, Muhlenberg was one of thirteen colleges and universities evaluated for a chapter. The College was visited, appraised, and recommended for a charter. Late in August, 1967, the Phi Beta Kappa Triennial Council approved this recommendation. Thus another milestone in the forward progress of a Greater Muhlenberg has been reached.

Dr. Jensen's statement, concluding an impressive list of things accomplished, restates the challenge: "We must be realistic, we must study our past, and chart our future. We must measure the challenge ahead accurately. The record of the past five years is good. With God's Blessing, and with the work and prayers of our friends, the next five years will be better."

This is not "The End" to the Muhlenberg story. Rather, like an unfailing stream, it continues to broaden and deepen. When the next chronicler takes up his pen to revise and to continue the story, may he find evidence of continued progress, hopefully accelerated progress, and a future of even brighter prospects.

Appendices

College Presidents
Dr. Frederick Augustus Muhlenberg, 1867–76
Dr. Benjamin Sadtler, 1877–85
Dr. Theodore Lorenzo Seip, 1886–1903
Dr. William Wackernagel, Acting President, 1903–04
Dr. John A. W. Haas, 1904–36
Dr. Robert C. Horn, Acting President, 1936–37
Dr. Levering Tyson, 1937–51
  Five-man Committee (Quinity), 1951–52
Dr. Morris Greth, Acting President, 1952–53
Dr. J. Conrad Seegers, 1953–61
Dr. Erling N. Jensen, 1961–

Deans of the College
Dr. George T. Ettinger, 1904–30
Dr. Robert C. Horn, 1930–46
Mr. Sherwood Mercer, 1946–54
Dr. Henry M. M. Richards, 1954–62
Professor Thad N. Marsh, 1962–66
Dr. Edwin R. Baldrige, Jr., Acting Dean, 1966–67
Dr. Philip B. Secor, 1967–

Presidents of the Board of Directors
The Honorable Robert E. Wright, 1867–76
The Reverend William Rath, 1876–86
Dr. George F. Spieker, 1886–1912
Enos R. Artman, 1912–13
Dr. Reuben J. Butz, 1913–51
Dr. George B. Balmer, 1951–60
The Reverend Dr. Lester E. Fetter, 1960–

Board of Trustees (1966–67)
  I. Elected by the Eastern Pennsylvania Synod:
    Alfred O. Breinig (Rydal)
    Ralph Deetz, Jr. (Philadelphia)
    The Reverend George R. Deisher (Kutztown)

The Reverend Paul C. Empie, D.D., L.H.D., LL.D., Th.D.
(Upper Montclair, N.J.)
The Reverend Lester E. Fetter, D.D. (Glenside)
The Reverend Theodore L. Fischer (North Wales)
The Reverend Frank Flisser (Bethlehem)
The Reverend Maynard C. Hallock, D.D. (Pottsville)
Alan M. Hawman, Jr. (Wyomissing)
The Reverend Edward T. Horn III, D.D., Litt.D.
(Philadelphia)
The Reverend Arnold F. Keller, Jr., D.D. (Allentown)
The Honorable Kenneth H. Koch (Allentown)
W. Raymond McGonigle (Wyomissing)
Frank Martin (Philadelphia)
Raymond W. Norton (Southampton)
The Reverend John H. P. Reumann, Ph.D. (Philadelphia)
Otto F. Wiedemann (Dunedin, Florida)
Mrs. Wilbur E. Zieger (Philadelphia)

II. Elected by the Slovak-Zion Synod:
The Reverend Albert A. Ursin (Torrington, Conn.)

III. Elected by the Board of Trustees:
John A. Deitrich (Summit, N.J.)
John F. Emhardt (Oreland)
Russell Fulford (Allentown)
Jacob L. Hain (Reading)
William S. Hudders (Allentown)
William S. Miller (Westfield, N.J.)
John H. Repass (St. Davids)
Morris Senderowitz, Jr. (Allentown)
Clifford H. Trexler, M.D. (Allentown)

IV. Elected by the Alumni Association:
Donald G. Carpenter (Allentown)
Donald B. Hoffman (Allentown)
Clyde H. Kelchner, M.D. (Allentown)

V. *Ex Officio:*
Erling N. Jensen, Ph.D., President of the College
The Reverend Samuel E. Kidd, D.D. (Norristown)
President of the Eastern Pennsylvania Synod of
the Lutheran Church in America
The Reverend John Zornan, D.D. (Pittsburgh)
President of the Slovak-Zion Synod of the
Lutheran Church in America

VI. Life Trustees:
George B. Balmer, LL.D. (Wyomissing)
The Reverend William C. Berkemeyer, D.D. (Drexel Hill)
Frederick G. Erb (Pottstown)
W. Bruce MacIntosh (Miami Beach, Fla.)
Donald P. Miller, Sc.D. (Allentown)
Harry I. Oxenreider (Reading)
The Honorable Henry V. Scheirer (Allentown)
The Reverend Bela Shetlock, D.D. (Philadelphia)
The Reverend Corson C. Snyder, D.D. (Allentown)
The Reverend Frank M. Urich, D.D., LL.D. (Philadelphia)
W. Gordon Williams (Forty Fort)

OFFICERS OF THE BOARD:
The Reverend Lester E. Fetter, D.D., Chairman of the Board
Russell Fulford, Vice-Chairman
Howard M. MacGregor, Secretary-Treasurer

EXECUTIVE COMMITTEE OF THE BOARD:
The Reverend Lester E. Fetter, D.D., Chairman
Alfred O. Breinig
John A. Deitrich
The Reverend Theodore L. Fischer
Alan M. Hawman, Jr.
The Honorable Kenneth H. Koch
John H. Repass
Clifford H. Trexler, M.D.
Erling N. Jensen, Ph.D., *Ex Officio*

Muhlenberg College Faculty–1867-1967

William F. Adams, B.A., M.A., 1965–67
Psychology
Helen Adolf, Ph.D., 1963–66
German
Guerney F. Afflerbach, '16, Ph.B., M.S., 1917–20
Chemistry
Roderick E. Albright, A.M., M.D., 1897–99
Biology
Colin C. Alexander, A.B., A.M., 1910–12
English
C. Spencer Allen, E.E., M.S., 1923–29
Physics
Hugo E. Anderson, A.B., A.M., 1920–21
Mathematics, Physics
Stephen L. Angell, B.S., M.A., 1959–61
Sociology
Gunars J. Ansons, '55, A.B., B.D., M.A., Th.D., 1965–
Religion
Henry W. Aplington, A.B., A.M., Ph.D., 1946–53
Biology
Aurelia M. Arre, A.B., M.A., 1958–65
Romance Languages

Kingsbury M. Badger, A.B., A.M., 1936–46
English
J. Frederick Baier, A.B., 1926–27
Mathematics
Harry D. Bailey, A.B., A.M., D.Sc., 1909–28
Biology
Edwin R. Baldrige, Jr., A.B., M.A., Ph.D., 1957–
History
Roger Baldwin, B.A., M.A., Ph.D., 1962–
Sociology
Preston A. Barba, '06, A.B., M.A., Ph.D., Litt.D.
   1922–51   *German*
   1951–   *Emeritus*

Clyde E. Barker, A.B., 1946–49
Physical Education
Delbert Barley, A.B., A.M., 1952–53
Sociology
William A. Barrett, B.S., M.S., Ph.D., 1963–66
Physics
Westbrook Barritt, A.B., 1946–47
Romance Languages
Robert A. Battis, B.S., A.M., Ph.D., 1956–59
Economics
Howard W. Baughman, B.S. in Ed., M.A., 1949–51
Physical Education
John A. Bauman, '73, A.B., A.M., Ph.D., D.D.
   1885–1923   *Natural and Applied Sciences, Physics, Meteorology, Mathematics, Astronomy*
   1923–33   *Emeritus*
William A. Beates, '72, A.B., A.M., 1872–77
Tutor
Charles S. Bednar, B.A., M.A., Ph.D., 1962–
Political Science
Robert E. Behler, '44, B.S., D.D.S., 1945–46, 1956–57
Biology
Samuel T. Beidleman, '63, B.S., 1965–
Physical Education
Harry A. Benfer, A.B., A.M., 1925–65
Religion
J. Kenneth Bennett, B.S., 1925–26
Romance Languages
William C. Berkemeyer, '29, A.B., B.D., S.T.M., 1946–47
Religion
Frank James Bernhard, Jr., B.A., M.A., 1963–64
English
Ralph Bieber, '14, A.B., Ph.D., 1918–19
History
Paul G. Billy, '57, A.B., 1960–62
Physical Education
James R. Bloomfield, '57, B.A., M.A., 1959–61
History, Political Science
Walter A. Blue, '63, B.A., M.A., 1966–67
Foreign Languages—French
Robert K. Bohm, '63, A.B., B.D., 1966–
Classics
E. Philip Bollier, '43, Ph.B., 1946–47
English

Alfred Borneman, B.A., M.A., Ph.D., 1948–50
Economics
C. J. Bornman, B.A., B.D., M.S., Ph.D., 1957–59
Sociology
Robert K. Bosch, '47, A.B., 1946–47
History
James H. S. Bossard, '09, A.B., A.M., 1911–17
History, Economics, Sociology
J. Gysbert Bouma, Ph.B., M.A., Ph.D., 1956–
English
Philip J. Bourque, A.B., A.M., 1954–55
Economics
John H. Bowen, A.B., A.M., 1954–55
Psychology
Glen Bowersox, A.B., M.S., 1948–51
Chemistry
Charles B. Bowman, A.B., B.D., A.M.
   1921–42   *Economics, Sociology*
   1942–59   *Emeritus*
Carl Wright Boyer, '23, A.B., A.M., Ph.D., 1926–61
Education
Robert A. Boyer, A.B., M.A., Ph.D., 1941–
Physics
Walter H. Brackin, B.S. in Ed., A.M., Ph.D., 1954–
Psychology
George H. Brandes, B. Chem., Ph.D., 1925–62
Chemistry
William E. Brandt, A.B., B.S., 1939–40
Biology
Marcia Lea Brazina, A.B., M.A., 1964–65
English
David H. Bremer, A.B., B.D., Ph.D., 1952–
Religion
Dewey L. Brevik, B.A., B.D., 1963–
Director of Admissions
John D. M. Brown, '06, A.B., A.M., Litt.D.
   1912–49   *English, English Literature*
   1949–50   *Emeritus*
Thomas M. Brown, B.S.E.E., 1930–32
Physics, Mathematics
Thomas G. Bruni, B.S., M.A., 1966–67
Foreign Languages
John W. Brunner, A.B., M.A., Ph.D., 1955–
German

Richard K. Brunner, 1964–
   1965–66   *English*
A. Éric Bubeck, '44, B.S. in Ed., A.M., 1947–52
  History
John E. Bulette, A.B., A.M., 1954–62
  English
Andrew S. Bullis, A.B., A.M., 1950–55
  Political Science
Elizabeth Z. Burkhart, A.B., M.A., Ph.D., 1965–66
  Biology

Joseph F. Cantieni, A.B., M.A., 1947–52
  Art
John Louis Cardinal, B.S. in Ed., M.A., 1949–51
  Physical Education
Donald G. Carpenter, '33, Ph.B., C.P.A., 1940–45
  Accounting
Frank G. Carrino, A.B., M.A., 1947–48
  Romance Languages
Anne Marie F. Carter, A.B., A.M., 1961–62
  Romance Languages
Minotte M. Chatfield, A.B., M.A., Ph.D., 1953–
  English
L. B. Clapham, U.S.A., 1919–20
  Military Science and Tactics
John R. Clark, B.A., M.A., Ph.D., 1965–66
  English
Calvin Claudel, A.B., M.A., Ph.D., 1946–47
  Romance Languages
William D. Coder, B.S., A.M., 1927–35
  English
Alfred J. Colarusso, B.S., M.A., M.F.A., Diploma, Academy of Fine
  Arts, Florence, 1960–
  Art
Robert J. Conklin, B.H., M.A., Ph.D., 1935–36
  English
Christopher W. Convery, Jr., B.A., M.A., 1966–
  Psychology
Anthony S. Corbière, '20, Ph.B., A.M., Ph.D.
   1920–62   *Romance Languages*
   1962–   *Emeritus*
Alex Corriere, B.A., M.A., 1946–48
  Romance Languages

H. P. C. Cressman, '13, A.B., A.M.
  1919–21   *History, Sociology, Religion*
  1926–43   *Religion, Sociology*
  1943–52   *Emeritus*
Carl S. Criswell, B.S., M.A., 1946–50
  English
Robert C. Currie, Jr., A.B., A.M., 1947–48
  English

John S. Davidson, A.B., M.A., B.S. in L.S., 1940–
  Librarian
Luther J. Deck, '20, A.B., A.M.
  1921–64   *Mathematics, Physics*
  1964–   *Emeritus*
Roland W. Dedekind, Jr., B.S., M.S., 1959–
  Mathematics
Anna Marie de Gorbea, B.A., B.S., M.A., 1960–66
  Romance Languages
Aida H. C. de Rivas, Diplome, Française, Diploma, English Studies,
  1966–67
  Foreign Languages
Ana Maria Diaz, Maestro Normal, Ed.D., 1966–
  Foreign Languages
Claude E. Dierolf, '43, A.B., A.M., Ph.D., 1952–
  English
Heimtraut Dietrich, A.B., A.M., 1957–58
  Dean of Women
Richard L. Dively, '48, B.S., 1948–49
  Biology
John W. Doberstein, A.B., B.D., Litt.D., 1943–47
  Religion
Robert B. Doll, '40, B.S., LL.B., 1949–51
  Pre-law Seminar
Philip Dowell, A.M., Ph.B., Ph.D., 1897–1902
  Natural and Applied Sciences
LeGrand R. Drown, B.S., A.M., 1946–48
  History, Economics
Griffith Dudding, B.A., A.M., 1962–
  English

H. Milton Ellis, A.M., 1909–11
  English
Andrew H. Erskine, A.B., M.A., Ph.D., 1942–
  English, Speech, Drama

George T. Ettinger, '80, A.B., A.M., Ph.D., Litt.D., LL.D.
 1892–1936   *Pedagogy, Latin*
 1936–49   *Emeritus*
Ephraim B. Everitt, A.B., A.M., 1927–47
 English
Robert C. Eyerly, B.S., 1947–48
 Biology

Joseph Frederick Fahs, 1867–69
 History
Howard A. Farrands, A.B.. A.M., 1955–57
 History
Albert C. H. Fasig, '09, A.B., M.S., 1912–38
 Chemistry, Physics, Geology
Joseph Federico, '59, A.B., M.A., 1959–
 1959–65   *Physical Education*
George F. Freeman, '51, B.S., M.S., Ph.D., 1954–59
 Physics, Mathematics
F. Ernest Fellows, '42, Ph.B., A.M., 1946–56
 Physical Education
John M. Ferguson, A.B., M.A., Ph.D., 1959–60
 Economics
William A. Flamish, B.S., 1956–
 Physical Education
Edward J. Fluck, '30, A.B., A.M., Ph.D., 1936–47
 Latin
Sten G. Flygt, A.B., A.M., Ph.D., 1952–53
 German
Richard E. Fox, B.S. in Ed., M.S., 1954–55
 Physical Education
Herbert W. Fraser, A.B., M.A., 1956–59
 Economics
William M. French, A.B., Ph.D., 1953–
 Education
Robert R. Fritsch, 1900, A.B., A.M., D.D.
 1907–46   *German, Modern Languages, English Bible,*
                  Religion
 1946–60   *Emeritus*
George A. Frounfelker, Jr., '41, Ph.B., A.M., Ed.D., 1947–
 Psychology
Mary A. Funk, B.S., M.S., 1939–
 Assistant Librarian, Mathematics

Davis Garber, A.M., Ph.D., 1869–97
Mathematics, Astronomy, Physics, Geology
Paul J. Gebert, '17, A.B., 1939–53
History
Alfred Gemmel, A.B., M.A., 1947–49
History
Franklin Gergits, B.S., 1955–56
Music
Helen M. Gibbons, B.A., M.A., 1966–67
German
George W. Gibbs, A.B., 1963–
Director of Development
Russell W. Gilbert, '27, A.B., A.M., 1929–30
German
Arthur T. Gillespie, B.S., 1924–26
English, History, Debating
Robert J. Goeser, B.A., B.D., 1946–47
Religion
Margaret T. Goettler, B.S., M.S.W., 1966–67
Sociology
Helmut J. Golatz, A.B., M.A., 1946–49
History
Margaret Gonzalez, '62, A.B., M.A., 1965–66
French
Camilla Görlich, Berlin Universities, 1966–67
German
Ralph S. Graber, A.B., M.A., Ph.D., 1953–
English
William A. Green, B.S., M.S., Ph.D., 1945–56
Biology
Morris S. Greth, '22, A.B., B.D., A.M., Ph.D., Litt.D.
1945–65   *Sociology*
1965–   *Emeritus*
John A. Griffin, B.S., M.A., 1948–49, 1957–61
Romance Languages
Alice T. Griffith, B.S., M.S., 1958–
Chemistry
David T. Grimsrud, B.A., M.S., Ph.D., 1966–
Physics
John A. Growich, '46, B.S., M.S., 1949–51
Biology
Charles Gruber, B.S. in Ed., 1943–45
Mathematics

William B. Guenther, A.B., M.S., Ph.D., 1954–56
Chemistry
John R. Gustavson, B.A., M.A., 1959–60
English

C. Hess Haagen, A.B., A.M., Ph.D., 1950–54
Psychology
John A. W. Haas, A.B., A.M., B.D., D.D., LL.D.
 1904–36 *President, Religion, Philosophy*
 1936–37 *Emeritus*
George N. Haasz, A.B., 1907–09
History, English
John C. Hadder, B.S., M.Ed., Ph.D., 1957–62
Biology
Charles Hagelman, A.B., A.M., 1946–51
English
Francis Baker Hague, B.S. in Ed., M.S., 1962–64
Education
Eugene M. Hamory, A.B., 1946–48
Chemistry
Richard V. Hamory, A.B., 1946–50
Economics
Roland F. Hartman, '31, B.S., Ph.B., A.M., 1931–47
Business
Gerard J. Hasenauer, A.B., M.A., 1946–50
Romance Languages
Eugene C. Hassler, B.S., M.B.A., C.P.A., 1958–59
Economics
Richard C. Hatch, Sc.B., Ph.D., 1962–
Chemistry
William A. Hausman, Jr., B.S., M.S., M.D., 1902–05
Biology
Ralph C. Hauze, '42, B.S., 1946–48
Chemistry
Jean Hecht, B.S., M.S., 1957–
Physical Education
Walter F. Heintzelman, '27, B.S., 1927–28
Biology
Milton C. Henninger, '74, A.B., 1874–75
Tutor
Charles W. Hepner, B.A., B.D., M.A., Ph.D., D.D., 1946–52
Religion
Elizabeth Anne Herbert, A.B., M.S., 1964–65
Chemistry

Henry H. Herbst, '78, A.M., M.D., 1892–1905
Physical Culture, Physical Education, Hygiene, Human Anatomy, Embryology
Ralph L. Herbst, '43, B.S., 1945–46
Chemistry
William S. Herbst, M.D., 1874–81
Botany
John K. Heyl, '28, A.B., M.Arch., 1943–45
Engineering, Drawing
Marc Heyler, B. ès L., D.E.S., C.A.P.E.S., 1962–
Romance Languages
Richard E. Hibbard, B.Ed., A.M., 1938–43
Political Science
Robert C. Hicks, B.S. in Ed., 1953–54
Physical Education
Lee L. Hill, B.S., 1963–67
Physical Education
Reuben A. Hill, A.M., 1876–80
Greek
Ellis O. Hinsey, A.B., A.M., 1947–48
English
Carl B. Hoffman, A.B., A.M., 1947–48
History
William R. Hofford, A.M., D.D., 1867–68
Latin
Philip R. Hoh, A.B., B.D., 1946–49
Religion
Charles Hollister, B.A., M.A., 1946–50
History
George R. Holstrom, '23, B.S., 1926–33
Coach
Everett W. Holt, A.B., M.S., 1946–51
Mathematics
Edward T. Horn, '07, A.B., A.M., D.D., 1945–52
Bible and History
Robert C. Horn, 1900, A.B., A.M., Ph.D., Litt.D.
1904–52   *Greek Language and Literature*
1952–59   *Emeritus*
Helene H. Hospodar, B.S. in Ed., M.S., 1963–
Physical Education
James L. Howell, B.A. in Ed., 1943–45
Mathematics
Ivan Huber, A.B., 1966–
Biology

Philip Hultman, B.A., M.F.A., 1966–
Art
Jerry D. Hunter, B.A., M.S., Ph.D., 1965–66
Biology
Rheiner T. Hutchins II, A.B., M.A., 1964–67
English
Charles A. S. Hynam, D.I.C.T.A., M.S., 1961–62
Sociology

Joseph S. Jackson, A.B., A.M., Ph.D., 1926–40
History
Charles M. Jacobs, A.M., 1904–09
History
Harvey F. Janota, B.S., Ph.D., 1963–
Chemistry
Stuart E. Jenness, B.Sc., 1949–51
Geology
Earl W. Jennison, Jr., B.A., M.A., 1965–
History
Erling N. Jensen, A.B., A.M., Ph.D., Litt.D., 1961–
President
Victor B. Johnson, A.B., A.M., Ed.D., 1952–53
Education
Victor L. Johnson, B.S., A.M., Ph.D., 1937–
History
Allen H. Jones, A.B., M.A., 1946–47
English
Alvin B. Julian, B.S., 1936–45
Coach

Wayne R. Keck, '44, B.S., 1946–47
Chemistry
Winfield Keck, B.A., M.A., 1941–46
Physics, Mathematics
John C. Keller, B.S., Ph.D., 1927–46
Chemistry
Norman F. Keller, A.B., M.A., 1946–49
History
Robert M. Kelly, A.B., A.M., 1947–49
English
Ralph Kemmerer, 1955–66
Music
Perry F. Kendig, A.B., A.M., Ph.D., 1938–52
English

Thomas Kennedy, A.B., A.M., 1938–41
Economics
Herbert Ketcham, A.B., M.A., Ph.D., 1948–49
Romance Languages
Elmer K. Kilmer, A.B., M.A., Ph.D., 1942–50
Education
William L. Kinter, A.B., A.M., Ph.D., 1946–62
English
Albert A. Kipa, B.A., A.M., 1966–
German, Russian
Howard R. Kistler, '15, B.S., M.S., 1921–26
Chemistry
Clifford C. Klick, '39, A.B., 1940–41
Physics
John R. Kline, '12, A.M., 1914–16
Philosophy
Homer C. Knauss, '32, B.S., M.S., 1934–37
Physics, Mathematics
Kenneth H. Koch, '32, Ph.B., LL.B., 1943–47
American Government
Truman Koehler, '24, B.S., A.M., Ph.D., 1927–
Mathematics
Edward J. Koons, A.M., 1867–69
Physics, Mathematics, Astronomy, Geology, Physics
Martin Kopf, B.A., M.A., 1962–67
Romance Languages
Adnah G. Kostenbauder, A.B., M.A., Ph.D., 1962–
Mathematics
James D. Kozlowski, B.S. in Ed., 1956–60
Physical Education
Henry Krauskopf, B.B.A., A.M., 1952–54
Economics
Adeline E. Kreinheder, B.S., M.A., Ed.D., 1959–
Education
George F. Kribbs, '73, A.B., 1873–74
Tutor
Constance Kunda, B.S., 1966–
Physical Education
Charles T. Kuntzleman, '62, A.B., M.Ed., 1962–67
Physical Education

Carl Stevens Laise, B.A., 1965–
Philosophy

J. Ann Lanz, A.B., M.S., 1958–59
Psychology
Donald K. Lauer, '55, A.B., M.A., Ph.D., 1960–65
Psychology
George E. Lawson, '28, Ph.B., 1947–58
Physical Education
John Lear, A.M., M.D., 1899–1909
Biology, Physical Education
George A. Lee, A.B., B.D., M.A., Ph.D., 1964–
Sociology
Stewart S. Lee, B.A., M.A., Ph.D., 1963–
Political Science
Rowland W. Leiby, '12, B.S., Ph.D., 1955–56
Biology
Ludwig Lenel, Diploma, Hochschule für Musik, Cologne; Diploma, Conservatory of Music, Basel; M.M., 1952–
Music
Bengt S. Liljeroot, B.A., 1949–50
Biology
Thomas B. Lloyd, B.S., M.S., Ph.D., 1947–54
Chemistry
Charles Lohman, '48, B.S., 1948–49
Physics
Thomas F. Lohr, B.A., M.A., Ph.D., 1955–
Psychology
Robert E. Lorish, '41, A.B., A.M., Ph.D., 1948–53
Political Science
Frank Lough, B.S., 1945–49
Physical Education
Walter E. Loy, Jr., '55, B.S., M.S., 1960–
Physics
Marianne P. Lynch, A.B., LL.B., M.A., 1966–67
Psychology

Robert McClurkin, A.B., A.M., 1940–41
Economics
Ralph G. McConnell, A.B., A.M., 1946–51
English
Frank J. McVeigh, B.S., M.S.I.R., 1966–
Sociology

John C. MacConnell, B.S., M.A., 1960–
Education

Sara B. MacGowan, B.A., 1965–67
French
Vasant V. Mainkar, B.Sc., M.Sc., M.S., 1966–
Physics
Theodore Maiser, B.S., Ed.M., Ed.D., 1957–
Psychology
Clement A. Marks, Mus.D., 1904–12
Music
Harold K. Marks, '07, A.B., Mus.D.
   1913–51   *Music*
   1951–   *Emeritus*
Thad N. Marsh, A.B., M.A., B.Litt., 1962–66
English
Robert J. Marshall, A.B., B.D., 1947–53
Religion
R. Ransom Mattoon, B.S., 1946–48
Physics
Sherwood R. Mercer, A.B., A.M., 1946–54
Dean
Thomas R. Meredith, '42, Ph.B., A.M., 1946–51
English, History
George William Merkle, B.S., A.M., 1927–31
Business Administration
Charles L. Merwin, Jr., B.A., M.A., 1936–37
Business
Heinrich Meyer, Ph.D., 1947–64
German
Alburtus L. Meyers, LL.D., 1956–
Music
Bessie Michael, A.B., M.A., 1958–64
English
George F. Miller, A.M., 1873–77
German
Harold E. Miller, B.Sc., M.Sc., 1929–40
Biology
Orlando Miller, '47, A.B., A.M., 1948–49
History
John Misz, A.B., 1947–48
Geology
Earl R. Mohn, B.S. in Ed., 1947–52
English
J. Michael Moore, A.B., A.M., 1946–51
German

Charles E. Mortimer, '42, B.S., M.S., Ph.D., 1950–
Chemistry
Joanne S. Mortimer, A.B., A.M., Ph.D., 1957–
History
Anna L. Motto, B.A., M.A., Ph.D., 1965–66
Classics
Charles E. Mowry, B.S., A.M., 1947–51
Romance Languages
Kenneth T. Moyer, B.S., M.A., 1960–
Physical Education, Health
Henry R. Mueller, '09, A.B., A.M., Ph.D., 1920–37
History, Political Science
Ernest A. Muhlenberg, '68, A.B., A.M., 1870–72
Tutor
Frederick Augustus Muhlenberg, A.M., D.D., 1867–76
President, Greek, Mental and Moral Science, Evidences of Christianity
Paul B. Myers, Jr., A.B., M.S., Ph.D., 1966–67
Geology
Richmond E. Myers, A.B., A.M., Ph.D., 1937–51
Geology

William A. Nagle, '63, A.B., M.A., 1965–67
English
John I. Nassar, B.A., M.A., Ph.D., 1966–
Mathematics
Thorman A. Nelson, B.S., M.Ed., 1946–51
Mathematics
Bernard Neumeyer, '43, B.S., 1946–48
Physics
Henry M. Noel, M.A., 1947–49
Romance Languages
German
Fred. William A. Notz, Ph.D., 1869–72
Anne Graham Nugent, Ed.B., M.A., 1958–
Education

Solomon E. Ochsenford, '76, A.B., D.D., 1899–1909
English Language and Literature, Mental and Social Science
Nils A. Olsen, A.M., 1909–10
History
Carl S. Oplinger, '58, B.S., M.S., Ph.D., 1963–
Biology

Stephen J. Osofsky, B.A., LL.B., M.A., 1966–67
Political Science
Gustav K. Osterhus, A.B., 1917–18
History, Economics
Samuel H. Ottinger, '46, B.S., 1946–49
Mathematics
Robert Parke, Jr., A.B., M.A., 1956–59
Sociology
Harold P. Parker, A.B., M.A., 1953–56
Sociology
Lawrence Pasel, A.B., M.A., LL.B., 1960–61
Economics
Bertha Paulssen, Ph.D., 1942–43
Sociology
Mary H. Perry, A.B., M.S., Ph.D., 1964–
Chemistry
Charles H. Pershing, A.B., A.M., 1944–47
Romance Languages
Arthur C. Peters, Jr., '46, B.S., 1946–49
Chemistry
Joseph Petro, '42, Ph.B., 1955–56
Physical Education
Luther A. Pflueger, '06, B.A., M.A., Ph.D., 1946–52
German
Samuel Philips, A.M., 1867–68
Rhetoric, Logic, English Literature, Political Economy
Manly J. Powell, B.S., M.S., Ph.D., 1956–60
Chemistry
Pinapati Prabhudas, B.S., M.S., Ph.D., 1967
Chemistry
W. Kendrick Pritchett, A.B., A.M., Ph.D., 1946–48
Classics

Conrad W. Raker, '34, A.B., B.D., D.D., 1949–50, 1953–55
Sociology, Bible, Religion
William B. Ramsdale, B.A., M.A., 1943–45
Physics
Arnold C. Rapoport, '54, A.B., LL.B., 1966–
Political Science
Jacob B. Rath, A.M., 1868–71
German, History
Harry L. Raub III, B.S., Ph.D., 1947–
Physics

David A. Reed, A.B., M.A., Ph.D., 1958–
Philosophy
John J. Reed, A.B., A.M., Ph.D., 1948–
History
Harold D. Reese, A.B., M.A., 1945–46
Mathematics
William H. Reese, Ph.B., M.S., D.Sc., 1904–17
Natural and Applied Sciences
Harry Hess Reichard, A.B., A.M., Ph.D.
   1925–46   *German*
   1946–58   *Emeritus*
Frances R. Reichman, B.A., M.A., 1965–66
Sociology
Robert F. Reiff, A.B., 1946–49
Art
Lawrence J. Reimert, '32, B.S., 1932–34
Physics, Mathematics
Walter L. Reinhard, '38, B.S., M.S., 1940–41
Chemistry
D. Irvin Reitz, '26, Ph.B., A.M., 1946–58
Accounting, Economics
Jesse B. Renninger, '31, A.B., B.D., S.T.M., 1946–49, 1957–
German, Religion
Stephen A. Repass, D.D., 1892–1905
Christian Evidences
Matthias H. Richards, A.M., D.D., 1867–73, 1876–98
  *Latin, Rhetoric, English Language and Literature, History, Political
  Economy, Logic, Mental and Social Science*
Henry M. M. Richards, '32, A.B., M.B.A., Ph.D., 1954–
Economics
Ursula M. Richter, 1949–50
Music
Werner Richter, Ph.D., Th.D., LL.D., 1947–50
Philosophy
William H. Rickert, '68, A.B., 1867–68
Tutor
George Rickey, B.A., M.A., 1941–49
Art
Henry N. Riis, 1867–68
German
Rodney E. Ring, M.A., Ph.D., 1950–51, 1955–
Religion
William S. Ritter, '16, B.S., A.M., 1919–53
Physical Education

Frederick Robinson, 1955–
Music
Anne E. Rodda, B.A., M.A., 1961–67
German
Jessie A. Roderick, B.S., M.A., 1965–67
Education
Jesse N. Roeder, A.B., M.A., Ph.D., 1958–62
Education
Bruce R. Romig, '46, B.S., 1948–51
Biology
E. Dudley Ross, Ph.M., 1910–11
History
Edward Rothstein, B.S., M.A., Ph.D., 1964–65
Sociology
Alice Routch, B.S., 1960–67
Music
Robert J. Ruhf, '41, B.S., M.S., 1947–51
Chemistry

Benjamin Sadtler, D.D., 1876–85
President, Mental and Moral Science, Evidences of Christianity
Peter T. Sardo, B.S., M.A., 1960–
Geography
Alice M. Savage, A.B., Ph.D., 1962–67
Biology
Arthur M. Schaefer, A.B., 1955–56
Economics
Robert L. Schaeffer, Jr., B.S., Ph.D., 1954–
Biology
Benjamin W. Schmauck, A.M., 1877–80
German
Arthur J. Schneider, B.S., 1948–49
Art
Karen C. Schneider, B.S., Certificat de Français, Sorbonne, 1964–65
Biology
Robert Schultz, B.A., B.D., Th.D., 1965–66
Religion
Edward J. Schurr, A.B., M.B.A., 1961–62
Economics
Floyd B. Schwartzwalder, B.S., M.S., 1945–49
Physical Education, Coach
Walter J. Scott, A.B., 1948–51
Physics

Walter L. Seaman, B.L., A.M.
1926–45   *Romance Languages*
1945–52   *Emeritus*
J. Conrad Seegers, '13, A.B., A.M., Ph.D., Litt.D., LL.D., L.H.D.
1953–61   *President*
1961–   *Emeritus*
Theodore L. Seip, A.M., D.D., 1867–1903
German, Greek, Latin, President, Mental and Moral Science, Natural Theology
Charles Seivard, '59, B.A., B.D., 1965–66
Religion
Wilson N. Serfass, Jr., B.S., M.B.A., C.P.A., 1959–
Economics
John V. Shankweiler, '21, B.S., A.M., Ph.D.
1921–64   *Biology, Zoology, Botany*
1964–   *Emeritus*
Wilbert P. Shanor, '77, A.B., 1876–77
Tutor
William A. Sharkan, B.A., M.A., D.Ed., 1966–
Education
Stewart A. Shaw, B.A., Ph.D., 1963–
Philosophy
Donald E. Shay, B.S., M.S., 1940–45
Biology
Leon F. Sherman, A.B., M.A., 1966–
History
Alfred L. Shoemaker, '34, A.B., Ph.D., 1946–47
German
Clarence A. Shook, A.B., A.M., Ph.D., 1965–66
Mathematics
Austin Short, B.S., 1957–60
Physical Education
Albert D. Simpson, '40, B.S., 1940–41
Mathematics
Stephen G. Simpson, A.B., A.M., Litt.D., 1911–42
English
Rohini P. Sinha, I.Sc., B.A., M.A., Ph.D., 1965–
Economics
Vimla Sinha, B.Sc., B.A., M.A., Ph.D., 1965–
Psychology
John H. Slater, B.S., 1926–27
English
G. N. Russell Smart, B.Sc., Ph.D., 1947–
Chemistry

Roy E. Smeltzer, C.L.U., 1940–52
Insurance
Edgar F. Smith, Ph.D., 1881–83
Natural and Applied Sciences
Fred H. Smith, A.B., 1937–40
Physics
Robert M. Smith, A.M., 1909–10
English
Frank Smoyer, A.B., 1947–54
English
Henry L. Snyder, '15, Ph.B., LL.D., 1946–48, 1961–66
Political Science
Jerome Snyder, B.B.A., M.B.A., 1947–51
Economics
David K. Spelt, A.B., Ph.D., 1946–51
Psychology
George F. Spieker, D.D., 1887–94
Hebrew
Rudolph J. Sprenger, A.B., M.Litt., 1948–51
German
Hagen A. K. Staack, M.S., S.T.M., Ph.D., 1954–
Religion
Janet Stamm, A.B., A.M., Ph.D., 1958–65
English
Melville F. Stark, B.S., M.S., 1957–60
Art
Robert L. Stauffer, '26, Ph.B., 1930–31
Biology
David N. Stehly, B.S., M.S., 1960–
Chemistry
Jacob Steinhaeuser, D.D., 1894–1904
Christian Evidences
Milton H. Steinhauer, '26, B.S., M.A., Ph.D., 1947–51
Education
Harold L. Stenger, Jr., A.B., A.M., Ph.D., 1946–
English
Edward B. Stevens, A.B., Ph.D., 1947–65
Classics
George R. Stevens, A.B., M.A., Ph.D., 1965–
Geology
Eugene H. Stevenson, A.B., 1926–27
English
Russell W. Stine, '22, A.B., A.M., B.D., S.T.M., Ph.D., 1927–58
Religion, Philosophy

Herbert G. Stinson, B.A., M.A., 1955–57, 1966–
Romance Languages
Eleanor Stuart, A.B., A.M., 1961–62
Romance Languages
Robert K. Stump, '54, B.S., M.S., 1959–
Mathematics
Margaret W. Sullivan, B.A., M.Ed., 1959–62
Physical Education
James Edgar Swain, A.B., A.M., Ph.D., LL.D.
1925–67   *History, Political Science*
1967–   *Emeritus*
Franklin P. Sweetser, A.B., A.M., 1954–55
Romance Languages
W. Warren Swenson, '44, B.S., 1946–47
Chemistry
Luther A. Swope, '68, A.B., A.M., 1867–72
Tutor
Alice P. Tallmadge, A.B., A.M., 1961–62
Classics
David E. Thomas, A.B., B.D., Th.D., 1959–
Sociology
N. Wiley Thomas, Ph.D., 1883–85
Natural and Applied Sciences
George N. Thompson, A.B., B.D., 1947–50
Religion
Robert B. Thornburg, A.B., A.M., Ph.D., 1951–53, 1962–
English
S. Francis Thoumsin, Jr., A.B., M.S., 1945–51
Geology
Richard H. Timberlake, Jr., A.B., A.M., 1947–51
Economics
Edward S. Tinley, B.S., M.S., 1946–47
Physics
James H. Tinsman, Jr., A.B., M.A., 1960–61, 1962–65
Philosophy
Horace Townsend, Jr., B.S., A.M., 1952–56
Economics
Robert R. Townsend, '44, B.S., M.A., 1943–45, 1957–59
Physics, Mathematics
Donald S. Traill, M.A., S.T.M., 1947–53
History
John E. Trainer, '35, B.S., M.S., Ph.D., 1939–
Biology

Charles D. Trexler, '03, A.B., M.A., D.D., Litt.D., LL.D., L.H.D., 1946–49
Religion
Thomas Triplett, B.S., 1949–50, 1953–55
Physical Education
Lynda Sue Trutt, B.A., M.A., 1966–67
English
Levering Tyson, A.B., A.M., Litt.D., LL.D., 1937–51
President

Paul T. Ulrich, A.B., 1946–47
Mathematics
Katherine S. Van Eerde, B.A., M.A., Ph.D., 1961–
History
Lee G. Van Horn, '43, A.B., 1946–49
Romance Languages
James R. Vaughan, '52, B.S., M.S., Ph.D., 1956–
Biology
Hermann F. Vieweg, B.Chem., Ph.D., 1924–27
Chemistry
Nelvin L. Vos, B.A., M.A., Ph.D., 1965–
English
John G. Voyatzis, LL.B., M.A., 1956–
Economics

William Wackernagel, A.M., D.D., LL.D.
    1880–1920   *German, French, Modern Languages, History*
    1920–26   *Emeritus*
Robert J. Wagner, B.S., M.S., 1961–
Mathematics
William C. Walker, B.S., M.S., Ph.D., 1946–47
Chemistry
William Ward, '41, A.B., A.M., B.D., 1946–53
Sociology
Francis W. Warlow, A.B., A.M., 1946–47
English
Thomas H. Weaber, Jr., '36, B.S., M.D., 1942–
Hygiene
Paul W. H. Weaver, Jr., '51, B.S., M.S., 1952–55, 1958–
Biology
Kenneth Webb, A.B., Ph.D., 1946–
Romance Languages
Kurt H. Weber, B.S., 1943–45
Physics

Adolph Wegener, '48, A.B., A.M., Ph.D., 1956–
German
Revere F. Weidner, '69, A.B., A.M.
   1868–70   *Tutor*
   1874–76   *Rhetoric, English Literature, History, Political Economy*
Frederick W. Wetzel, B.S., 1964–65
Biology
Raymond J. Whispell, B.S., 1956–
Physical Education
William R. Whitehorne, Ph.D., 1902–04
Sciences
Donald E. Wieand, A.B., LL.B., 1954–56
Economics
Matthew I. Wiencke, A.B., B.D., 1945–46
Religion, Philosophy
William C. Wilbur, Jr., A.B., Ph.D., 1940–60
History
Frank R. Wilgruber, B.S., M.A.F.A., 1965–66
Art
Norman B. Wilkinson, '38, A.B., A.M., 1942–47
History
Earl L. Williams, A.B., A.M., 1925–26
Mathematics, Physics
Phillip H. Williams, B.S., LL.B., 1956–58
Economics
Cyrus Williston, 1908–09
Science
Stanley Wise, '48, B.S., 1948–50
Chemistry
Benjamin F. Wissler, '26, B.S., 1927–30
Physics
Karl F. J. Wittrich, B.S., M.S., 1941–52
Economics
Rollin Wolf, B.S., M.Arch., 1943–45
Engineering Drawing
Harry D. Wood, A.B., A.M., 1953–61
Political Science
Ralph C. Wood, A.B., M.A., Ph.D., 1945–56
German
John M. Woolford, Ch.E., M.A., 1946–49
Mathematics
Leslie J. Workman, B.A., 1960–67
History

Frederick H. Worsinger, '19, A.B., 1919–21
Biology
Clayton W. Wotring, A.B., A.M., Ph.D., 1945–47, 1951–52
History
Isaac Miles Wright, B.S., Pd.M., Pd.D.
   1917–45   *Philosophy, Pedagogy, Education*
   1945–47   *Emeritus*

Theodore Conrad Yeager, M.D., 1867–73
Chemistry, Botany, Physiology
John M. Yetter, M.E., A.B., 1898–99
English
Donald H. Yoder, A.B., B.D., Ph.D., 1948–49
History

Ira F. Zartman, '23, B.S., M.S., Ph.D., 1929–48
Physics
Arvids Ziedonis, Jr., '55, A.B., B.D., S.T.M., 1963–
Russian
Louis Ziemand, LL.D., A.M., 1954–55
German
Robert T. Zuch, A.B., M.A., 1965–67
History

Bibliography

PUBLISHED WORKS

Danforth Commission on Church Colleges and Universities, *Eight Hundred Colleges Face the Future* (Preliminary Report, 1965).

Leonard, R. J., Evenden, E. S., and O'Rear, F. B., *A Survey of Higher Education for the United Lutheran Church in America* (3 vols., Teachers College, Columbia University, 1929).

Lineberry, W. P., *Colleges at Cross-Roads* (New York, 1966).

Martian, J., *Education at the Cross Roads* (Yale University, 1964).

Ochsenford, S. E. (editor), *Muhlenberg College: A Quarter-Centennial Memorial Volume; Being a History of the College and a Record of its Men* (Muhlenberg College, 1892).

Rudolph, F., *The American College and University: A History* (New York, 1962).

Sack, S., *History of Higher Education in Pennsylvania* (2 vols., The Pennsylvania Historical and Museum Commission, 1963).

Seip, T. L., *Muhlenberg College* (Lutheran Publication House, 1887).

Tappert, T. G., "Two Hundred Years of the Ministerium of Pennsylvania" (*Minutes of Ministerium*, 1948).

MONOGRAPHS

Horn, Robert C., "Muhlenberg College: History of One Hundred Years, 1848–1948." (Typewritten copy in Muhlenberg Library.)

Jensen, Erling N., "Years of Change, Years of Growth, A Five Year Report" (University Press, Buffalo, 1966).

"Muhlenberg College: The Future" (Report of Committee on future of the College, Dr. Conrad Seegers, Chairman, 1961).

"Muhlenberg College, Report on Evaluation by Commission of Institutions of Higher Learning of the Middle States Association" (1965).

"Muhlenberg College, Report of Self-Evaluation Submitted to the Middle States Association of Colleges and Secondary Schools, Commission on Institution of Higher Learning" (Dr. Harold L. Stenger, editor, 1965).

Nixon, Austin and Ireland, Corporation, "Report of Service" (Campaign Fund observations, 1960–62).

MUHLENBERG PUBLICATIONS

The Ciarla (1893–).
College Catalogs (1867–).
Muhlenberg College Alumni Quarterly (1936–38).
Muhlenberg Alumni Magazine (1938–).
The Muhlenberg College Monthly (1883–89).
The Muhlenberg (1889–1914).
The Muhlenberg Weekly (1914–).

CALL-CHRONICLE NEWSPAPERS

MINUTES AND RECORDS

Minutes of the Board of Trustees (1867–).
Minutes of the Executive Committees of the Board of Trustees (1867–).
Minutes of the Faculty (1867–. There are many gaps.)
Minutes of the Executive Council of Alumni Association (1927–).
Minutes of Student Council (1940–).
Minutes and Records of Muhlenberg Woman's Auxiliary (1924–. One volume missing).
Minutes of the Women's Council of Muhlenberg College (1958–).
Minutes of Euterpean Literary Society (1874–1878).
Minutes of Sophronian Literary Society (1871–1895).
Reports of the Presidents of Muhlenberg College to Board of Trustees.
Reports of the Ministerium of the Evangelical Lutheran Church of Pennsylvania and Adjacent States (1945—).

Index

Academic freedom, 96
Academic Regulations and Standards Committee, 98
Adams, Henry, 56
Administration, reorganization, fall (1962), 112
Administration building, constructed, 33; fire, 78
Admission, requirements for (1867), 45; (1891), 62
Admissions policy, 122
Adult education, 164–166
Afflerbach, Gurney F., 60
Allentown Atlantic League, 50
Allentown Collegiate Institute, 6
Allentown Collegiate Institute and Military Academy, 6
Allentown Female College, 65
Allentown Preparatory School conversion, 72
Allentown Seminary, founding of (1848), 6
Alpha Kappa Alpha, 64
Alsace, 1
Alumnae Association, 166
Alumni, 161–164; annual fund, 163; House, 100; Scholarship fund, Haas, 67; Secretary, Fasig, 60
Alumni Association (1911), 53; on coeducation, 93
American Association of University Professors, on academic freedom, 97
American Civil Liberties Union, on student constitution, 83
American Council on Education, survey on coeducation, 83
American Society of Church History, 18
Amherst College, 23

Antioch College, 64
Arcade, student control of, 123
Arre, Aurelia, 93
Athletics, 133–135; Afflerbach, 60; Committee on, 128; nineteenth century, 27; new program (1961), 129
Augsburg Confession, 83
Augustus Church, Trappe, 3

Background, of Haas, 37; of Jensen, 103–104; of Muhlenberg, F. A., 10; of Sadtler, 14; of Seegers, 88; of Seip, 16; of Tyson, 70
Bagger, Henry H., 135
Baillie, John, 80
Baldwin, Roger, ACLU, 83
Balmer, George B., 103, 107; Future of College Committee, 110; Quinity, 87
Barba, Preston A., 43; *Deutscher Verein,* 63; reaction to new location, 34
Barnard College, 65
Barzun, Jacques, 154
Bauman, John, 140
Bausch, Mrs. Elmer H., 161
Benfer, Harry A., 72; on athletics, 128
Berkemeyer, Mrs. William C., 161
Berks Hall, constructed, 33
Bernheim, Oscar, 72, 143
Bernheim House, 100
Bibliography, 203
Board of Associates, 106
Board of College Education and Church Vocations, 116
Board of Directors, Presidents of, 177

Board of Trustees, on curriculum, 114; meeting (December 11, 1953), 88; officers of, present, 179; organization of, 105; present members, 177–178; -Faculty retreat, 112

Bossard, James H. S., 43, 81

Boyer, Robert A., Future of College Committee, 110; non-credit courses, 165

Brandes, George, 43

Brandt, William E., 81

Breinig, A. L., 26

Bremer, David H., Future of College Committee, 110; Monograph, 126

Brobst, Samuel K., 5–7

Brown, John D. M., 43, 64, 81, 135; library, 158; 200th anniversary celebration, 74

Brown, Richard L., 158

Brown University, 23

Bryan, William Jennings, 55

Butz, Reuben J., 41, 87, 107, 151

Bylaws, amendment on faculty (1934), 98; amendment (1959), 99; (1966), duties of President, 107

Byrd, Richard, 58

Campaign, Greater Muhlenberg (1938), 73; (1954), 88; fire damage, 78; Secretary, Afflerbach, 60

Campus, new (1904), 33

Cardinal and Gray Annual (1921–22), 63

Carlson, Edgar M., 162

Carnegie Foundation, 102

Carpenter, Donald G., 75

Cedar Crest College, on coeducation, 83; "Gentlemen's Agreement" with, 65

Centennial (1948), 80

Chapel building, 151–153; compulsory (1925–28), 62; construction of (1931), 59

Chaplain, role of, 151

Chaplin, Charlie, film, 96

Chatfield, Minotte, 165

Christian Education Appeal (1951), 83

Christian Higher Education Year (1949–50), 78

Churchill, Winston, 86

Ciarla (1893), 25; coeducation in staff, 93; student control of, 123

Civil Aeronautics Authority, 75

Civil War, 6

Coeducation, Dr. Haas on, 64–66; survey on (1946), 83; adoption of, 90–94; athletics, 129

College Band, 64

College Choir, 64

College Council (1962), 112

Collegian, 27

Commencement (1892), 19

Commons Building, construction of (1915), 53

Coolidge, Calvin, 58

Cooper, Charles J., 28

Cooper, Prentice, 73

Cooperative Store, 76

Corbière, Anthony S., 43, 64

Curriculum (1867), 12; (1960–64), 113–117; alterations (1920–30), 60–61; approval by Board of Trustees, 113; faculty approval, 115; on physical education (1899), 48; Tyson on, 71

Danforth Fellowships, 125

Danforth Report, on Admissions, 122; on teachers, 117

D'Ascenzo Studios, 152

Deans of the College, 177

Decade of Dedication Campaign, 130

Deck, Luther, 43; Quinity, 87

Degree, Bachelor of Philosophy (1909), 45

Dempsey, Jack, 58

Department of Public Instruction, 166

Depression (1873), 12; (1929), 60

Deutscher Verein, 63

Development Committee, Board of Trustees, 106
Development Office, 113
Dickinson College, 4
Dierolf, Claude E., on coeducation, 92; Future of College Committee, 110
Dietrich, Heimtraut, 91
Director of Church Relations, 105
Durham, Mrs. Hannah, 81

Eastern Pennsylvania Synod (1963), 105; appropriation, 130
Ebert, Sister Anna, 93
Ecumenical Council, 169
Eichorn, George F., Jr., 105
Eisenhower, Dwight D., 85
Endowment Fund (1868), 12; (1874), 12; (1915), 52; Mosser-Keck, 15; Asa Packer, 15; Rehrig, 64; Saeger, 64; Trumbower, 131
Enrollment (1867), 11
Eta Sigma Phi, 64
Ettinger, George, 140
Euterpea Society, 24–26
Evangelical Lutheran Ministerium of Pennsylvania, 17; and Adjacent States, 7
Executive Committee, Board of Trustees (1966), 179; organization of, 106
Executive Council of College, 112
Extension Division, organized, 46
Extension School, coeducation, 65
Extracurricular organizations, 64

Faculty (1867–1967), 180–202; first meeting, 8; House, 100; meetings, 118; purpose, 95–97; Senate, 98; -Student baseball game, 27
Fasig, Albert C. H., 60
Federal Education Act, 102
Fegley, Charles K., 80
Ferguson, Homer, 80
Fetter, Lester E., 97, 103, 107
Field Secretary, Afflerbach, 60
Finances (1857–58), 6; (1886), 18; (1900's), 27; (1915), 52; (1952–53), 88

Financial Campaign, post World War I, 59
Fischer, Emil E., 80, 151
Fister, Gordon, 72
Fletcher, Sir Angus, 74
FonDersmith, gift to athletics, 51
Ford Foundation grant, 89
Francke, Augustus Herman, 2
Francke, Gottlieb August, 2
Francke Institute, 2
Franklin, Benjamin, 44
Franklin College, 4
Franklin Society, 26
French, William M., 165
Fretz, Barbara, 91
Fringe benefits, present, 119
Fritsch, Robert, 143
Fulford, Russell, 103
Fuller, Mrs. Dewey, 161
Funk, Mary, 93
Future of the College Committee (1959), 110
Future Planning Committee (1959), 106

Garber, Davis, 35
Gearhart, Ethan Allen, 81
Gebert, George, 26
General Council of Pennsylvania, 5
General Foods Corporation, grant, 89
"Gentlemen's Agreement," 66
Gettysburg College, 4; Seminary, 5
G.I. Bill of Rights, 78
Gibbs, George W., 106
Gifts and grants, 131
Gilbert, Mrs. Karl B., 161
Glee Club, 64
Goethe, 109
Grange, Red, 58
Greth, Morris, Acting President, 87; faculty services, 106
Griswold, Alfred W., 154
Gross, Mrs. Walter H., 161

Haas, John A. W., 14; on athletics, 51–52; on coeducation, 64–66; concern for successor, 70; library, 158; new president, 36–40;

Haas, John A. W. (*cont.*)
retirement, 69; on students' religious affiliation, 62; teacher training, 47; 200th anniversary celebration, 54
Haas, Mrs. John A. W. bequest, 67
Hagan Field, 90
Hamilton College, 23
Harter, Mrs. Stanley L., 161
Hartzell, Mrs. G. W., Chapel gift, 59
Harvard University, 22–23; seal, 36
Hauser, John R., 80
Haverford College, 48
Health Center, 90
Hecht, Jean, 92
Heil, J. B., 26
Hemingway, Ernest, 70
Henninger, James F., on faculty, 118; on President Jensen, 104
Hillel, 126
Hillman, James N., 155
History of Ideas, 116
Hock, Donald V., 81
Hoffman, Donald, 64
Honor System, 122
Honors Program (1964), 115
Hoover, Herbert, 69, 85
Horn, Robert C., 41, 60, 81, 87
Horn, Mrs. Robert C., 158
Howatt, George, 82
Howe, Harold II, 170
Hudders, William S., 103
Hutchins, Robert, 155

Inauguration, Haas, 38; Jensen, 104; Muhlenberg, 10; Sadtler, 14; Seip, 16; Tyson, 70
Intercollegiate athletics, approval of (1900), 50
Interfraternity Council, 94

Jacobs, Charles M., 51
Jacobs, Rear Admiral, 75
Jefferson, Thomas, 101
Jensen, Erling N., on athletics, 129; on curriculum, 116; on future of college, 176; on long-range planning, 112; new president, 103; on summer school, 165
Jessup, Walter, 70
Johns Hopkins University, 23
Johnson, Lyndon B., 102
Johnson, Victor L., 103
Junior Oratorical Contest (1922), 63

Kappa Phi Kappa, 64
Katz, William L., 89
Keck, Thomas, endowment, 15
Keiter, Ernest R., 136
Keiter, F. T. L., 26
Kelly, Thomas, 133
Kendig, Perry F., 92
Kennedy, John F., 101
Klick, Richard C., 110
Klinglers' Band, 134
Koehler, Truman, 75
Kopf, Martin, 165
Korean War, 79
Kostenbader, Dorothea, 161
Knubel, Frederick H., 73
Kreinheder, Adelaide, 93
Kunze, J. C., 3

LaFaver, Jon F., 172
Lafayette College, 23
Lambda Epsilon Delta, 93
Lear, John, 137
Lehigh Valley, 1
Librarian, Board appointment of (1911), 53
Library, 156–159; building constructed, 59
Life Magazine, on coeducation, 91
Lilje, Hans, 80
Lindbergh, Charles, 58
Lohr, Thomas F., Future of College Committee, 110; on liberal arts, 156
Long-Range Planning Committee (1961), 106; (1963), 113
Luther, Martin, 19
Luther, Martin, dormitory, 90
Lutheran Church in America, relation to College (1963), 105; role in education, 150

Lutheran College for Women (1921), 65
Lutheran Synod of Pennsylvania, 3

MacGregor, Howard M., 87
MacLeish, Archibald, 154
Madison Square Garden, 76
Magnificus, Rector, 54
"Man-of-War," 58
Mandolin Club, 64
Mann, Horace, 64
Marks, Clement A., 81
Marks, Mrs. G. Donald, 161
Marks, Harold K., 81
Marsh, Thad N., 165
Marshall, George, 86
Marshall, John, Club, 64
Martin, Frank, 113
Mask and Dagger, 64
Mathematics Club, 64
M. Book (1939–40), 81
McCarthyism, 96
McClelland, George W., 80
McGrath, Earl J., on athletics, 128; on college future, 171; on liberal arts, 156; report, 114; on summer school, 165
Memorial Hall, 90
Men's Dormitory Council, 94
Mercer, Sherwood, 87
Meyer, Heinrich, 165
Middle Atlantic Conference (athletics), 129
Middle Atlantic States Association (1955), 89; Evaluating Committee on library, 158; on student body, 123
Miller, Mrs. Richard G., Sr., 161
Millerheim, 100
Ministerium, assumes responsibility of College (1874), 13; on coeducation, 64–66; on faculty religious affiliation, 96; meeting (December 11, 1953), 88; Orphan's Home, support of, 13; at Philadelphia (1769), 3; plea for new location, 33; Publication House,

support of, 13; subscription (1919), 59; Theological Seminary, support of, 13
Missionary Society, 26
Monmouth College, 77
Moore, Dale H., 81
Morrill Act, 148
Mortimer, Charles E., 110
Mortimer, Joanne Stafford, 93
Mosser, Charles, 73
Mosser, Mrs. George K., 160
Mosser, James K., endowment, 15
Moyer, William, 103
Mueller, Henry R., 43; library, 158; John Marshall Club, 64
Muhlenberg, Frederick Augustus, on inauguration of Seip, 16; new president, 6; on Quarter-Centennial, 29; resignation, 14
Muhlenberg, Frederick Augustus Conrad, 3
Muhlenberg, Gotthilf Henry Ernest, 3
Muhlenberg, Henry Melchior, 2–5; 200th anniversary of arrival in America, 73; 200th anniversary of birth, 54
Muhlenberg, John Peter Gabriel, 3; dedication of statue, 55
Muhlenberg, William F., 54
Muhlenberg, The, first college paper, 25
Muhlenberg Christian Association, 126
Muhlenberg College, named, 6
Muhlenberg Monthly, The, 26
Muhlenberg News, The, on coeducation, 93
Muhlenberg Weekly, The, student control of, 123; on student government, 94; student opinion on faculty, 96; supervision of, 62
Murray, Gilbert, 175

National Council for Accreditation of Teacher Education, 166
National Defense Act, 173

National Defense Education Act, 131; fellowships, 125
National Science Foundation awards, 125
New Hanover church, 3
New York University, 27
Newman Club, 126
Non-credit courses, 165
Normal schools, Pennsylvania, 46
Notre Dame University, 58
Nugent, Anne, 92

Oberlin College, 64
Oberly, F. C., 26
Oberly, Sherman, 81
Ochsenford, S. E., 19
Omicron Delta Kappa, 93
Oxenreider, Harry, 103
Oplinger, Carl, 165
Oratorical contest, 135–137

Packer, Asa, endowment, 15
Palatinate, 1
Paulssen, Bertha, 93
Pembroke College, 65
Pennsylvania, University of, 23, 27
Pennsylvania Germans, 1
Pennsylvania Reserve Defense Corps, 75
Pennypacker, Samuel K., 54
Phi Alpha Theta, 64
Phi Beta Kappa, 176
Phi Sigma Iota, 64
Philadelphia English Conference (1904), 33
Philadelphia Lutheran Seminary (1864), 5–7; Ministerium Campaign, 73
Power House constructed, 33
Pre-Medical Club, 64
Presidents of the College, 177
Princeton University, 23
Prohibition, 57
Prosser, Dr. and Mrs. Harrison, 93
Prosser Hall, 93

Quarter-Centennial Memorial Volume, 19
Quinity, 87

Radcliffe College, 65
Radio Station WMUH, student control of, 123
Rahn, Earl F., 80
Raker, J. H., 26
Rausch, J. C., 60
Rayburn, Sam, 73
Reed, David A., 165
Reed, John, 94
Reese, William H., in athletics, 50; in Extension Division, 46; in Summer School, 165
Rehrig, W. N., endowment, 64
Reichard, Harry H., 43; *Deutscher Verein*, 63
Reimert, William D., 172
Reisner, Walter, 134
Reno, Claude T., 81
Repass, John, 103
Reserve Officers Training Corps, World War I, 57
Richards, Henry M. M., on faculty services, 106; on student council, 94
Richards, Matthias Henry, 35
Rickmers, Mrs. Harold J., 161
Rickover, Hyman G., 155
Ring, Rodney, 165
Rochester University, 23
Rockefeller Foundation gift, 59
Rockne, Knute, 58
Roosevelt, Franklin D., 69, 85; 200th anniversary celebration, 73
Roosevelt, Mrs. Franklin D., 73
Roosevelt, Theodore, 49, 54
Root-Tilden Law School scholarship, 125
Ruhe, Percy B., 81

Sadtler, Benjamin, new president, 14; Quarter-Centennial, 29; retirement, 16
Saeger, Florence T., endowment, 64
St. Michael's Church, Philadelphia, 3
St. Stephen's Lutheran Sunday School, 26

Salary comparison (1911–16), 53
Sardo, Peter, 165
Scherer, Paul, 74
Schlenker, Luther F., 89
School and Society, on athletics, 52
Schweitzer, Albert, 109
Science building, constructed, 59
Seegers, J. Conrad, on Chaplin film, 96; on coeducation, 93; on internal administration, 99; new president, 87; resignation, 100
Seegers Union, 100
Seidel, Charles, 81
Seip, Theodore Lorenzo, death, 35; early work for College, 12; new president, 16; plea for new location, 31
Self-Evaluation report, 155
Shankweiler, John V., on athletics, 128; new appointment, 43; Pre-Medical Club, 64
Shankweiler, Mrs. L., 160
Simpson, Stephen, first librarian, 53, 141
Sinclair, Upton, 58
Singmaster, J. Walter, 51
Slovak-Zion Synod, 105; appropriations, 131
Smart, G. N. Russell, 172
Smith, Edgar Fahs, 15, 35
Smith, Warren S., 141
Snyder, Corson C., 80
Snyder, Harvey C., 81
Snyder, Henry L., on athletics, 134; on oratory, 135
Snyder, LeRoi, 72
Society for Propagation of Christianity and Useful Knowledge among Germans in America, 4
Sophronia Society, 24–26
Spanish-American War, 49
Spieker, George F., 35
Sputnik, Russia's, 103
Staack, Hagen, 165
Stagg, Alonzo, 133
Stamberg, Baron von, 54
Stenger, Harold L., Jr., 110

Student Army Training Corps, World War I, 57
Student body activities, early years, 137–144; characteristics, current, 120–123; government (1938–40), 81–83; organization (1920–30), 62
Student Council, on Chaplin film, 97; character of, 94–95; on coeducation, 93
Student departmental organizations, 64
Student Honors Court, 94
Summer School (1913), 46
Susquehanna University, 83
Swallow, William, 81

Tau Kappa Alpha, 64
Teacher Training, 164–166
Teachers College survey, 67
Tennis courts, 90
Texas Christian University, 58
Thomas, David E., 106
Thomas, N. Wiley, 15, 35
Tilden, William, 58
Trexler, Clifford H., 110
Trexler, Harry C., visiting professorship, 131
Trumbower, Peter S., endowment, 131
Two Hundredth Anniversary Celebration of Muhlenberg's arrival in America, 73; birth, 55
Tyson, Levering, on arrival of V12 unit, 75; "Greater Muhlenberg" Campaign, 73; impact of resignation, 87; new president, 69; on postwar problems, 77; resignation, 84; on student body, 81

Uhl, Frederick E., 81
Union College, 23
United Lutheran Church, C.H.E.Y., 78; funds for coeducation, 65
United States Office of Education, 174
U.S. Steel Foundation gift, 89

V5 Military Unit, 73
V12 Military Unit, 73

Van Eerde, Katherine S., on college future, 171; women faculty, 93
Virginia, University of, 22
Visiting Professorship, Trexler foundation, 131
Volstead Act, 125
Voorhees, Donald, 81

Wacker, Henry, 134
Wackernagel, William, Acting President, 35; "Old Faculty," 137; St. Stephen's Sunday School, 26
Watson, Frank R., 152
Weaber, Thomas H., Jr., 72
Weiser, Anna Maria, 3
Weiser, Conrad, 3
Whispell, Raymond J., 110
Who's Who in American Colleges and Universities, on coeducation, 93
Wickersham Report (1931), 57

William II, Emperor, 54
Wilson, Woodrow, 85; honorary degree, 54; on peace, 57; fellowships, 125
Woman's Auxiliary, 159–161; contribution (1949–50), 78
Women, in Extension Division, 47
Women's Council organized, 93–94
World War I, 56; Post, on curriculum, 61
Wright, Isaac M., Extension Division, 46; fund, 166
Würtemberg, 1

Yale University, 23

Zartman, Ira F., honorary degree, 81; new faculty, 43
Ziegenfus, Mrs. Charles, 160
Zinzendorf, Count, 3
Zion Church, Philadelphia, 3

A HISTORY OF
MUHLENBERG COLLEGE
1848-1967

James E. Swain

The year 1967 is noteworthy for Allentown: it is the centennial of the naming of Muhlenberg College, of the incorporation of the city by the Commonwealth of Pennsylvania, and of the founding of Cedar Crest College; and it is the bicentennial of the transfer of the land on which the city was built from Judge William Allen to James Allen.

Allentown and Muhlenberg College grew up together—the city from a small town to a thriving metropolis and Muhlenberg from a defunct preparatory school to a thriving and highly respected educational institution.

The Muhlenberg story is one of doubt and insecurity but with enough success to keep the institution alive. In the early years, agony overshadowed ecstasy, yet faith, ultimate belief in its purpose, and hard work eventually shaped the College as it is today.

This account is more than just a history of Muhlenberg College. It also includes its participation in the broader areas of national growth, particularly in reference to private school education, church relationship, and liberal arts committed to excellence.

The seventy-five years between Muhlenberg's quarter centennial and centennial have been years of change and years of growth.

In his quarter-centennial presidential address (1892), Dr. Theodore L. Seip had a vision of improved buildings and equipment that would permit the College to enlarge its "sphere of influence."

Today Dr. Seip's vision is reality. But Dr. Erling N. Jensen, Muhlenberg's President, also has dreams for the College's future. They include the educational program as well as the expansion of the physical plant and an increase in endowment.

To achieve this, Dr. Jensen believes: "We must study our past, and chart our future. We must measure the challenges ahead accurately. The record of the recent past is good. With God's blessing, and with the work and prayers of our friends, the future will be even better."